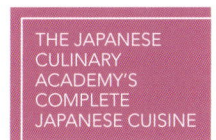

THE JAPANESE
CULINARY
ACADEMY'S
COMPLETE
JAPANESE CUISINE

MUKOITA I
Cutting Techniques
—Fish

MUKOITA I

Cutting Techniques

| Fish

JAPANESE CULINARY ACADEMY

SHUHARI INITIATIVE

C O N T E N T S

Copyright © 2016 Shuhari Initiative Ltd.
Photograph and Text Copyright © 2016
Non-Profit Organization
Japanese Culinary Academy
Shuhari Initiative Ltd.
Photograph Copyrights © 2016
Saito Akira, Yamagata Shuichi

Published by Shuhari Initiative Ltd.
info@shuhariinitiative.jp
shuhariinitiative.jp
2-11-2 Ginza, Chuo-ku, Tokyo, 104-0061,
Japan

All rights reserved. Printed in Japan
First Edition, 2017
23 22 21 20 19 18 17   10 9 8 7 6 5 4 3 2 1

ISBN 978-4-908325-06-9

The jacket features the work of Yoshioka Sachio, the fifth generation in a lineage of Kyoto master dyers. Yoshioka is known for his traditional vegetable dyeing techniques. The jacket of this book displays *fukaki-murasaki*, a dark purple that expresses one of the deepest, richest hues of this color.

NOTE: Japanese names in this book are given in traditional order, surname first.

PREFACE

MURATA Yoshihiro

Director, Japanese Culinary Academy

Surrounded by ocean and blessed with an abundant supply of fresh water, Japan is a place where the culture of eating foods in their raw, natural state goes back to antiquity. In the clear waters they were so blessed with, people cleansed fish and vegetables and presented them as offerings to the gods. Afterwards, in eating the foods thus offered they felt they were receiving the power of life from the gods. People's confidence in the quality of their water led to the development of cutting techniques for serving sashimi and preparation methods like *arai* for tightening the flesh of sea bream or carp in ice water. No matter how fresh, the raw consumption of fish and shellfish involves risks, such as spoilage or parasites. The wisdom of using wasabi and daikon for their antiseptic properties arose to counter such risks, and today they are among much-favored garnishes for sashimi. This history and cultural milieu are why cutting (of raw ingredients) comes first in the list of the "five techniques" (along with grilling, simmering, steaming, and deep-frying).

I once put a group of children to a test, showing them cucumber cut to various lengths: Which ones would you call "ingredients"? I asked. Which one is "food"? Interestingly enough, the children called the piece cut about bite size "food." The way ingredients are cut and how big the pieces are change the way we look at food. The reason that cutting is so important is that food is eaten with chopsticks in Japan, and serving portions that are easy to eat represents thoughtfulness. Flavors are best enjoyed when the bite taken is just right. The volume of the mouth is about the same for most people, and since the opening of the mouth is about 3.3 centimeters high and wide, that is roughly the size of a "bite-sized" piece. The optimal weight of a bite is about twelve grams, and based on that wisdom, the usual sashimi slice is twelve to fifteen grams. *Mukozuke* dishes are thus designed to hold five slices of twelve grams each for sixty grams in all.

Sashimi is a simple dish, and only if the fish is cut skillfully, will it retain its fine texture, freshness, and flavor. Enjoyment of fish in its raw state depends greatly on the feel and texture of the flesh, so the relatively springy white meat of fish like sea bream and flounder is sliced thin, while the soft, red meat of tuna and bonito is cut thick, and the tough and chewy flesh of seafood like squid is made into slender strips. Other special slicing techniques, such as *hegi-zukuri* (diagonal, shaved-off slices) and *hoso-zukuri* (thin, slender slices), have been developed for particular fish and preparations. In addition to techniques like *arai*, there are ways, as with *kobujime*, to bring out the inherent flavor of the ingredients.

Work in the kitchen of a traditional-style Japanese restaurant is customarily handled by a team of specialists: for sashimi, simmered foods, grilled dishes, and so on. The *mukoita* position in this team, named after the cutting board (*ita* means "board"), handles mainly the sashimi and other dishes that contain raw fish. In most cases the main chef takes the *mukoita* position and supervises all of the other positions for preparing the courses of a meal. The sashimi (served in a vessel called a *mukozuke*) is a very important part of the meal. The *mukoita* chef is expected not only to prepare sashimi with practiced skill but to be capable of overall good judgment and management of other aspects, including proper care and storage of fish and supervision of the preparation of fish dishes other than sashimi. This book is devoted to explaining the techniques of carving fish, which is the main work of the *mukoita* chef. Few books present photographs and step-by-step instructions in as much detail as will be found here and in *Mukoita II*, the next book in this series, which treats cutting techniques for seafood, poultry, and vegetables.

The techniques and processes of filleting and cutting may differ from one chef to another and for different types of dishes. We hope that in the pages that follow, the reader's understanding of these techniques will be furthered by our systematic treatment from *ikejime* spiking through preparation of the parts of the fish for filleting to finally the slicing of sashimi.

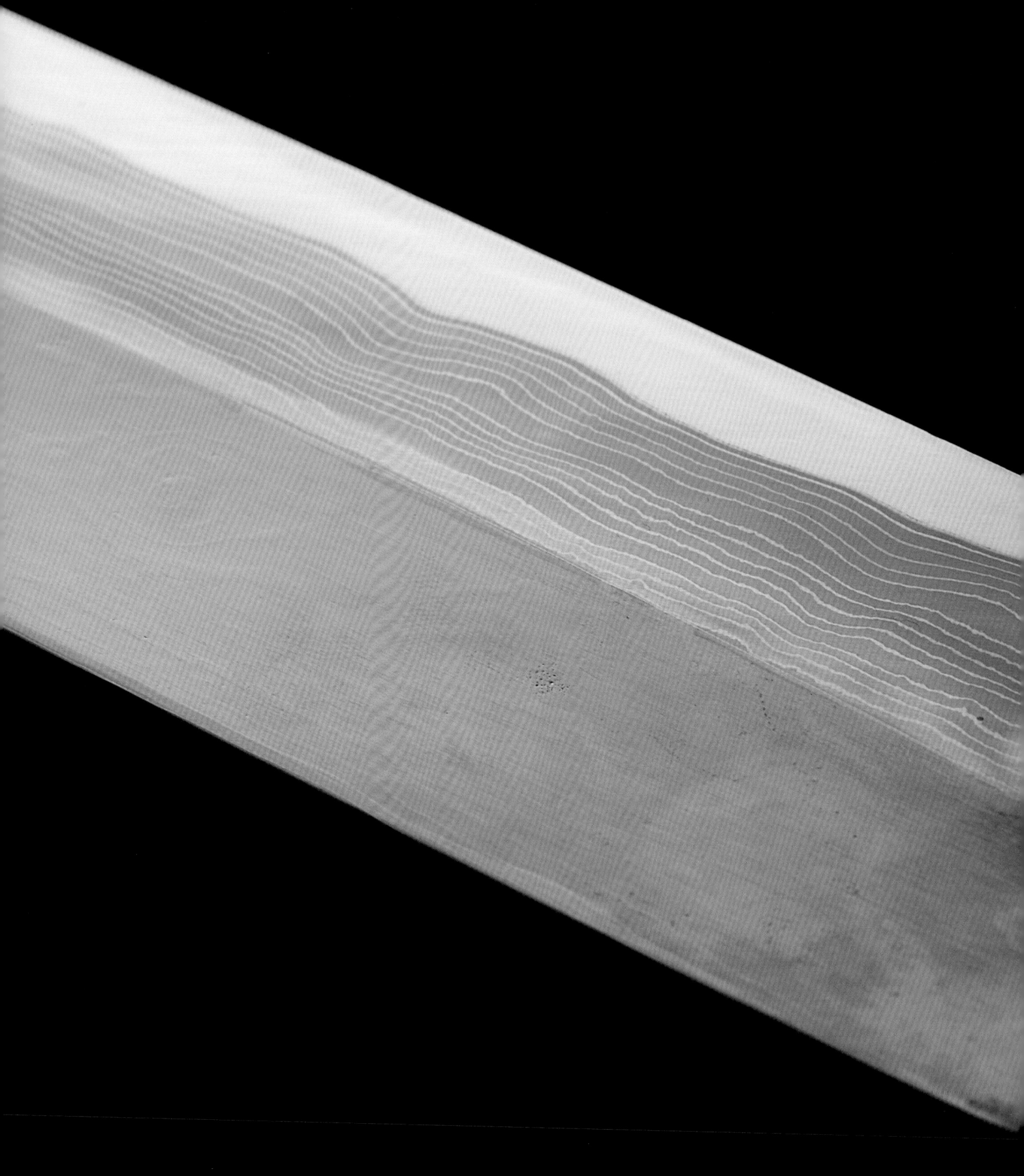

Chapter 1

The Basics

Blessed with an abundance of fish and seafood as well as vegetables and fruit throughout the four seasons, Japan has nurtured a culture of enjoying foods in their raw state and preparing them so as to draw out the inherent flavor of ingredients to best advantage. This, combined with the traditional emphasis on the aesthetic qualities of food that is served, means that great respect and refinement have historically been accorded to expert cutting techniques. This chapter presents basic knowledge of the history and culture of Japanese kitchen knives (*hocho*) along with their types and applications.

Mukoita and the Arts of Sashimi

Chefs in a traditional Japanese restaurant are divided into those assigned to the *nimono* simmered dishes, *yakimono* grilled course, sashimi, and so on. The highest status belongs to chefs entrusted with preparation of sashimi, the arts of which are known as *mukoita*—from *muko* for the *mukozuke* course, which almost always features sashimi, and *ita* or "board," for cutting board. The *mukoita* chef often doubles as head chef and is responsible for overseeing the entire cuisine. Such is the central position accorded to the *mukozuke* (sashimi) course in washoku cuisine.

The consumption of raw fish is the greatest distinguishing feature of Japanese cuisine. Although historically the practice of eating sliced raw meat or fish with vinegar or other condiments existed in ancient China, where it was known as *kuai* (Jp. *namasu*), for hygienic reasons, over time it was largely replaced by heated food. In Japan, however, *namasu* developed into sashimi, which, thanks to today's sophisticated seafood distribution systems, reigns as the veritable star of washoku.

Sashimi neatly encapsulates washoku's defining characteristics. It involves seemingly little preparation, yet in actuality conceals a tremendous amount of effort to select ingredients and enhance flavor without compromising freshness, as well as precision skills wielding knives honed to perfection. This reflects the aesthetics of Japanese cuisine, which—unlike other styles that entail adding various flavors to ingredients—expends great energy on unseen tasks while making it all look effortless. The philosophy of drawing out natural flavors through minimal intervention is evident in dashi and *nimono* as well, and is why Japanese cuisine is sometimes characterized as an art of subtraction.

The Special Place of Sashimi in Japanese Cuisine

Sashimi holds high status in Japan, where it is regarded with special gravity and expectation. In sashimi, the intrinsic taste and aroma and texture of each fish come forth. Heating, by contrast, robs the flesh of its moistness, bringing out the chewiness; simmering in sauce makes the seasonings seep in, to the loss of the fish's natural, fresh flavor. Meanwhile, the *aburi* or "seared" style of briefly charring the surface of the flesh, which is also often seen nowadays, is a variation on raw serving and may look similar to but is different in conception from rare-done steak.

In washoku it is thought to be a shame to cook fish that is fresh enough to be enjoyed raw. For example, although sardines, saury, horse mackerel (*aji*), and *saba* mackerel are inexpensive and not considered particularly high class, they can be served raw only while very fresh. As sashimi, then, their value goes up significantly.

The Techniques That Support Sashimi

Cooking rightfully begins with sourcing the ingredients. To prepare sashimi, the chef must ready fish of exacting high quality, rigorously choosing only those that are fresh enough to be eaten raw.

Sashimi needs to be not only fresh, but also flavorful. For this reason fish are matured as appropriate for a short time while the adenosine triphosphate (ATP) in the muscles breaks down into inosinic acid, contributing to the umami of the dish. The key is to offer the fish at just the right level of increased inosinic acid content; otherwise with time the compound will decompose further into hypoxanthine and other substances lacking in umami.

Umami enhancement through maturation is particularly important for white-fleshed fish such as sea bream and flounder, which are light in flavor. Aging these fish over a few to about a dozen hours at a low temperature (about 34°F or 1°C) heightens umami but detracts from freshness, so that experience comes into play in determining suitable timing. Given that flesh progressively stiffens after death, a skilled chef must also be able to gauge the optimum balance between umami and texture.

In the area of supply and distribution, one technique practiced to ensure catch quality is spiking, or *ikejime* (see pp. 40–43), in which fish are paralyzed so as to be transported live from the sea to the kitchen. The brain is directly destroyed with the spike, and a long needle may be inserted from the tail through to the spinal cord, disabling the motor nerves. Advanced systems for live shipping likewise answer to the vigorous demand for raw fish consumption.

The Importance of the Knife

The sharpness of the knife is an important determining factor in the flavor of sashimi. The contours of Japanese kitchen knives are subtly shaped to keep fish flesh from cleaving to the blade during cutting. There are several types of specialized sashimi knives, most of which have an exceedingly sharp, single-ground edge. To maintain superior performance, chefs hone their knives on a whetstone both before and after use. The cleanness of the cut makes for fine differences in sensation that can be appreciated on the palate (see pp. 36–37).

Knives in the History of Japanese Cuisine

In early times, the art of cutting held pride of place in Japanese cuisine. Culinary masters were famed for their skills with the *hocho*, the kitchen knife, and their virtuosity was the object of appreciation.

Already in the late Heian period (ca. 1000–1192) we have evidence of aristocrats who were *hocho* adepts, including Fujiwara no Ienari (1107–1154), who appears in the story anthology *Konjaku monogatari*. According to one anecdote, Ienari was once commanded to fillet a carp in the presence of the emperor. He demurred at first, but, on being urged by the emperor himself, was obliged to obey and performed to the awed admiration of all.

Later, the growth of warrior culture gave rise to professional chefs called *hocho-nin*, who carved not only carp but also game such as crane and wild boar. These men used as their tools sharp, metal-tipped cooking chopsticks and a knife forged by a swordsmith and perfected techniques for cutting fish and fowl on a large board without ever directly touching the fish or fowl. The sixteenth-century *Shuhanron emaki* (Sake and Rice Debate Illustrated Handscroll) depicts a *hochonin* wearing a formal *eboshi* hat and wielding his knife at the head position in the kitchen. The act of cutting was indeed a measure of culinary prowess.

Knife skills were not the preserve of kitchen professionals alone: there were also experts among the daimyo lords of the provincial domains of the sixteenth to seventeenth century. The detailed accounts of Japanese culture in *História da Igreja do Japão* (The History of the Church in Japan) by the Portuguese interpreter João Rodrigues (1561–1633) include a list of ten accomplishments esteemed by aristocrats and warriors, the third of which—carving food with a kitchen knife—Rodrigues describes as a refined and accustomed task among the members of those classes.

The daimyo Hosokawa Sansai (1563–1646), who was versed in this art, once filleted a carp in front of the tea master Sen no Rikyu. After it was over, Rikyu expressed his compliments but also noted that the cutting board seemed slightly thinner than it should be. While the anecdote is chiefly meant to celebrate Rikyu's discriminating eye as revealed by his ability to discern a few millimeters' insufficiency in a board more than seven centimeters thick, it also illustrates that the display of culinary dexterity was always conducted before a fitting audience.

Such traditions survived in the Edo period (1603–1867) in the form of "impromptu" cuisine using fish kept live in water inside the restaurant so as to be filleted and prepared before diners' eyes. In sum, cutting performances have been an aspect of Japanese cuisine for well over a millennium.

Today the *kappo* style of Japanese fine dining features over-the-counter cuisine by a chef preparing sashimi and other offerings at a workstation set directly across from patrons. No such custom of showing work in progress is found in fine classi-

A valuable document for learning about the history of food culture, this detail from the sixteenth-century *Shuhanron emaki* (Sake and Rice Debate Illustrated Handscroll) painted by Kano Motonobu depicts scenes of both the preparation of food and its consumption. Note the men seated in the upper left (in the honored *kamiza*-position in the room), one wearing an *eboshi* hat, who are in charge of cutting the fish and fowl for the cooks.

cal restaurants in the West, which keep their kitchens and dining spaces strictly separate. Cooking as performance in Japan owes its existence to the long-standing tradition of culinary masters demonstrating their *hocho* skills before an audience.

Those traditional skills live on in the *hocho-shiki* food-carving ceremonies performed by several schools. Among them is the Shijo, which was founded by the aristocrat Fujiwara no Yamakage (824–888) and carried on by the Takahashi family of court chefs. The school's seminal treatise, the late fifteenth-century *Shijo-ryu hochosho*, specifies that cutting boards should be of *hinoki* cypress and measure two *shaku* seven *sun* five *bu* (82.5 centimeters) long by one *shaku* six *sun* five *bu* (49.5 centimeters) wide by two *sun* five *bu* (7.5 centimeters) thick. The source also calls for the knife to be sword-shaped with a blade eight *sun* (24 centimeters) long, indicating that the kitchen knives of the time, while large, were not single- but double-ground in the same way as Japanese swords. Single-ground knives of the type commonly seen today probably developed later on in the Edo period.

In the late fourteenth century the Okusa and Shinji schools emerged from the warrior class, and various treatises were produced on the style of each. Another school, the Ikama, continues in Kyoto; its archives include illustrated handscrolls of foods cut and presented according to ancient techniques.

The Hygiene for Food Eaten Raw

In Japanese cuisine, which often features ingredients prepared without heating or cooking, proper hygiene in the kitchen is particularly important. The hygienic practices not only of suppliers all along the food supply chain but of individual restaurants should give high priority to the principles of hazard analysis and critical control points (HACCP), the international management system for food quality control. HACCP provides for analysis of possible hazards that might occur along the path from food production to consumption and identifies essential points for control and monitoring. Japan has its own Food Sanitation Act, which spells out regulations and other measures relevant to food safety from the viewpoint of public health. HACCP similarly aims to protect consumers of food, but in contrast to such conventional regulations, which focus mainly on culinary professionals and kitchen conditions such as cooking tools, or counters and cutting boards, its system offers broad, overall guidelines ranging widely from sanitation during food production and distribution to the washing and handling of ingredients in the kitchen, as well as refrigeration temperatures, shelf life, and other considerations for safe consumption.

Good judgment regarding the quality of food ingredients and the temperature at which they are kept is crucial, of course, but those engaged in cooking must also practice the fundamental principles of good hygiene. They must maintain careful track of food quality and temperature, keep their hands clean, and be scrupulous about their personal care as well, including hair, fingernails, and clothing. Thorough attention to all of these things, no matter how basic, is the first step to introducing HACCP.

The professional chef is constantly conscious of the following three key principles for a safe and healthy kitchen:

Safe Handling of Food

Seafood, meat, and vegetables carry all sorts of bacteria at the time of purchase. The best way to safeguard food and the kitchen is to always select fresh ingredients, wash them carefully in plenty of clean water, place them in clean containers, and keep them in refrigeration of at least 46°F (8°C). Those handling ingredients and preparing food should make it a habit to thoroughly wash their hands with soap, not only before cooking, but after contact with different ingredients as well as after activities outside the kitchen.

Keeping Bacteria at Bay

Take care to keep all foodstuffs at the proper temperature. With raw ingredients, especially, care should be taken to store them at around 40°F (4°C) and not leave them at room temperature. Foods left standing after being made ready to eat are prime sites for the propagation of bacteria and so should be served as soon after preparation as possible.

Clean and Disinfect

Bacteria on meat, eggs, etc. can be killed by sufficient application of heat. Kitchen cloths, dishcloths, cutting boards, knives, and other utensils will harbor bacteria if not carefully disinfected. Especially after contact with meat, fish, eggs, etc. they should be thoroughly washed with detergent and sterilized by either chlorination or boiling water.

Putting these three principles into practice translates into not only personal cleanliness but good health and fitness. The conscientious chef, moreover, will be aware of the temperature in the kitchen and in the storage of ingredients and be careful to judge whether they are safe to be eaten raw or should be prepared by heating instead. Sensitivity to even the slightest concern about spoilage will protect kitchen and customers from food poisoning.

The pursuit of good flavor and the safety of food may seem quite different things, but the professional chef will always have food safety in mind in the creation of fine cuisine.

The eyes of fish indicate freshness, as in this freshly caught yellowtail. The eyes of fresh fish are round and clear in color. Clouded and bloodshot eyes signal that freshness has passed.

Knives in the Japanese Kitchen

The kitchen knife, the *hocho*, is the most important tool in Japanese cookery. The word *hocho* (Ch. *paoding*) is said to come from the name of a legendary court cook, Pao Ding, described in the ancient Chinese philosophical treatise *Zhuangzi*. Later, the story goes, his name was applied to knives for preparing fish, meat, and vegetables. Great value is accorded to the *hocho*, to the extent that it is often likened to the "soul" of a chef, and much can be known about a chef's abilities simply by looking at his knife. Particularly in Japanese cuisine, where cutting skills are paramount, knives must answer to the demand for razor-sharpness and nuanced control.

Western knives are typically steel or stainless steel and double-ground, that is to say sharpened on both sides of the blade. By contrast, most Japanese knives have a single-ground blade in one of two types: *hon-yaki*, which is 100 percent high-carbon steel, and *kasumi* (also *awase*), or high-carbon steel forged onto soft iron. *Hon-yaki*, a high-end product crafted of the same material as traditional Japanese swords, boasts a sharp edge that keeps well, but because of its hardness takes longer to hone. The more commonly available *kasumi* consists of a steel edge to perform the actual cutting jacketed onto a body of soft iron. It cuts well and is more affordable and easier to maintain than *hon-yaki*, but suffers in terms of edge retention.

Whereas double-ground Western knives are made mainly to cleave food, dividing it left and right, single-ground Japanese *hocho* are efficiently designed to slice foods thinly without crushing the delicate tissue. The back side of the blade is curved to keep food from sticking, further enhancing cutting capability.

The three major kinds of *hocho* are *usuba*, *yanagiba* (sashimi), and *deba* (pp 18–21); together, these will serve most tasks in Japanese cooking. There is a varied array of other knives for custom purposes, including the *ai-deba*, which is made lighter than a *deba* for use on smaller foods; *hamo honegiri* knives, used in Kyoto cuisine to cut up the fine bones of *hamo* pike conger; sushi knives; knives for filleting *unagi* eel; and many more.

blade cross section

hon-yaki (single-forged steel)

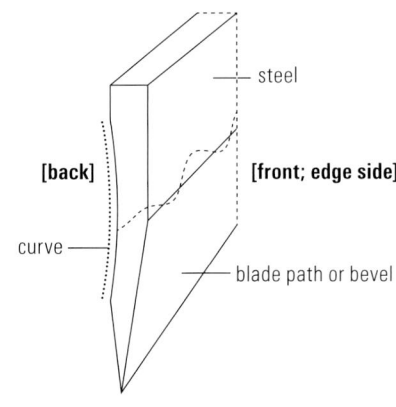

steel

[back]　　[front; edge side]

curve

blade path or bevel

kasumi (steel-jacketed soft iron)

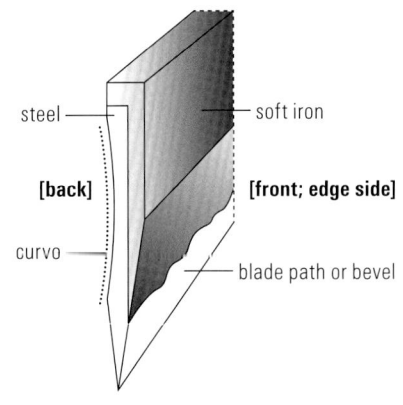

steel　　soft iron

[back]　　[front; edge side]

curve

blade path or bevel

Parts of a *Hocho*

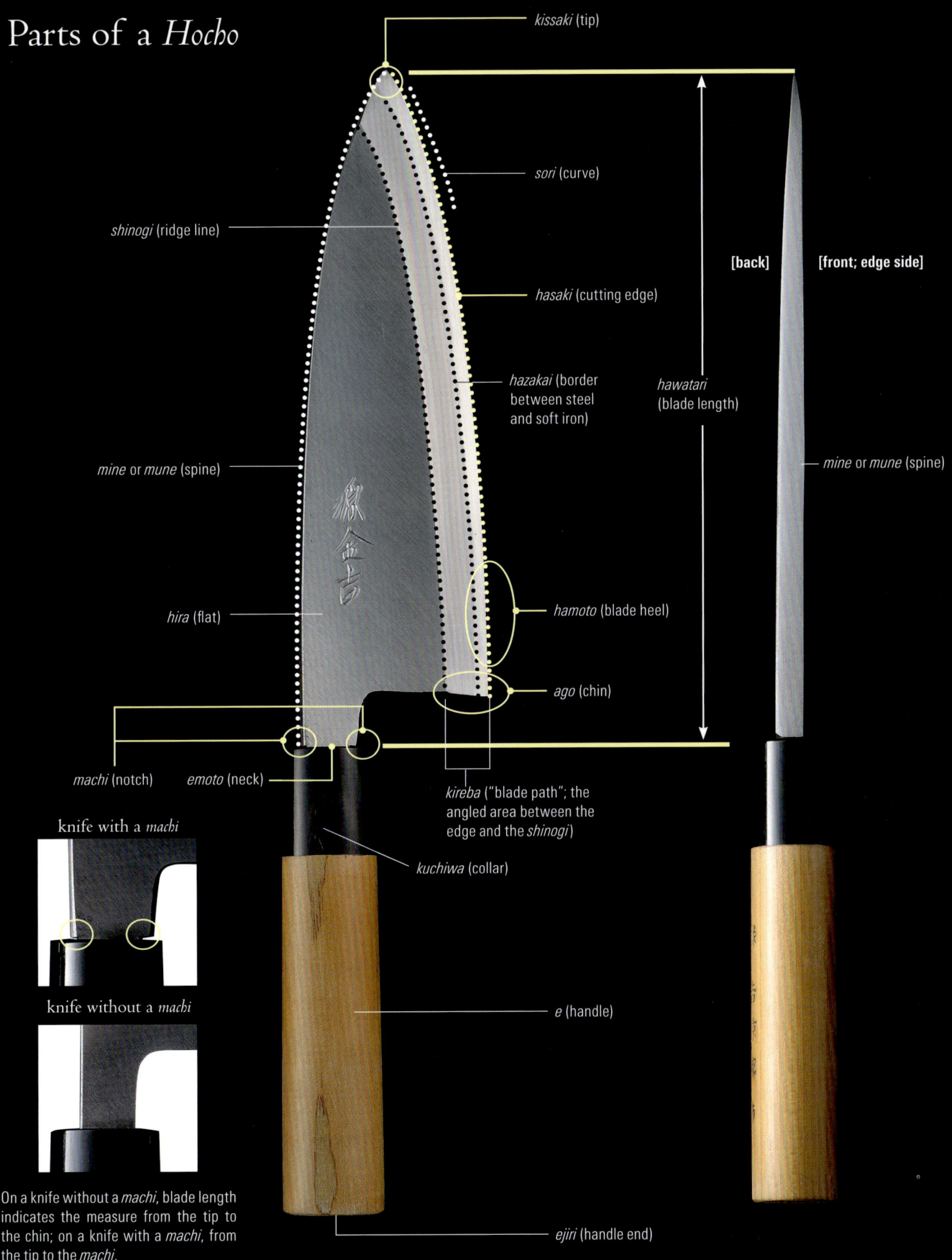

kissaki (tip)

sori (curve)

shinogi (ridge line)

hasaki (cutting edge)

hazakai (border between steel and soft iron)

mine or mune (spine)

hira (flat)

hamoto (blade heel)

ago (chin)

machi (notch)

emoto (neck)

kireba ("blade path"; the angled area between the edge and the *shinogi*)

kuchiwa (collar)

e (handle)

ejiri (handle end)

hawatari (blade length)

[back]

[front; edge side]

mine or mune (spine)

knife with a *machi*

knife without a *machi*

On a knife without a *machi*, blade length indicates the measure from the tip to the chin; on a knife with a *machi*, from the tip to the *machi*.

Types of *Hocho*

usuba

yanagiba

Shown here are the three basic types of *hocho*—*usuba*, *yanagiba*, and *deba*. *Deba* knives are further classified into *shomi-deba* ("true" *deba*; also *hon-deba*) and *ai-deba* depending on blade width. Each category of knife is available in varied blade lengths—e.g., five *shaku* five *bu* (approx. 167 millimeters), six *sun* (approx. 180 millimeters), and so on—measured in the traditional units: *shaku* (approx. 300 millimeters), *sun* (approx. 30 millimeters), and *bu* (approx. 3 millimeters).

deba: shomi-deba

deba: ai-deba

Uses of *Hocho*

Hocho come in many different shapes, sizes, edges, and thicknesses tailored to their purpose and the foods they are to cut. All knives in this book are single-ground, or sharpened on one side of the blade only. The characteristics of the three basic types of *hocho* are described below.

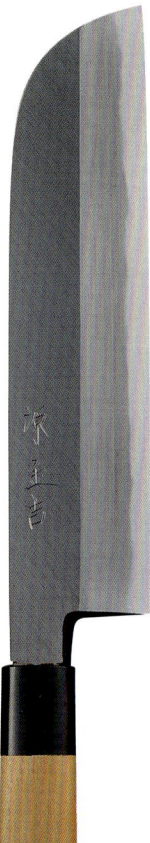

Usuba

Usuba knives from the Kansai (Kyoto-Osaka) area have a rounded head, for which they are also known as *kamagata* ("sickle-shaped"; see left). *Usuba* from Kanto (Tokyo and its environs) have square top corners. Primarily for use with vegetables, *usuba* are equipped with a thin blade that offers little resistance and is suited to skinning or to fine work such as *katsuramuki* rotary peeling and decorative cutting. Slicing is done using the entire length of the blade; mincing or julienning, the area from the tip to about the middle; and peeling, the heel. To cut straight on thick foods, direct the force toward the front (side facing right) of the blade. In terms of orientation, the front (*omote*) side of the blade is called the "outside" while the back (*ura*) side is the "inside."

Yanagiba

Yanagiba knives are named for their likeness to the tapered leaves of the willow (*yanagi*). They are also called sashimi knives after their purpose, although in the Kanto area the *takobiki*, another *hocho* characterized by a blade of uniform width from heel to tip, is sometimes used to make sashimi. The long blade of the *yanagiba* slices as it pulls, without crushing the tissue; its thinness minimizes resistance, ensuring a clean cut surface. Aside from sashimi, the *yanagiba* can be used to fillet meat as well as small fish with soft bones.

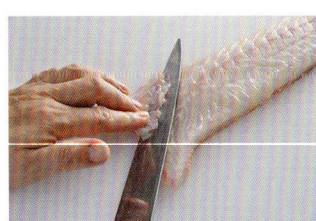 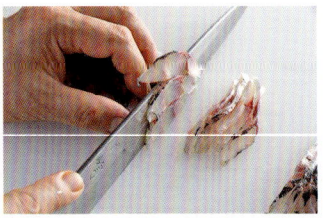

Deba

The hefty blade of the *deba* knife is designed to fillet fish and meat and to cut through tough bones. The blade is made extra thick along the spine to support greater pressure, in contrast to the tip, which is kept thinner for more precision work. Chopping bones and other hard materials is done with the part from the heel to the center of the blade, and filleting with the top half from the center to the tip. A range of knife dimensions accommodates foods of different sizes and thicknesses.

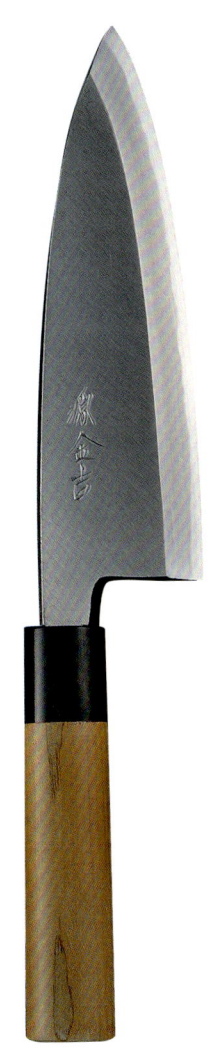

Ai-deba

Ai-deba knives are somewhat narrower in width than *deba* knives. Lighter and easier to handle, they are excellent for skinning or slicing fish but not as well suited to chopping through things like large bones. To cut hard objects using an *ai-deba*, place the edge against the surface and drive the blade in by pushing on the spine with the left hand.

Posture and Grip

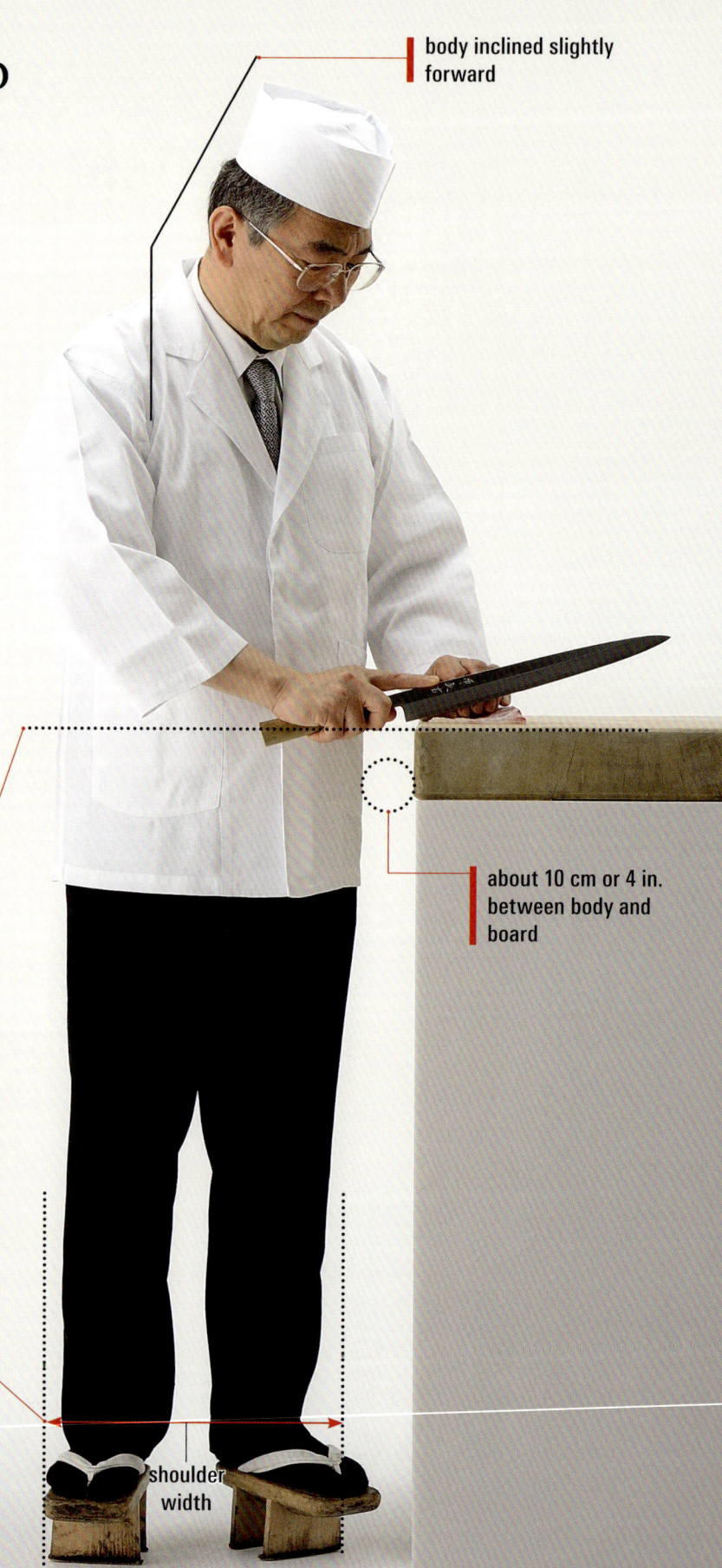

body inclined slightly forward

When using a *hocho*, it is important to stand at a proper distance from the cutting board and maintain correct posture to facilitate smooth movement. A correct hold is the key to skillful manipulation. Some chefs wear tall *geta* clogs in the kitchen in order to adjust their height in relation to the board and also to make it easier to serve food to customers sitting across from them at a counter.

In the most basic technique, the knife is inserted perpendicularly into the food; the illustration here shows this basic stance. Depending on where the cut is to be made, adjust your own position by pulling your right foot backward or forward.

about 10 cm or 4 in. between body and board

cutting board at level of navel

feet apart at shoulder width

shoulder width

NOTE: The directions given in this book are intended for handling of right-handed knives. For handling of left-handed knives, reverse the directions given. (The chef at right is photographed without an apron to better show the position of his feet.)

Basic Posture

- Stand at an angle from the cutting board. Set your feet shoulder-width apart, pulling your right foot half a step backward so that the blade can be positioned to enter perpendicularly when making a cut.
- Place the cutting board at the height of your navel and hold the knife perpendicular to the board.
- Keep your body at about a fist's length (approximately 10 cm or 4 in.) away from the board.
- Incline yourself slightly forward and direct your gaze to the inside (back) of the blade.

Hand position

- Hold the food in place by curling your left hand over it into a light fist as though cupping an egg inside.
- Rest the first knuckle of your left middle or index finger against the flat of the knife and shift the hand away from the blade as you cut.

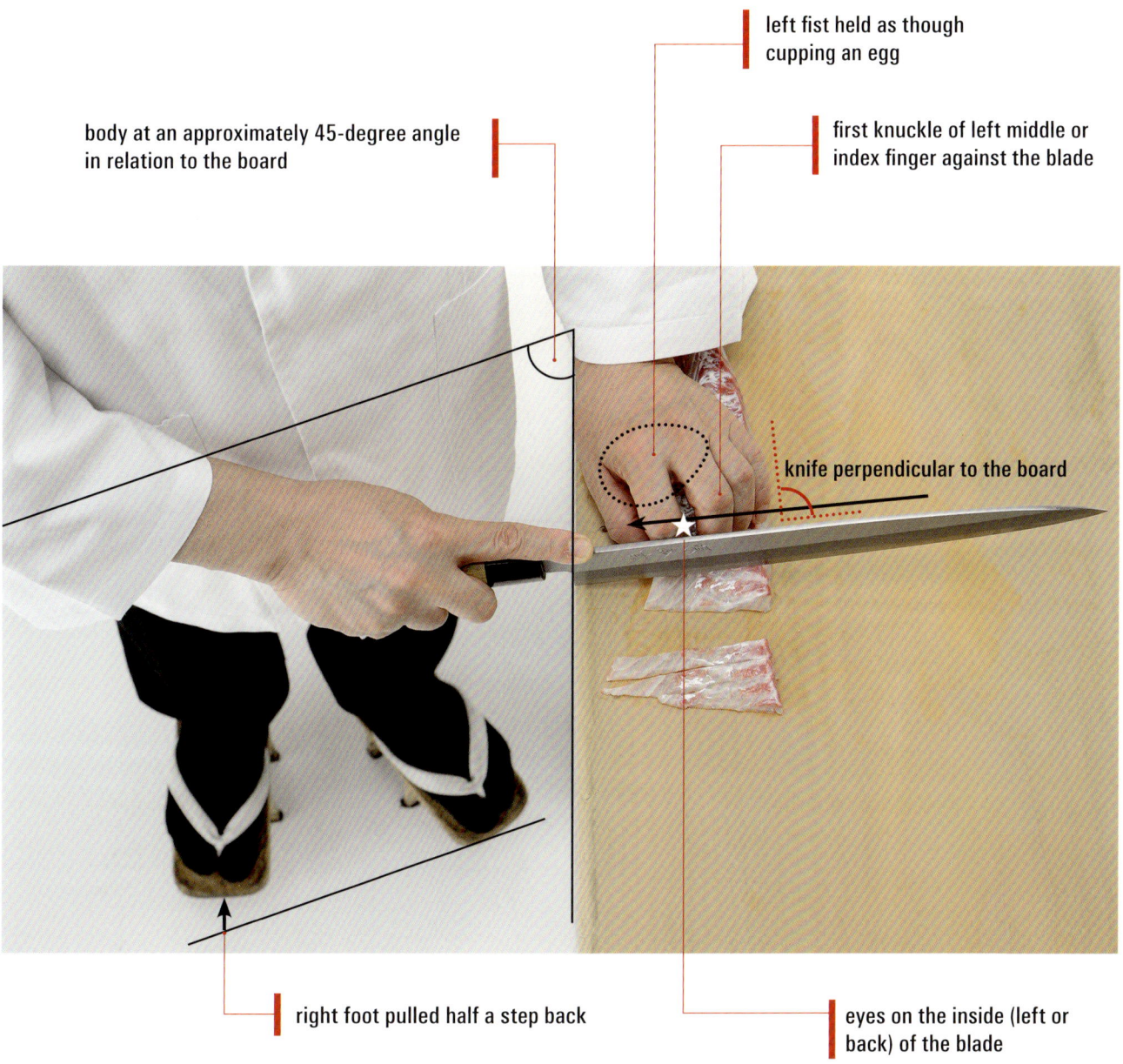

left fist held as though cupping an egg

body at an approximately 45-degree angle in relation to the board

first knuckle of left middle or index finger against the blade

knife perpendicular to the board

right foot pulled half a step back

eyes on the inside (left or back) of the blade

Basic Grip

Regardless of type, all *hocho* are held in basically the same way. Mastering the correct grip is essential to cutting precisely and efficiently with minimum force.

Usuba

edge side

back

Mincing

With the *hocho* spine-side up, take the area near the heel of the blade between your thumb and index finger; lightly wrap your other fingers around the handle. Firmly gripping with the thumb and index finger helps stabilize the blade, making this the optimum hold for mincing and skinning vegetables.

Peeling

For *katsuramuki* rotary peeling or decorative cutting, hold the *hocho* as described at left but with the blade held horizontal to the surface to be peeled, as shown.

Yanagiba

Start by holding as you would an *usuba* knife. When filleting fish, extend the index finger over the spine; this allows you to sense the blade all the way to the tip and also stabilizes the knife, ensuring smooth, straight slicing.

Deba

Filleting fish

Start by holding as you would an *usuba* knife. Place your index finger along the spine as with the *yanagiba* but further forward, pushing your fist up near the root of the blade. This stabilizes the center of gravity and makes it easier to work while filleting fish and meat.

Chopping

Hold the handle lightly near the end. Grasping the end helps exert more force on the heel—which is heavier compared with the rest of the blade—thus imparting the power necessary to cut through tough bones or chop flesh finely.

Knife Maintenance

The Whetstone

Japanese kitchen knives must be regularly sharpened on a whetstone to refresh the blade, which dulls with repeated use.

Whetstones are classified into two types according to whether they are from natural quarried stone or synthetic abrasives. Japan being a land of frequent volcanic and other geological activity, it has historically been blessed with an excellent supply of natural stone. Stones believed to have been used for whetting blades have been uncovered from archaeological sites dated to the Jomon period (ca. 10,000 B.C.–ca. 300 B.C.); eighth-century documents from the Shosoin treasury in Nara include references to whetstones from different parts of the country, and a whetstone quarry appears in the *Jingoji ezu* (Pictorial Map of Jingoji Temple), from 1230. Today, since the number of quarries has been declining, synthetic whetstones are most common, and high-quality natural whetstones are extremely expensive.

Natural whetstones vary greatly according to geological source and environment; type and hardness will differ depending on locale and even on where the stone was mined within a particular locale. High-quality whetstones are usually named after their source, for example *Tanba aoto* (from Tanba in Kyoto prefecture) or *Amakusado* (from Amakusa, Kumamoto prefecture). *Awasedo*, a finishing whetstone produced from slate that, due to geological factors, can only be obtained near Kyoto, is especially esteemed for the fineness of its particles.

Both natural and synthetic whetstones are available in three grades—*arato* (coarse), *nakato* (fine), and *shiageto* (finishing)—each fit for its own purpose. Grain size is measured in "grit" (#), with higher grit index indicating progressively finer grain. *Arato* ranges from about #120 to #600 and, being quite coarse, is primarily used to repair chipped blades. *Nakato* is for daily sharpening; those of about #1200 are suitable for *hocho*. To make edges keep longer, chefs further refine them with the *shiageto*, which usually measures above #4000. These last two grades are the ones a chef should procure for day-to-day maintenance.

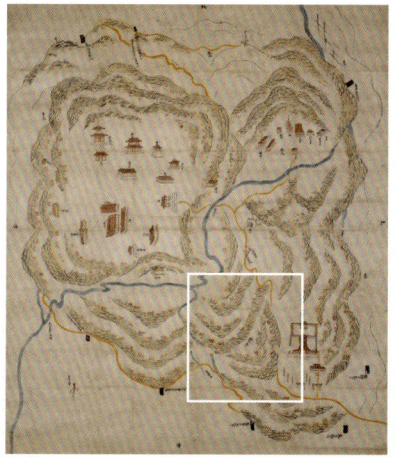

Top: *Jingoji ezu* (1230)
Bottom: Detail showing location of quarry, labeled 砥取峯 ("whetstone-quarry mountain")

A natural *shiageto* (above) and *nakato* (right). The *nakato* is made of *aoto*, a rare slate quarried only in Kyoto that is highly prized for its fineness. Finishing with a *shiageto* enhances both sharpness and edge retention.

The Sharpening Process

The cutting performance of a chef's knives is considered key to the quality of the cuisine. A uniformly thin and keen edge enters food smoothly with little resistance, producing cuts that bring out the best in the ingredients. A knife should be sharpened until its edge is perfectly smooth.

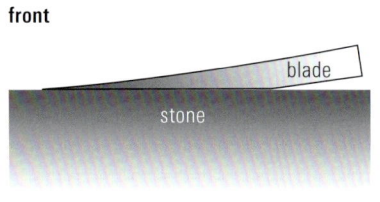

front

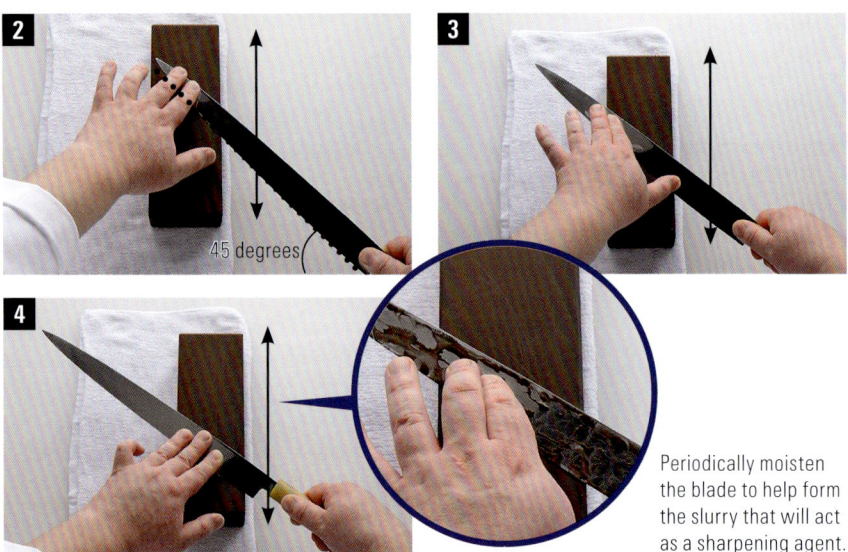

Periodically moisten the blade to help form the slurry that will act as a sharpening agent.

back

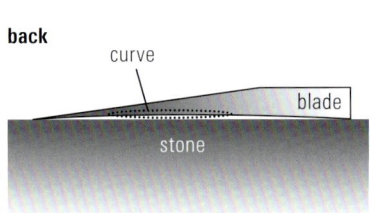

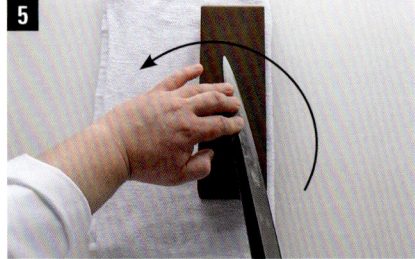

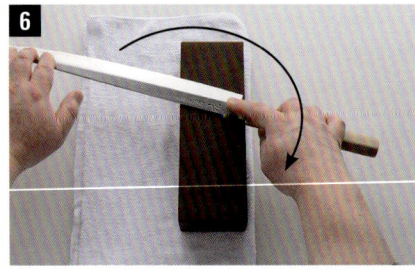

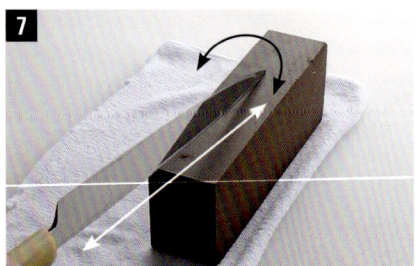

Sharpening

1 Soak the whetstone in water for about an hour beforehand, because the friction of whetting a blade on a dry surface may cause the edge to chip. Giving the stone plenty of water also allows this water to mix with the grit that shaves off against the blade, forming a slurry that acts as a sharpening agent.

2 Place a damp, well-wrung-out towel under the stone, both to prevent the stone from drying out and to hold it in place. Lay the stone on the towel with the shortest side facing you at a distance of about one fist. Start working on the beveled side of the blade (the front) from the tip end, keeping it at a 45-degree angle from the vertical axis and holding down with the fingers so that the bevel of the blade fits flush against the stone.

3 As you slide the blade across the stone, grasp the handle firmly with your right hand and with the fingers of your left hand press down on the blade (be careful not to press too hard and injure yourself).

4 Whet the upper part of the blade about ten times, then the middle part ten times, and finally the lower part ten times. For long knives such as the *yanagiba*, work a quarter of the length at a time, ten times each.

5 Turn the blade over to work the back side. Be careful not to sharpen this side too much, since doing so will reduce the back curve (see p. 16). Run the blade gently over the stone, circling it around to the left as you move from tip to heel.

6 Once you have made a semicircle, reverse the process and rotate the blade back down toward the right. Flip the knife over and sharpen the front again three more times, sprinkling water as you go to wash away the slurry.

7 Roll the stone over on its side and slide the knife tip and spine straight against it, back and forth. Then slide the spine back and forth again while tipping to either side (this restores the bevel on the spine that was flattened out when it was first rubbed). Knives are sharpened several times a day, as needed, maintaining the blade, the tip of the spine, and tip of the blade, for best performance.

A polisher made from a rolled-up old dishcloth bound with kite string. A regular dishcloth or sponge may also be used.

Polishing

1 After the blade has been sharpened, it needs to be polished. Place the knife on a cutting board, front side up. Apply cleansing agent to a dishcloth and polish the blade from the heel toward the tip. Scrub hard to completely remove the slurry caught deep in the fine scratches on the blade.

2 Repeat step **1** on the back side.

3 Repeat again along the spine.

4 To polish the wood of the handle, switch to cleansing agent and a scrubbing brush. (Do not polish the collar, since it may scratch.)

5 Finally, clean the base of the blade near the handle using a sanding block or other solid abrasive.

6 Rub to remove dirt and rust.

7 Be sure to remove all soiling thoroughly to prevent rusting of the blade above the collar.

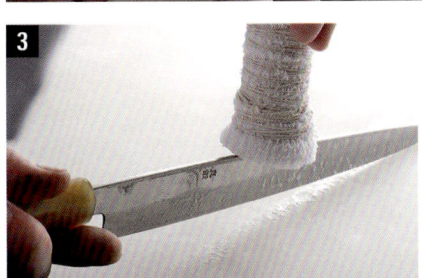

Caring for the Stone

1 The top center of the whetstone will gradually become concave with repeated use, requiring it to be periodically resurfaced. Resurfacing can be done using a concrete block or other hard, flat object. Moisten the stone and place it diagonally on the block, rubbing back and forth until the surface has evened out.

2 Bevel the edges of the stone (to prevent sharp corners against which the knife might hit, chipping the blade).

3 Finish the surface with a whetstone polisher.

4 Finish the bevels on the edges as well.

The Forging of *Hocho*

Kitchen knives are largely manufactured in one of three methods. *Uchiha-mono* knives are hammered from steel in traditional fashion, while die-cut knives lend themselves to mass production, and Western-style knives often use forged stainless steel. In *uchiha-mono*, steel and soft iron are heated and shaped with a hammer. The process encompasses dozens of steps that are mostly performed by hand, so that it takes months to produce a single knife. Instead of a die, artisans refer to a model to craft their desired shape. While not suited to mass production, *uchiha-mono* does carry the advantage of allowing knives to be created in a free variety of forms.

As discussed earlier (p. 16), traditional Japanese *hocho* may either be purely steel *hon-yaki* or the more commonly available *kasumi*. *Kasumi* knives combine keenness with durability by adopting hard steel (called *hagane*) for the cutting edge and more supple soft iron (*jigane*) for the remainder of the blade. The forging process starts by welding the *hagane* and *jigane* together, and then the *jigane* is hammered at a temperature of about 1650°F (900°C) (see photo). The whole is hammered and shaped while being kept at high heat. After cooling and several more steps, including careful refinements to the shape of the blade, the knife is put through *yaki-ire*, or "flame-hardening";

this tempering process involves heating the blade to roughly about 1500°F (800°C) and then rapidly quenching it again to take advantage of the material properties of steel, which hardens and strengthens when brought suddenly back down from a certain critical temperature. The blade is next hammered to correct the warps introduced during *yaki-ire*, and then the edge repeatedly ground to the proper thinness, the *jigane* polished, and the handle added before the knife is finally complete. Each and every task—more than twenty in the forging part alone—depends on the skills and experience of the artisan.

The forging process. The *jigane* is hammered at a temperature of about 1650°F (900°C).

A correctly sharpened blade shows a keen and uniformly thin edge. An unmaintained edge blunts and droops over time, to the detriment of performance.

Chapter 2

Red Sea Bream

Yellowtail

Bonito

Butterfish

Salmon

Standard Techniques

The basic method of carving fish is filleting, dividing the fish into three parts (*sanmai-oroshi*; upper and lower fillets and central bones). Fish that are thin or large may be divided into five parts (*gomai-oroshi*; upper dorsal, upper ventral, and lower dorsal, lower ventral fillets and central bones). This chapter explains mainly the three-piece filleting process for different kinds of fish, followed by instructions for slicing into sashimi.

By time-honored custom in Japan, marine fish are placed with the head facing left and the belly down. This rule is generally followed when working with fish on the cutting board as well as when serving it on the table. Following that left-facing orientation, the upper side of the fish is customarily called *uwami*, or upper flesh, and the lower side is called *shitami*, or lower flesh. Fish are lined up facing left at the time of catch and shipped in that same orientation, so the lower fillet is likely to lose its freshness first. When shipping time is short, which side is used for what purpose may not matter, but chefs have long fallen into the practice of using the *uwami* flesh for sashimi and the *shitami* side for cooked dishes.

The Secrets of *Tsukuri*

Tsukuri, as professional chefs call sashimi, is fish sliced thinly and eaten after dipping in some seasoning, such as salt or shoyu. Enjoyment of raw fish is made possible by an array of techniques developed not only by experienced chefs, but by fishermen, distributors of fish, and many others.

When fish die, the nucleotide adenosine triphosphate (ATP) that transports energy between cells in the muscles is converted to inosinic acid or inosine monophosphate (IMP), which is a source of umami taste. The peak of IMP production differs for each fish. In the case of yellowtail stored at 32°F (0°C), IMP begins to increase sharply about four hours after death and peaks in fourteen to sixteen hours. For tuna, the peak of IMP production is one day after death, and for *hirame* about two days. What the chef tries to do, in cooperation with the fishermen, the distribution chain, and local fishmonger, is to obtain fish that contains IMP and serve it in a timely manner. Shoyu contains large amounts of sodium glutamate, and the synergy of IMP with sodium glutamate can be utilized to further augment the umami of the fish.

When the concentration of ATP in the muscles of fish declines after death, the proteins in the muscle fiber begin to congeal, and the tissue stiffens (rigor mortis). The time it takes for the muscles to stiffen differs from one fish to another. If a fish struggles violently at the time it dies, its body temperature rises and the quality of the meat is reduced. The *ikejime* spiking technique (see p. 40) is designed to cut the spinal cord and prevent the fish from struggling, thereby suppressing the exhaustion of the ATP in the muscles and delaying the process of rigor mortis. It is also important to drain out the blood as soon as possible, not only for the sake of the appearance of the fish but to forestall the dispersal of proteins in the muscle by enzymes contained in the blood.

Other techniques for enhancing the umami of fish include *arai* (ice bath), which gives slices of fish like carp and sea bream a crisp, crunchy texture. *Arai* calls for carving the fresh fish quickly before the flesh stiffens and slicing it thinly, then plunging the slices into ice water in order to cause the muscles to contract and stiffen. The muscles will more easily contract in hard water, which contains plenty of calcium ions, than in soft water.

When cutting fish, the use of a well-sharpened knife assures the minimum loss of nutrients. The flesh is soft and the cut surface may stick to the knife. The Japanese knives for cutting *tsukuri* are single-ground so that when a slice is cut away from the face of the flesh, it does not flop against the remaining block. In addition, the blade is thinner toward its tip so that when the knife is drawn back, less force impinges on the fish, preventing damage to the muscle cells as it passes.

The toughness of flesh differs greatly from one fish species to another, and cutting techniques differ accordingly. Flesh that is harder to chew is sliced thin, while softer flesh is cut more thickly. The collagen contained in the fish muscle provides the much-valued texture of sashimi.

Tsukuri is served in attractive arrangements called *ashirai* (p. 72) with *ken* and *tsuma* garnishes and Japanese herbs for aroma and spice. The traditional reason for these garnishes is that they helped prevent the growth of bacteria and inhibited spoilage, but today they are more important for their fragrance and role in adding lively flavors.

The Merits of the *Yanagiba* knife

What makes a fillet of fish into the delicacy that is sashimi is, above all, the way it is cut—the *kirikuchi*. Slices that are smooth and lustrous—what the chefs and specialists describe as "clean cut" (*kirikuchi ga tatte iru*)—are essential to the quality of the dish. The aesthetically pleasing cut, delighting the eye when it is served, and the smooth yet chewy texture when savored on the palate—these are the qualities most prized in sashimi cuisine. What kind of knife is needed to cut sashimi with such qualities? What features of a knife enable it to perform that task? They are described here in relation to the structure of the Japanese knife (*wabocho*) blade.

The many types of knives used in Japanese cuisine have been presented above; here the main focus is on the *yanagiba*, the knife most often used to slice sashimi. Like other traditional Japanese kitchen knives, the *yanagiba* is single ground; it is made with a longer blade than other knives so that each slice of fish can be completed with just one pull of the knife, as described on page 54. The knife is exceedingly sharp along its entire length (see photo on p. 18), but the secret of the effectiveness of a professional chef's knife is best seen through a digital microscope (Figure 1).

The upper left-hand image shows the side of a freshly sharpened *yanagiba* blade and the lower left image—showing the thin, white line running vertically—is the cutting edge taken in frontal view. As the measurement scale shows, the thickness of the blade is no more than 2 or 3 micrometers at its edge. The action of cutting involves applying highly localized force to an object. The greater the force, or, alternatively, the smaller the surface area to which force is applied, the greater the effect of the force on the structure of the object. This explains why the *yanagiba*'s extremely thin blade slices easily through fish flesh in one stroke. The microscope's image also shows that the cutting edge of the *yanagiba* knife is not entirely straight and smooth but is actually jagged, with some indentations as deep as 4.38 micrometers (Figure 1, upper left). Since sashimi is sliced with the knife moving in one

direction only (*hiki-kiru*), these fine indentations on the blade edge act like saw-teeth, facilitating the knife's entry and passage. In other words, if we think on the scale of micrometers, the blade is acting like a high-precision saw, so these structural characteristics of the blade are what make possible precise slicing.

For comparison, an ordinary kitchen knife of the type found in most households was also photographed and studied. The knife was one that had been used for some time without sharpening. Like most Western kitchen knives, it is double-ground. The width of the cutting edge is between 18 and 19 micrometers (Figure 1, lower right), far wider than that of the *yanagiba*. Seen from the side, the blade edge does not show the slight indentations observed on the *yanagiba* blade (Figure 1, top right). Cutting a fillet of fish with such a knife will not result in a clean, smoothly cut slice. This is because the blade's cutting edge is relatively wider than that of the *yanagiba*, decreasing the force it applies to the flesh.

Even an ordinary kitchen knife, if carefully sharpened, can have a cutting edge of between 5 to 6 micrometers. The knife will also have the indentations observed on the *yanagiba*, but they are likely to be quite deep ones of a few dozen micrometers, which could result in damage to the flesh. The fine and relatively shallow indentations shown on the *yanagiba* at left are not present. An ordinary knife, therefore, does not cut lightly and smoothly into the flesh of the fish without damaging it. A clear conclusion from this data is that no matter how sharp a household knife is, it cannot be expected to cut the smooth-surfaced slices possible with a *yanagiba*.

Observing the slices of flounder cut by a professional chef using the *yanagiba* blade and the kitchen knife blade photographed above (Figure 2) provides further examples of this point. The slice were made using the *hegi-zukuri* cutting technique (see p. 116).

Slices cut with the ordinary kitchen knife (right side), cut by either technique, show numerous white-flecked spots. These are where the indentations on the flesh are

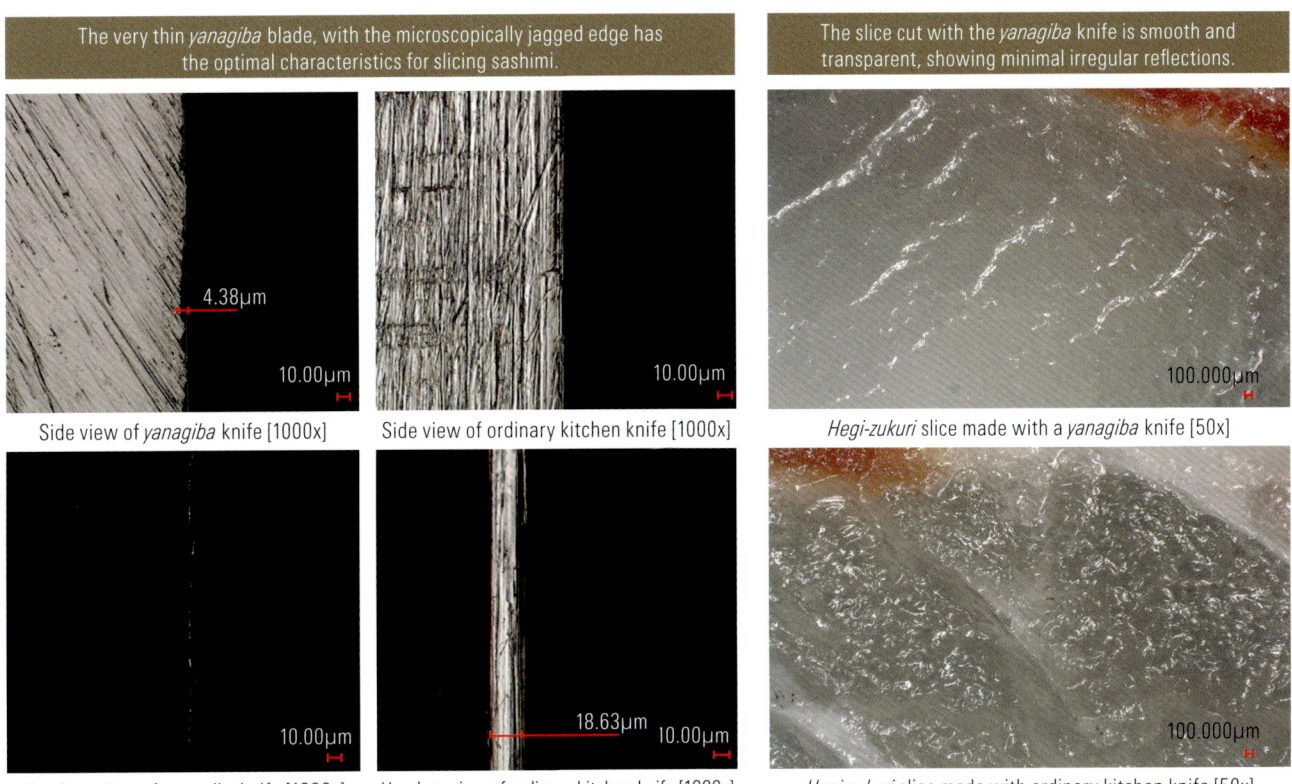

The very thin *yanagiba* blade, with the microscopically jagged edge has the optimal characteristics for slicing sashimi.

The slice cut with the *yanagiba* knife is smooth and transparent, showing minimal irregular reflections.

4.38μm

10.00μm

10.00μm

Side view of *yanagiba* knife [1000x]

Side view of ordinary kitchen knife [1000x]

100.000μm

Hegi-zukuri slice made with a *yanagiba* knife [50x]

10.00μm

18.63μm   10.00μm

Head-on view of *yanagiba* knife [1000x]

Head-on view of ordinary kitchen knife [1000x]

100.000μm

Hegi-zukuri slice made with ordinary kitchen knife [50x]

Figure 1: Comparison of *Yanagiba* blade and Ordinary Kitchen Knife Blades

Figure 2: Surface of Flounder Sliced with *Yanagiba* and Regular Kitchen Knives

pronounced, causing the light to reflect. In the *hegi-zukuri* image, large tears in the flesh are observed. The surface of sashimi cut with the ordinary kitchen knife is not smooth and clean, but reveals parts where the flesh has been torn and the cell structure damaged. What this demonstrates is that if a poorly maintained ordinary kitchen knife is used (the same being true for a regular, double-ground Western-style kitchen knife), even the skill of an experienced chef will not produce cleanly cut sashimi.

In the photographs of the slices made with the *yanagiba* blade, however, indentations on the surface and white-flecked reflections are few. Also, in the upper left photo showing the *hegi-zukuri* slice, the presence of fine lines of tissue are seen. These are visible because the cut is so clean and sharp that the tissue structure of the fish remains undisturbed. Looking at the image of sashimi cut with the ordinary kitchen knife, this delicate tissue is not

visible, whether because the refracted light blots it out or because the tissue has been crushed. As this shows, slicing with the same way, that done with the *yanagiba* knife clearly achieves a smoother, precisely cut surface.

Another factor thought to be essential to good sashimi is the way the slices pick up the dipping shoyu. Is the surface of sashimi cut with a *yanagiba* knife so smooth that shoyu does not adhere to it easily? The answer might seem to be straightforward, but according to the professional chefs, that is not always the case. The way sashimi chefs (*mukoita*) explain it, when fish is cut with a knife other than a well-sharpened *yanagiba*, the cell structure of the flesh is damaged, causing the cells to spill their content. Oils contained in the tissue can form a film over the slices that in some cases make it difficult to pick up shoyu when dipped. Such explanations await verification by scientific experimentation.

Fish Anatomy for Chefs

For the purpose of this book, we divide fish into three types: oval fish, flat fish, and round fish. Since the methods for cutting fish are fairly uniform for each of the three types, a good grasp of the fish's bone structure is the best way to understand the correct procedure for carving. Oval fish like sea bream, tilefish, and sea bass, flat fish like flounder and butterfish, and cylindrical fish like devil stinger and bartail flathead, respectively, have similar bone structures. In the diagrams, pink indicates hard bones and blue, soft bones.

Oval fish

Example: Red sea bream or snapper (*tai*/*madai*)

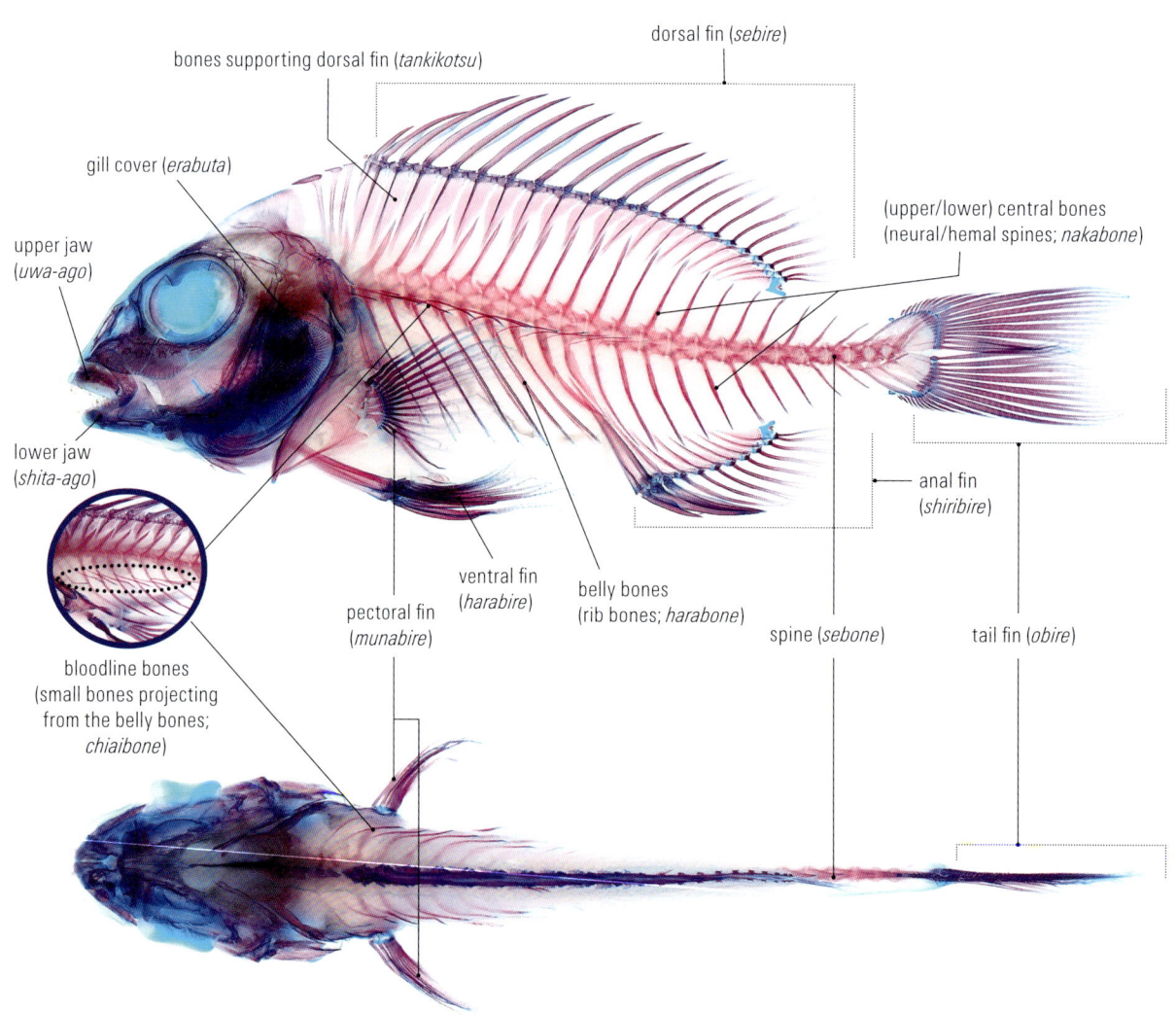

bones supporting dorsal fin (*tankikotsu*)

dorsal fin (*sebire*)

gill cover (*erabuta*)

(upper/lower) central bones (neural/hemal spines; *nakabone*)

upper jaw (*uwa-ago*)

lower jaw (*shita-ago*)

anal fin (*shiribire*)

ventral fin (*harabire*)

belly bones (rib bones; *harabone*)

bloodline bones (small bones projecting from the belly bones; *chiaibone*)

pectoral fin (*munabire*)

spine (*sebone*)

tail fin (*obire*)

Flat fish
Example: Flounder (*hirame*)

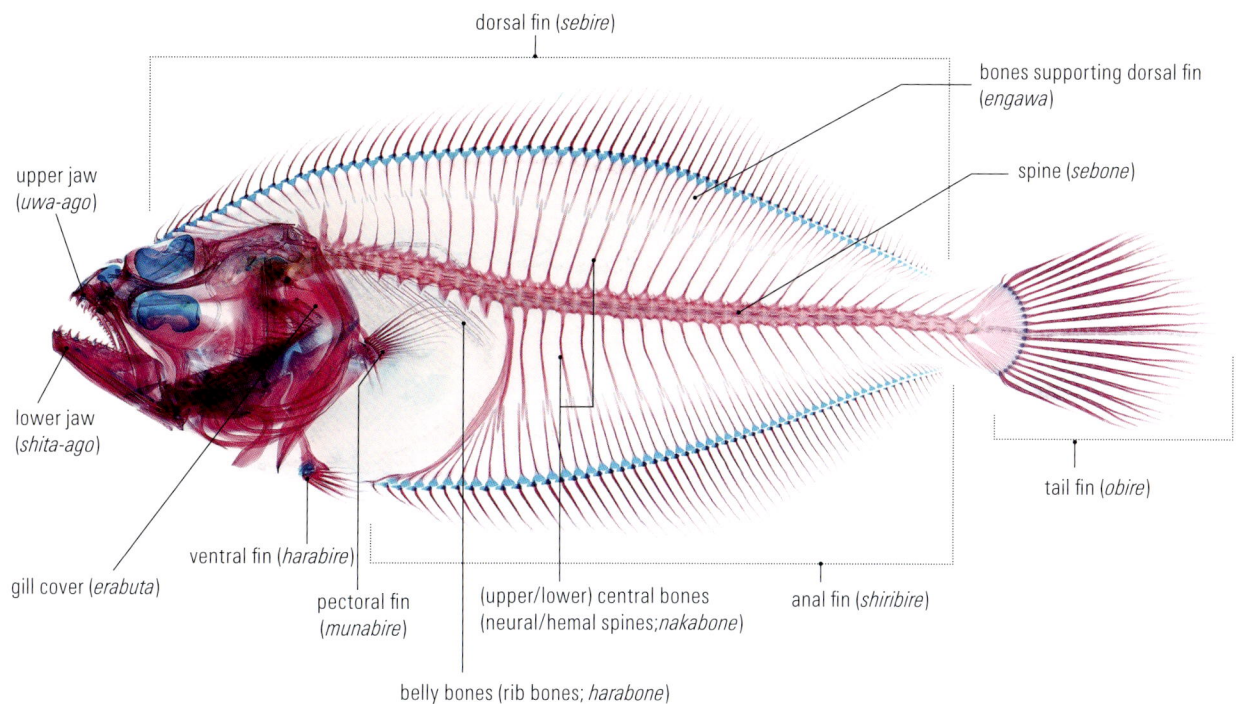

dorsal fin (*sebire*)

bones supporting dorsal fin (*engawa*)

spine (*sebone*)

upper jaw (*uwa-ago*)

lower jaw (*shita-ago*)

gill cover (*erabuta*)

ventral fin (*harabire*)

pectoral fin (*munabire*)

(upper/lower) central bones (neural/hemal spines; *nakabone*)

anal fin (*shiribire*)

tail fin (*obire*)

belly bones (rib bones; *harabone*)

Round fish (cylindrical)
Example: Bartail flathead (*kochi*)

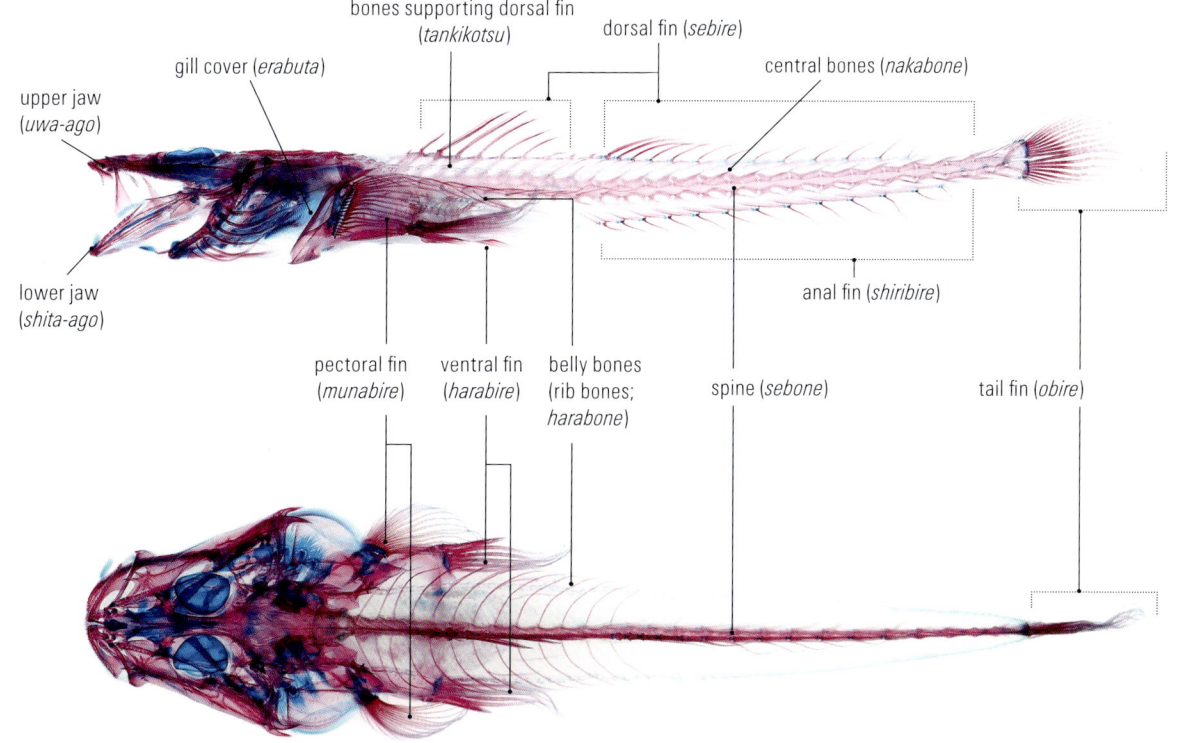

bones supporting dorsal fin (*tankikotsu*)

dorsal fin (*sebire*)

central bones (*nakabone*)

gill cover (*erabuta*)

upper jaw (*uwa-ago*)

lower jaw (*shita-ago*)

pectoral fin (*munabire*)

ventral fin (*harabire*)

belly bones (rib bones; *harabone*)

anal fin (*shiribire*)

spine (*sebone*)

tail fin (*obire*)

Spiking Fish

wire for neural spiking

Ikejime

Fishermen and chefs practice *ikejime*—spiking the brain and severing the spinal cord in order to best preserve the freshness of fish. By killing with dispatch and draining the blood, the process of rigor mortis can be delayed, thereby enhancing freshness. Nerve spiking (*shinkeijime*) is the method of running a thin wire through the medulla oblongata and the spinal cord after killing fish by *ikejime*. (For the procedure for *ikejime* and *shinkeijime*, see pp. 41–43) These techniques require know-how and experience and cannot be used for fish caught in large quantities like mackerel and sardines, which are either flash-frozen in ice or left to die naturally on fishing boats. Blood is not drained out, so the fish lose their freshness faster than in the case of *ikejime*. *Ikejime* involves handling fish one by one and is generally reserved for high-quality fish like sea bream, flounder, and *suzuki* sea bass. In Japan *ikejime* is generally performed by fishmongers before delivering fish to a restaurant.

gaff with a wooden shaft

Maturation

Many people think sashimi is best when it is so fresh that the flesh still twitches after filleting, as in the case of *ikezukuri* ("live" slicing), but the umami of the fish is actually stronger when a few to a few dozen hours (varying with fish species and size) have passed after the fish is spiked by the *ikejime* method.

Generally, the flesh of a live fish has a springy texture; after death, the process of rigor mortis soon sets in and the flesh begins to harden. *Ikezukuri* sashimi is enjoyed before rigor mortis for the springy and crunchy texture and umami flavor of the fish. After rigor mortis has passed, the flesh begins to mature. During maturation, the umami content increases and the flesh becomes soft again. Live fish does not have much umami content, but when it dies, the action of enzymes produces inosinic acid, a component of umami. Maturation, then, is the process of inosinic acid production. The speed of maturation varies depending on the moisture content and other characteristics of the flesh as well as the workings of enzymes, and therefore experience and skill are required to determine when the umami of the fish is at its height. *Ikejime* helps retain freshness for some time, allowing optimal time to enjoy the peak of umami. Once the process of rigor mortis (the period of maturation) has passed, the flesh will steadily lose its freshness.

Sea Bream *Ikejime*

To delay the process of rigor mortis, spike the brain, then sever the medulla oblongata and the spinal cord of the brain-dead sea bream. It is crucial to cut the cord swiftly and accurately. Drain out the blood thoroughly following spiking to prevent a bad odor from pervading the flesh. This rule applies to all fish.

1 Place the head to the right and, holding the body with the left hand, drive the spike of the gaff into the head just behind the eyes.

2 Turn the fish over and place the head to the left. Opening the gill cover, insert the knife and cut through the spine (the medulla oblongata) at the base of the collar.

3 Turn the fish over, placing the head away from you and the body slanting up toward the right. Insert the knife at the base of the tail and sever the spine (cut the bone only, leaving the tail attached).

4 Run the spiking wire into the spinal cord from the tail all the way to the head.

5 Soak the fish in cold water for 5–6 minutes to drain out the blood. Swish the fish in the water to check whether the draining is complete.

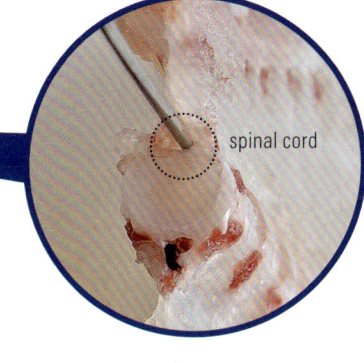

spinal cord

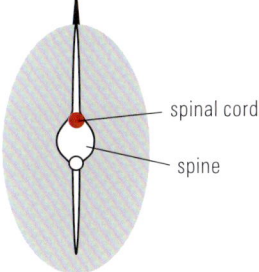

spinal cord

spine

Run the wire into the spinal cord, situated in the upper part of the spine.

Flounder *Ikejime*

Basically the *ikejime* of flounder is the same as that of sea bream, but since the flounder has a curved spine, it will be easier to run the wire into the spinal cord from the head side.

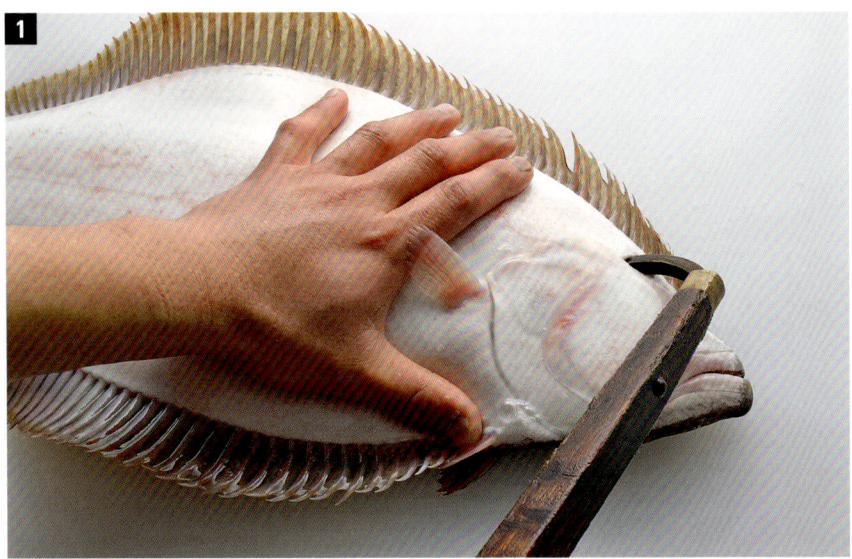

1. Turn the flounder over (face side on the cutting board), placing the head to the right. Drive the hook into the dorsal end of the gill cover.

2. Place the dorsal side facing you and the head to the left, with the body slanting upward toward the right. Insert the wire into the hole made by the hook in step **1** and run it through to the base of the tail.

3. Sever the spine (the medulla oblongata) at the dorsal side of the collar.

4. Soak the fish in ice water for 5–6 minutes to drain the blood.

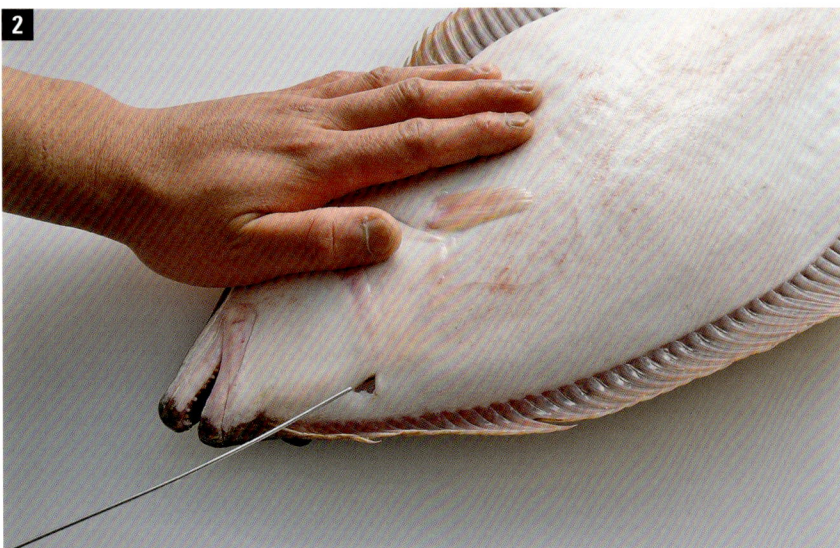

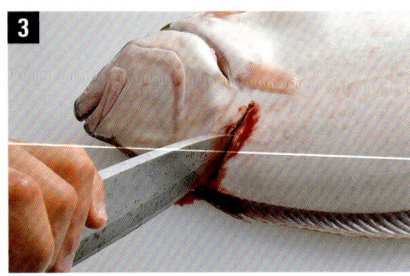

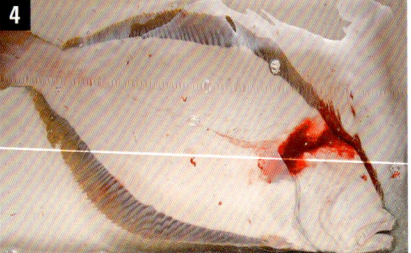

Devil Stinger *Ikejime*

Restaurants often purchase live devil stinger, the handling of which requires great care because of the poison-carrying spines in the fish's dorsal fin. The method of *ikejime* is the same as for sea bream, except that the wire is run in from the head side.

1. Wear a glove on the left hand to prevent injury from sharp spines. Holding the belly side with the left hand (avoiding the spines in the dorsal fin), drive the hook into the head (just behind the eyes).
2. Change the position of the fish and hold the head to face you. Insert the wire into the hole made in step 1 and run it through to the base of the tail.
3. Place the head to the left. Sever the spine (the medulla oblongata) at the dorsal end of the collar.
4. Soak the fish in ice water for 5–6 minutes to drain the blood.

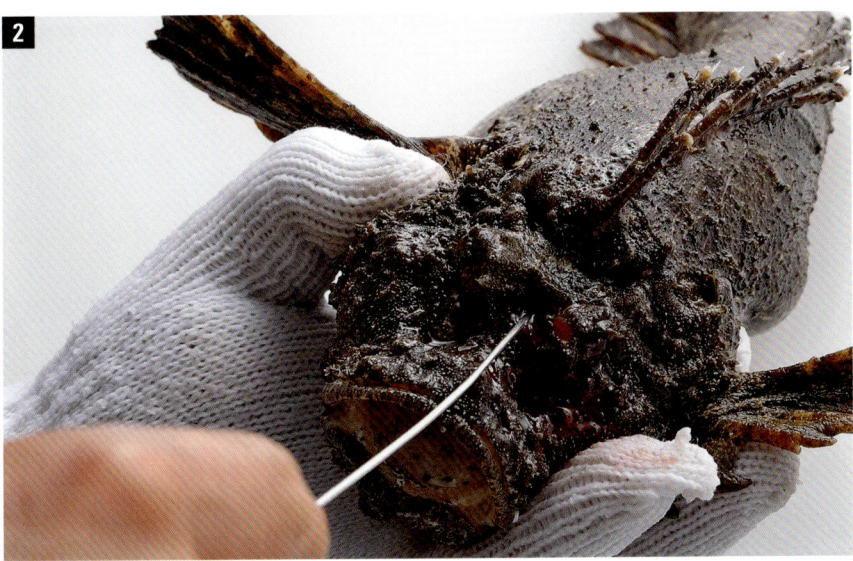

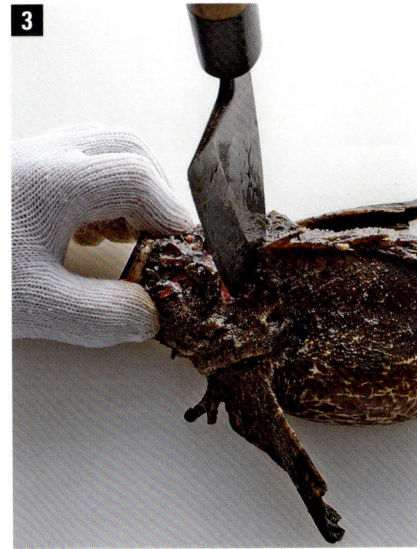

Madai
RED SEA BREAM
Pagrus major

An important member of the family Sparidae (order Perciformes), which includes breams and porgies, *madai* has long been favored in Japan for its appearance, color, and flavor. It is not only consumed as food but also has many other significant uses, including offerings to the gods. While there are more than one hundred species in the Sparidae family (Jp. *tai*), by strict definition the word *tai* used without modification can be assumed to be *madai* ("true" sea bream).

The fish is large, growing to as much as one meter in length, with a blackish red coat and cobalt blue spots on the back and elsewhere. It may also be identified by the blackish fringe on its anal fin. The deep blue streak above each eye grows darker during the spawning season. Wild *madai* are pink in color owing to their large diet of crustaceans such as shrimp and crab; farmed *madai* are raised in shallow enclosures and often appear darker as a result of greater exposure to the sun.

Wild sea bream weighing about two kilograms and measuring about thirty centimeters from below the eyes to the root of the tail are considered to look and taste the best and therefore command the best prices. Due to the tenderness of their flesh, female *madai* are generally more expensive than males.

There are two prime fishing seasons, one in spring and one in autumn. Females close to spawning in early spring turn a vibrant pink and are especially sought after as *sakura-dai*, or "cherry blossom bream"—a reference both to their appearance and to the flowers that also bloom at this time of the year. The spring season of the fish, which spans the time before, during, and after spawning, is from late February until April; the autumn season lasts through November from mid-September, when the fish begin to feed more, enhancing their flavor.

CUTTING RED SEA BREAM INTO THREE PIECES

Preparation

1 Insert the pectoral fin into the gill cover, so it will not be damaged.

2 Pectoral fin inserted into the gill cover. With dishes using the head or whole-fish sashimi (*sugata-zukuri*), keep the pectoral fins intact for an attractive appearance.

3 Grasping the head with the left hand, remove the scales with a scaler, in strokes moving from tail to head.

4 Remove the remaining scales around the fins and other areas by scraping with the tip of the *deba* knife. Be careful not to cut the skin or damage the fins.

5 Wash scales off the fish and blot dry with a cloth.

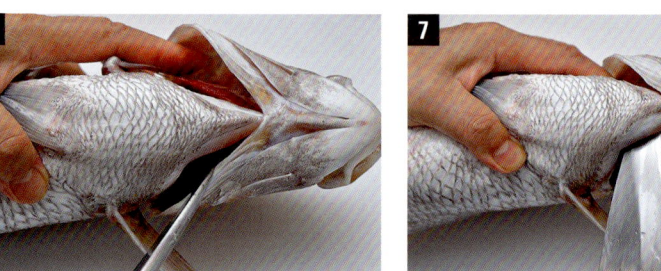

6 Place the fish with the head to the right and with the belly facing you. Open the gill cover with the forefinger of the left hand. Insert the tip of the knife into the gill cavity.

7 Insert the tip of the knife, blade facing right (*sakasabocho*), between the gills and the *kama* ("collar," the area between the gill cover and the pectoral fin) and cut the gill tip (at the base of the collar) away.

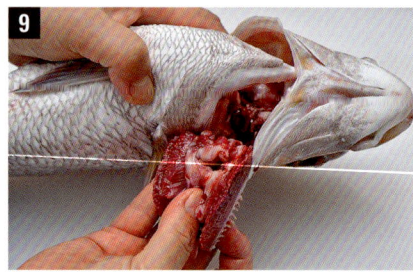

8 Cut away the gills where attached at the throat of the fish.

9 Insert fingers into where the gills were cut away and pull out the gills and attached organs.

10 With the head to the right and the belly facing you, firmly hold the fish as shown, with index finger in the gill slit; insert the knife at the incision made in step **8** above.

11 Cut to the left from the incision to a point between the ventral fins.

12 Reverse blade direction so that the knife faces the head (*sakasabocho*), insert blade tip into the vent, and cut to meet the incision of step **11**, keeping the knife insertion shallow in order to avoid slicing the internal organs.

13 Pull open the side of the fish slightly (as shown), and cut away the tissue holding the internal organs.

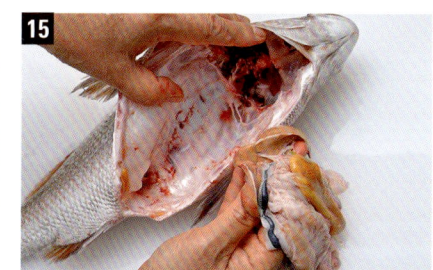

14 With the left hand, open the belly and gill cover and insert the fingers of the right hand under the internal organs.

15 With your fingers, carefully remove the internal organs.

16 With the blade facing the tail, make a shallow incision in the membrane under the spine that covers the swim bladder and blood pockets; be careful not to cut into the flesh.

17 Open the belly wide as shown.

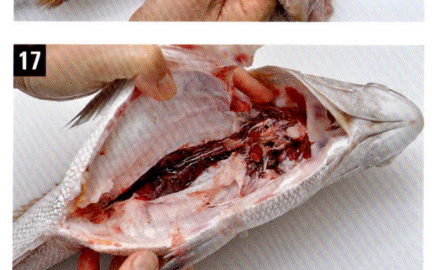

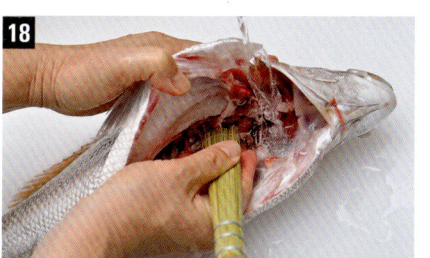
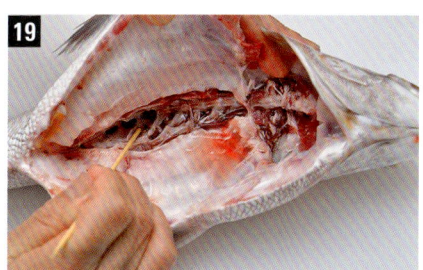

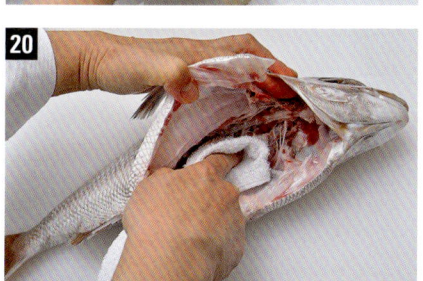
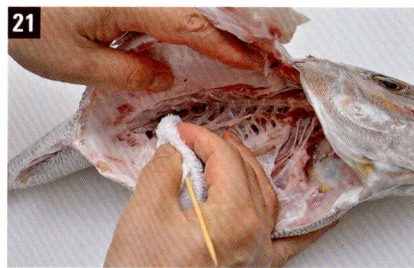

18 Under running water, use a *sasara* bamboo brush (or equivalent stiff-bristled brush) to clean out blood and debris.

19 With a bamboo pick or pointed skewer, clean out the last bits of the organs from the cavities.

20 Wash thoroughly and blot both the inner cavity and the outside of the fish dry with a cloth.

21 Wrap a bamboo pick with a cloth and remove any remaining bits of blood or debris.

Removing the head

1 Place the fish with the head to the left and the belly facing you. Insert the knife at the base of the pectoral fin.

2 Holding the head firmly, with thumb inside the head as shown, cut at an angle (roughly 45 degrees) with the blade pointing toward the front of the dorsal fin, as shown.

3 Lifting the head slightly and twisting it away from the body with the left hand, continue cutting diagonally toward the front of the dorsal fin until the knife strikes bone.

4 Turn the fish over, and as in step **1**, cut at an angle through the flesh at the base of the pectoral fin toward the front of the dorsal fin.

5 Continue the diagonal cut, as in steps **2**–**3**, and pull the head away to reveal its connection with the spine.

6 Cut through the skin and connection with the spine and remove the head. See pp. 58–59 for uses of the head.

Cutting the lower fillet

1 Place the fish with the tail at left and the belly facing you. Hold the fish with the left hand and cut in from the head end and over the central bones until the knife reaches the spine.

1

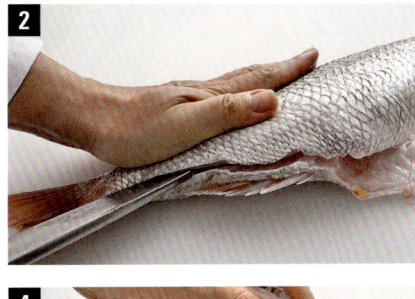

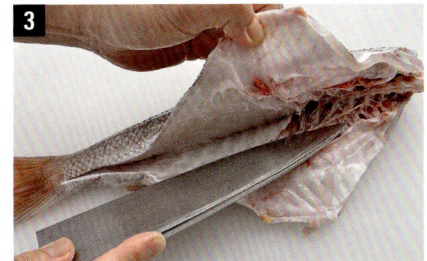

2 With the tip of the knife, make a shallow cut over the central bones and continuing as far as the base of the tail.

3 With the left hand, lift the flesh and cut in further from step **1** up to the spine.

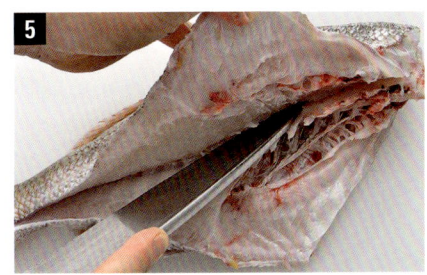

4 Holding the knife as shown, cut away the base of the belly bones from the spine.

5 Draw the tip of the knife along the spine, toward the tail.

6 Cut in as far as the tail.

7 Lifting the flesh with the left hand, slice 1–2 cm (½ in. to 1 in.) over the dorsal fin.

8 Close the fish and, with the knife flat, cut along the upper central bones beyond the spine, slicing over the dorsal fin.

9 Drawing the knife over the central bones, cut toward the tail. While you may open the fish to check the position of the knife, closing the fish keeps the knife in a horizontal position and prevents damage to the flesh.

10 At the midpoint of this cut, lift the fillet with the left hand (hold by the edge of the skin so as to avoid touching the flesh).

11 Continue cutting all the way to the tail.

12 At the tail, close the fish and cut the fillet from the base of the tail.

Cutting the upper fillet

1 Turn the fish over with the tail to the left and make an incision in the skin on the edge of the dorsal fin.

2 Lifting the flesh with the left hand, insert the knife at the incision and cut along the dorsal fin toward the tail.

3 Slice (dotted line) toward the base of the tail over the central bones as far as the spine.

4 Lifting the fillet with the left hand, cut into the base of the belly bones.

5 Cut over and along the spine all the way to the base of the tail.

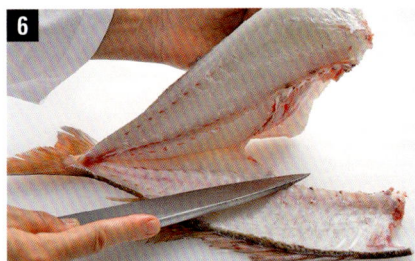

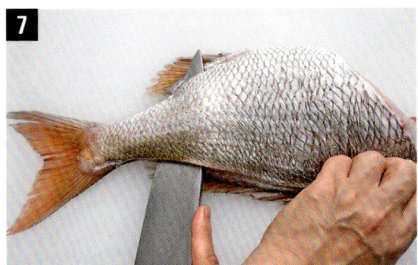

6 Lifting the fillet with the left hand and checking to assure the knife is over the spine, continue cutting inward.

7 Close the fish and cut through, running the knife along the central bones on the far side from the spine, above the anal fin.

8 Cut the fillet away at the base of the tail.

belly bones

belly bones

Removing the belly bones

1
2 Place the fillet so that the head end is at the upper right, skin-side down. Lightly steady the belly bones with the left hand. Holding the knife blade up (*sakasabocho*), insert the point as shown and cut along the inner edge of the belly bones.

3 Hold the fillet firmly with the left hand. With the blade facing down, slide it into the incision, drawing the knife toward you as you slice the belly bones away from the flesh.

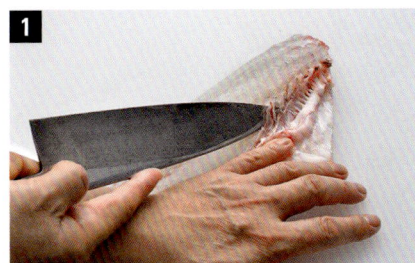

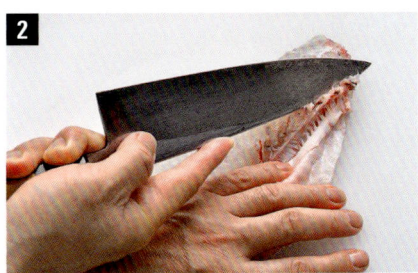

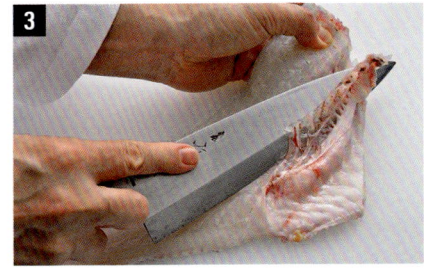

4 Place the fillet so that the head end is at the lower left and carefully slice off the belly membrane that connects to the flesh. Try to cleanly sever only the membrane and avoid cutting into the flesh.

5 Where the flesh adhering to the membrane becomes thinner, cut through the edge of the flesh, with the blade aligned vertically, cleanly removing the belly bones.

6 The fillet and the belly bones removed. Use the same steps to remove the belly bones from the second fillet.

bloodline bones (dotted lines)

Making *saku* blocks

1 Make incisions along both sides of the bloodline bones (*chiaibone*).

2 When cutting along the right side, tilt the knife to the right, and when cutting along the left side, tilt the knife to the left, forming a V shape (the V shape makes it easier to remove the bloodline and the small bones around it).

3 Separate the ventral and dorsal parts of the fillet (leave the bloodline part attached to the ventral part).

4 Now cut along the bloodline all the way
5 to the tail end and remove the bloodline.

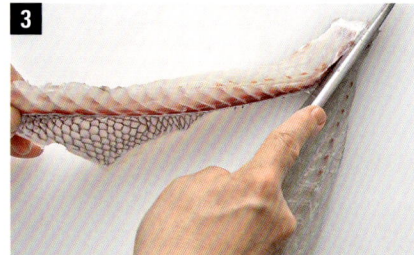

dorsal fillet (*semi*)

bloodline part (*chiai*)

ventral fillet (*harami*)

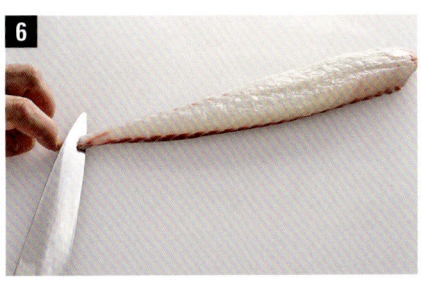

6 Change to a *yanagiba* knife. Position the dorsal fillet (to be used for the *tsukuri* sashimi dish) with the head end to the right, skin-side down. Make an angled cut, blade facing right (*sakasabocho*) at the base of the tail.

7
8 Slide the knife under the flesh of the fish, and, while pulling on the skin with the left hand, draw the knife between the skin and the flesh. Cut through at the tip. Take care to remove the skin only.

skin and dorsal fillet

Hira-zukuri

For *hira-zukuri*, one of the most widely used ways of cutting sashimi, the knife is held vertically—rather than angled diagonally—using the entire length of the blade from base to tip (see also p. 242).

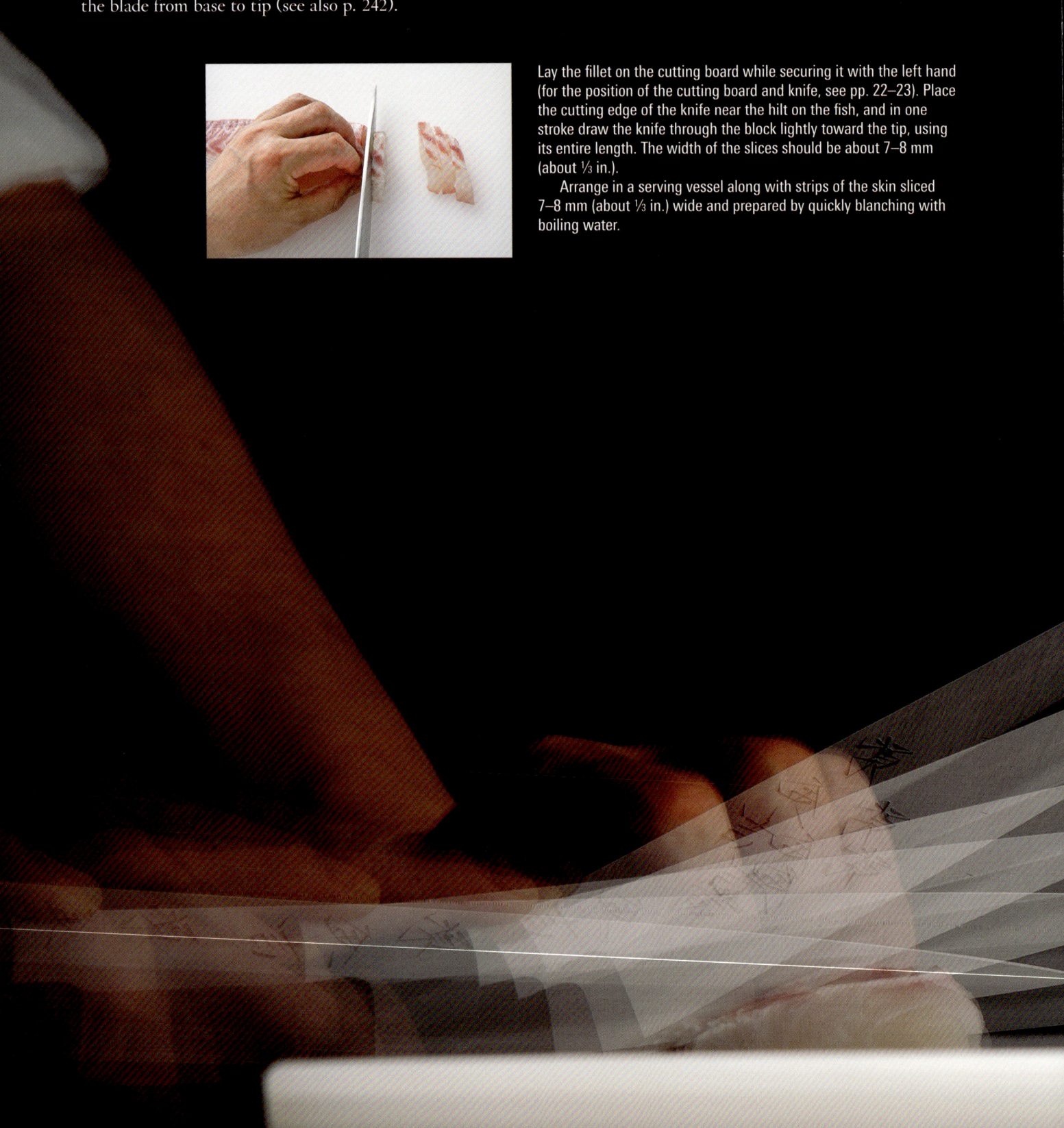

Lay the fillet on the cutting board while securing it with the left hand (for the position of the cutting board and knife, see pp. 22–23). Place the cutting edge of the knife near the hilt on the fish, and in one stroke draw the knife through the block lightly toward the tip, using its entire length. The width of the slices should be about 7–8 mm (about ⅓ in.).

Arrange in a serving vessel along with strips of the skin sliced 7–8 mm (about ⅓ in.) wide and prepared by quickly blanching with boiling water.

Red Sea Bream Rectangular Cut Sashimi

red sea bream blanched skin

finely julienned daikon

flower-petal *udo*

flower-petal carrot

shiso

wasabi

Hoso-zukuri

This technique is well suited for serving such delicacies as kombu-cured white fish, thin-flesh squid, *sayori* (halfbeak), or *kisu* (Japanese whiting). Using the knife on the vertical, cut thin slices. When the flesh is thick, slice blocks into two or three sheets and then cut into strips. Here we combine the recipe with the procedure for curing with kombu. Kombu-cured fish is sometimes made after the fish is sliced into sheets.

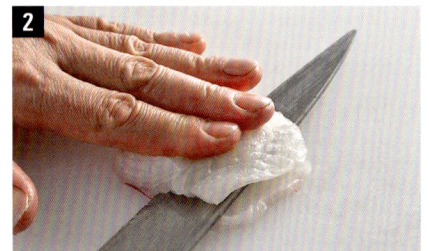

1 First cut the fillet into three or four blocks of equal length; strips cut from these blocks will be of uniform length.

2–**5** A form of butterfly slicing is used to make fillet blocks into sheets of uniform width and thickness.

2 Lay the knife flat and slice into the flesh from the belly side.

3 Open out from the incision and make another incision in the center of the thick part of the flesh.

4 Cut further into the flesh and open out.

5 The resulting sheets should be about 5 mm (¼ in.) thick.

6 Cut all the sheets into strips 5 mm (¼ in.) wide.

Curing with kombu

Red sea bream flesh carries a fair amount of moisture; it can be better enjoyed after curing in kombu, which removes excess water while enhancing the umami of the flesh (see p. 63).

1 Sprinkle salt (about 0.8 percent of the weight of fish) over 200 g (about 7 oz.) of fish that has been cut into narrow strips and leave for 1 hour. Add 1½ Tbsp. of sake, allowing it to blend well with the strips.

2 Prepare two 20 x 20-cm (7¾ in.) sheets of kombu, dampening them with 80–100 ml (scant ½ cup) of sake.

3 Spread one sheet of kombu in a tray and spread out the strips of sea bream so that all have contact with the kombu.

4 Cover with the second sheet of kombu.

5 Cover the container with plastic wrap.

6 Place a second tray of appropriate size on the kombu, press down lightly to facilitate the blending of the flavors, and refrigerate for 1 to 3 hours.

Kombu-cured Red Sea Bream Sashimi

hamabofu garnish cut with "anchor" curls

wakame

wasabi

basic vinegar flavoring (p. 245)

Carving the Head

A fish that is highly prized for its color, appearance, and auspicious associations ("tai" evokes *medetai*, "happy occasion"), sea bream is an indispensable part of the menu of any celebratory meal. Not only the meat of the fish but even its head will be used—grilled, simmered, in soups, and so forth. Here we present the procedure for cutting the head in preparation for making *tai ara-ni* (simmered sea bream bones).

1
2 Lay the head nose-up on the cutting board, and place the *deba* knife tip at the center of the upper lip. Push the knife in and cut into the skull.

3 Keeping the point deep into the head, push down, through the bone.

4
5 Cut all the way through the skull and open the head vertically.

6 The head divided in two. If not carving in the *kabuto* (samurai helmet) style (see box), cut the lower jaw to separate the two halves.

7 For each side of the head, insert the knife blade vertically, cutting along the gill cover.

8 Separate the collar (*kama*) from the head, leaving the pectoral fin and ventral fin attached to the collar.

9 Plunge the knife into the side of the head at the area under the nose. Make a cut from under the eye through to just above the pectoral fin.

10 Turn over and cut from the incision (in step **9**) down hard on the jaw area, cutting off the gill cover.

11 Cut the gill cover away from the collar bone.

12 Hold the knife vertically and chop down hard, dividing the mouth area into two parts.

13 Chop the collar removed in step **8** in the center, between the pectoral fin and the ventral fin, into two parts.

14 Shows division of the collar into two parts, with some flesh adhering to each part.

15 Carved head, showing pieces. The cavity is where the gill cover has been trimmed away. Follow the same steps for the other half of the head.

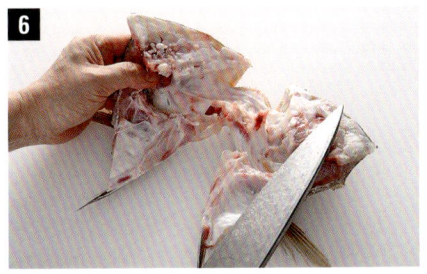

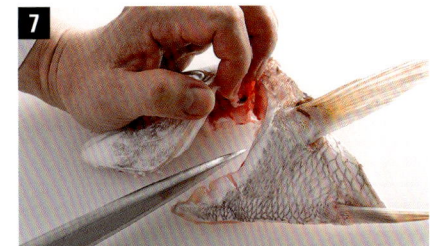

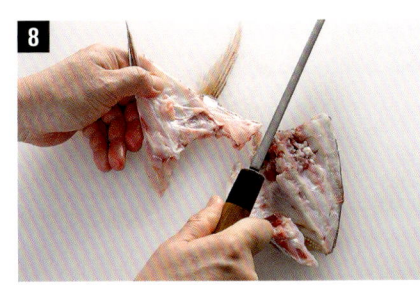

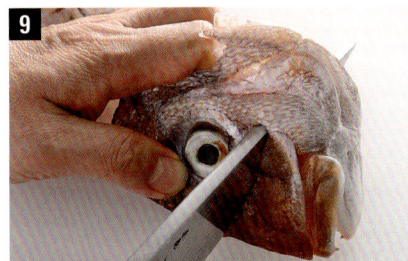

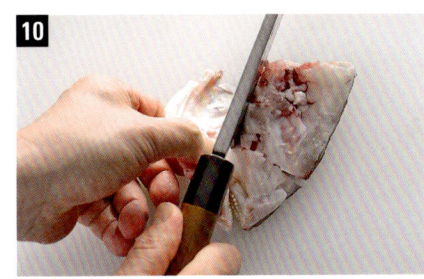

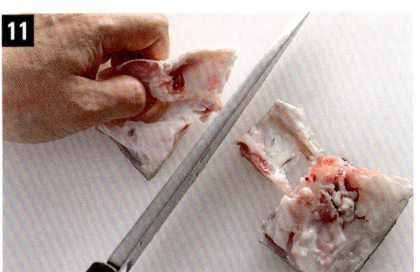

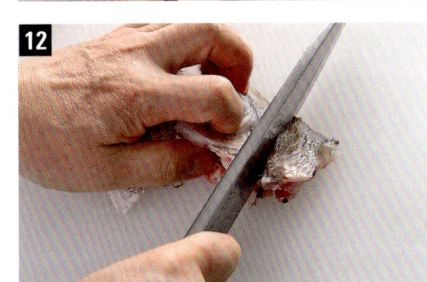

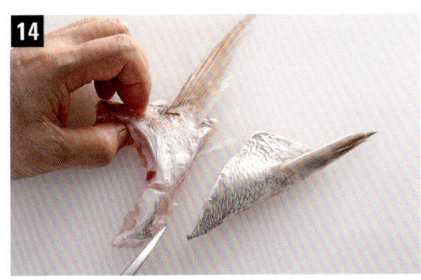

Sea Bream Head Dish for Children's Day

Held on the fifth day of the fifth month of the year, the Tango no Sekku is an annual festival held to drive away ill fortune and illness and pray for the healthy growth of children. Originally celebrated for boys, it was a samurai festival in olden times, and even today the symbols of the festival include helmets (*kabuto*), swords, and other accouterments associated with the samurai way of life. Among the foods served are auspicious dishes including *kabuto-yaki* (grilled sea bream head) or *kabuto-ni* (simmered sea bream head).

The opened-up head takes up space in the pot when simmering, so sometimes it is prepared separately and then added to the other parts of the simmered dish when served.

Ara-ni Simmered Sea Bream

Tai Ara-ni

The head, central bones, collar, and other edible parts remaining after filleting fish, called *ara*, make a tasty dish when simmered with seasonings for a sweet-salty flavoring. *Ara-ni* brings out the buried umami of the bones and remaining flesh for a dish rich in flavor.

Serves 4

Head of 1 sea bream, carved
  (see pp. 58–59)

100 g (3⅓ oz.) *gobo*

720 ml (3 cups) sake

140 ml (generous ½ cup) mirin

90 ml (scant ½ cup) shoyu

8 sprigs of *nanohana* mustard greens

20 sprigs of *kinome*

1 Bring pot of water to a boil and insert the prepared pieces of sea bream head.

2 Heat for about 10 seconds (until scales begin to stand on end).

3 Plunge the head parts into ice or cold water (*shimofuri*). Remove the scales. Remove from water when the pieces have cooled through.

4 Cut well-scrubbed *gobo* into seven or eight lengths and lay in the bottom of the pot (this helps prevent scorching of the fish). Lay the pieces of the head on the *gobo* pieces.

5 Add the sake and mirin and place over high heat.

6 Skimming off any foam that forms, cook on high heat for about 5 minutes, burning off the alcohol. After alcohol has burned off, add the shoyu.

7 Insert drop lid and simmer down at high heat.

8 As the liquid boils down, remove the drop lid and ladle the liquid over the head parts to bring out the glaze.

9 Boil until there is almost no liquid remaining. Remove the pieces of *gobo* and cut them into lengths of about 5–6 cm (about 2 in.) Blanch the *nanohana* greens to a bright green color and squeeze out the water. Arrange the sea bream pieces in a serving bowl and garnish with the *gobo*, *nanohana* greens, and *kinome*. Warm up the remaining liquid in the pot and pour it over the pieces of sea bream.

Curing Fish

The term *shimeru* (in suffix form, *-jime*; "bind" or "restrict") refers in Japanese cuisine to methods for dehydrating, dry-smoking, pickling, or otherwise firming up the flesh of ingredients by promoting a chemical change. Pickling foods in vinegar and dehydrating were originally employed for food preservation, but they also alter the texture of ingredients and add new flavors, and today it is for such qualities that these methods are most widely used.

Curing with kombu (*kobujime*) is done by lightly salting raw fish slices and placing them between dampened blades of kombu. The kombu tightens up the surface fiber of the fish, giving the flesh a distinctively moist but firm texture. At the same time, glutamic acid from the kombu seeps into the fish, enhancing its umami. Kombu curing is used mainly with white-fleshed fish like sea bream, flounder, and sea bass and with squid. The kombu blades must be dampened with water or sake before use in order not to draw too much moisture from the fish. *Shiroita* (planed) kombu is often chosen because it does not affect the color of the fish and yields flavor that does not alter with time; the curing kombu can also be served together with the fish and enjoyed as part of the dish.

Sujime, or pickling salted fillets or other fish parts by soaking them in vinegar or other low-pH acidic liquid is a means of preventing the propagation of bacteria. Fish cured in vinegar becomes very firm and chewy. The vinegar also reduces unpleasant smells by adding an aroma that masks as well as neutralizes the amines that produce these odors. Acidity denatures protein, so the use of vinegar alone would cause the protein to swell and become difficult to coagulate. This can be avoided by salting the fish first, thereby changing the salt-soluble proteins into gel and promoting coagulation. For thin-fleshed fish like Japanese halfbeak (*sayori*), the initial salting should be light and the vinegar-curing time shortened in order to prevent the flavor of the fish from being leached out. When the flesh is thick, as with mackerel (*saba*), the fish should be generously salted to draw out excess moisture. The liquid that drains out of the fish after salting will carry a strong odor and so should be wiped away before the addition of vinegar. If using only salt would produce too salty a result, the fish may be cured first with sugar and then with salt.

Hamachi
YELLOWTAIL
Seriola quinqueradiata

Yellowtail (order Perciformes) is called *hamachi* in Japanese at the middle stage of its life cycle when its length is about forty centimeters. The same fish is called *tsubasu* (or *wakashi*) as fry, *mejiro* (*warasa*), *hamachi* in midlife, and *buri* when mature. *Buri* grow quite large, reaching one meter in length.

Yellowtail is a member of the Carangidae family, but it does not have the hard spines characteristic of horse mackerel (*aji*) of the same family and is known for the yellow stripe stretching along its sides from head to tail. Farmed

yellowtail tend to be rounder of body than the wild fish; the tail fin is rounded and relatively short.

Farmed yellowtail is in plentiful supply and available all year round, but wild *hamachi* is tastiest between summer and autumn, when ample fat is on the flesh. It is served not only as sashimi, but grilled and in simmered dishes; yellowtail collar is considered a particular delicacy.

CUTTING YELLOWTAIL INTO THREE PIECES

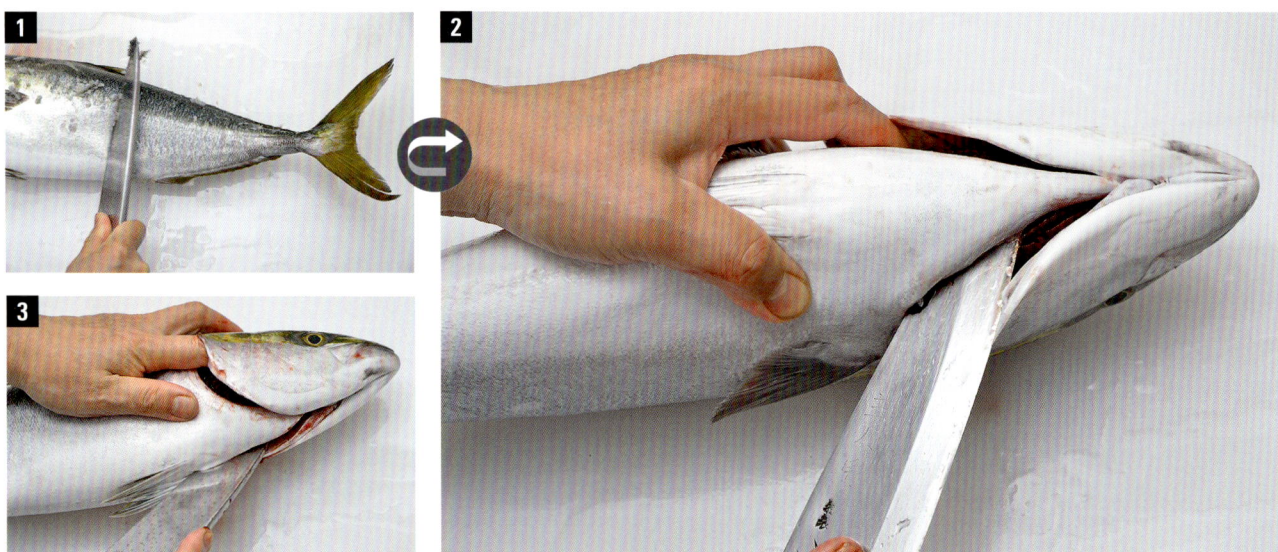

Preparation

1. The scales are small and thin and may be removed by lightly scraping the skin with a *deba* knife, the blade held vertically, in strokes moving from tail to head.

2. With the head to the right and belly facing up, grip the body, fingers in the gill slit as shown, knife facing up (*sakasabocho*). Insert the tip of the knife into the gill cavity and cut the attachment between the jaw and the gills.

3. With the head to the right and the belly facing you, insert the knife under the jaw and make an incision in the center of the belly down to the ventral fin.

4. Turn the knife over so the blade faces the head, insert the knife at the vent, and cut forward to meet the incision made in step 3.

5. Pull open the side of the fish slightly (as shown) and cut away the tissue connecting the gills to the collar. With the right hand, grip the gills and remove them along with the attached organs. Under running water, use a *sasara* bamboo brush (or equivalent stiff-bristled brush) to clean out blood and debris.

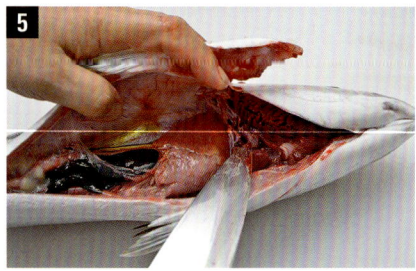

Removing the head

1 Place the fish with the head to the left. With the left hand lift the collar and insert the knife diagonally from the gill cover toward the back.

2 With the head to the left, turn the fish so that the dorsal side is facing you. Cut down at an angle from the base of the pectoral fin through the back of the fish.

3 Cut to meet the incisions made in steps **1** and **2**, separating the head and collar.

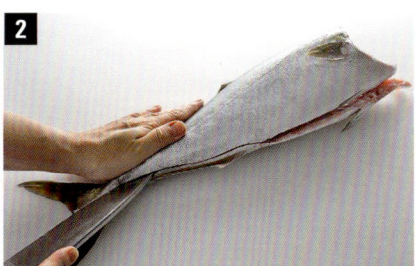

Cutting the upper fillet

1 Place the fish with the head end facing right and the belly toward you. Steady the back of the fish with the left hand and insert the knife in the slit made in step **3** on the facing page.

2 Leaving the fish closed and with the knife flat, cut in over the central bones and back toward the tail, separating the flesh from the bones.

3 Lifting the flesh with the left hand, cut the tissue connecting the flesh to the spine. Drawing the knife over the central bones, continue cutting inward and separate the flesh from the spine.

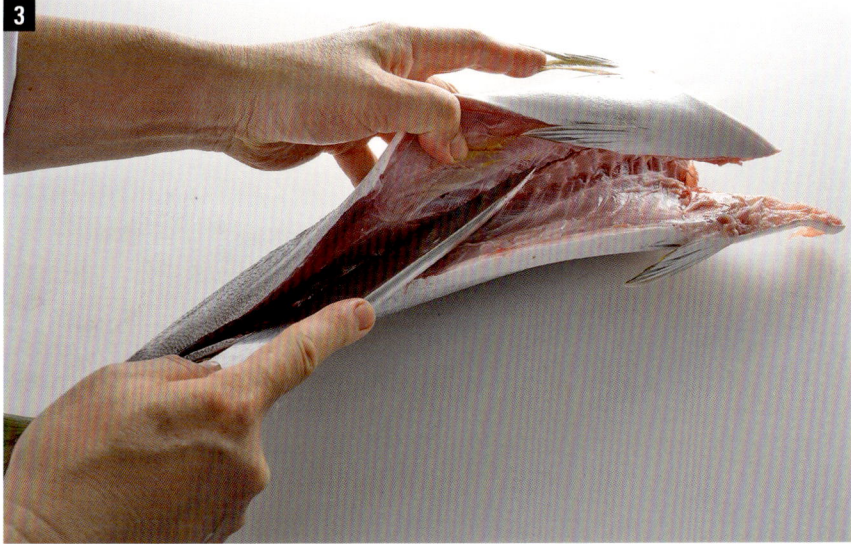

4 Place the fish with the head end facing right and the back toward you. Steady the belly of the fish with the left hand and make an incision just above the dorsal fin.

5 Sliding the knife over the upper central bones and along the edge of the dorsal fin, cut in all the way to the base of the tail. After checking the location of the spine, reinsert the knife and cut in behind the spine.

6 Place the head end to the left and the belly facing you. Insert the knife over the anal fin into the base of the tail (as shown).

7 Lifting the flesh with the left hand and checking the location of the belly bones, cut toward the head end, sliding the knife over the upper central bones.

8 Close the fish and, inserting the knife under the ventral fin, cut the fillet away from the belly bones.

the fish and the upper fillet after removal

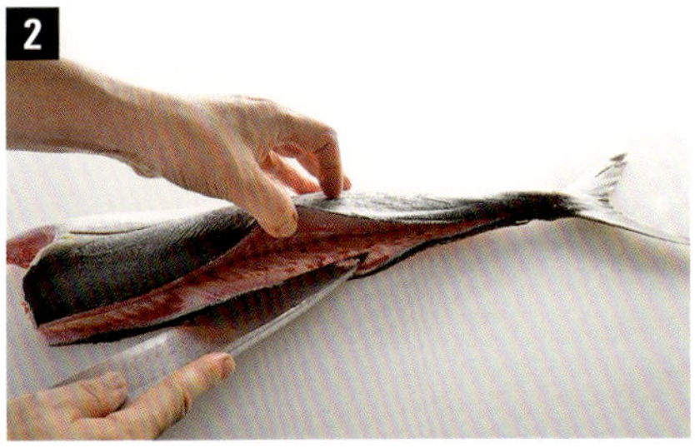

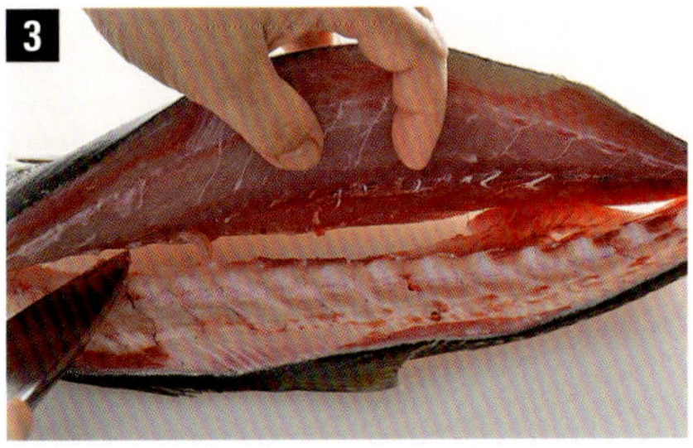

Cutting the lower fillet

1 Place the head end to the left, skin-side up. With the left hand holding the fish firmly in place at a spot close to the tail, cut in over the dorsal fin.

2 Lifting the flesh lightly with the left hand, continue cutting along the spine toward the head end.

3 Cut inward to the edge of the spine. Draw the knife over the central bones, using several passes to carefully part the flesh completely from the bones.

4 Close the fish and, with the knife lying flat, cut through at the base of the belly bones and separate the flesh from the spine.

to next page

completed fillets:
upper fillet (*uwami*)
central bones (*nakabone*)
lower fillet (*shitami*)

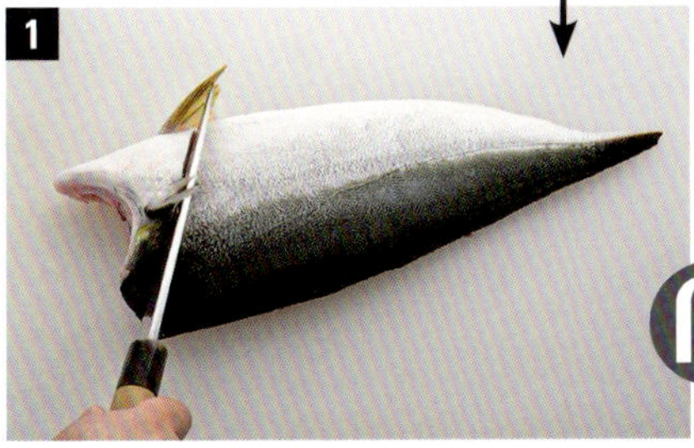

Removing the belly bones from the lower fillet

1 First, remove the collar. Angle the blade from the base of the pectoral fin to the back of the ventral fin (as shown) and cut through. (If using the fillet for sashimi, cut closer to the collar.)

2 With the blade facing up, slip the point into the crease between the belly bones and the flesh and make a shallow incision along the base of the bones.

3 Turn the fillet around so that the head end faces you. Holding the flesh lightly with the left hand, insert the knife in the incision made in step **2** and, sliding the knife from left to right, slice off the belly bones with as little flesh as possible.

the belly bones cut away from the lower fillet

from previous page

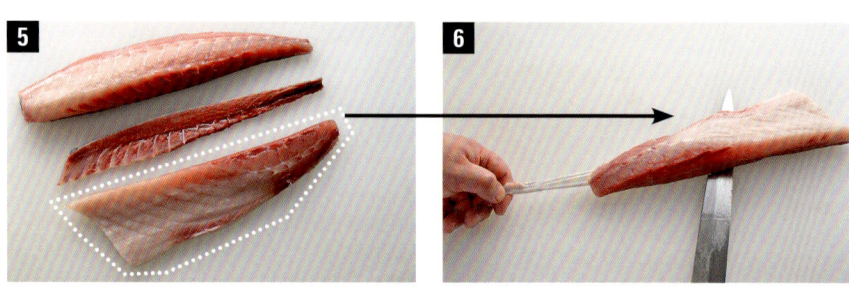

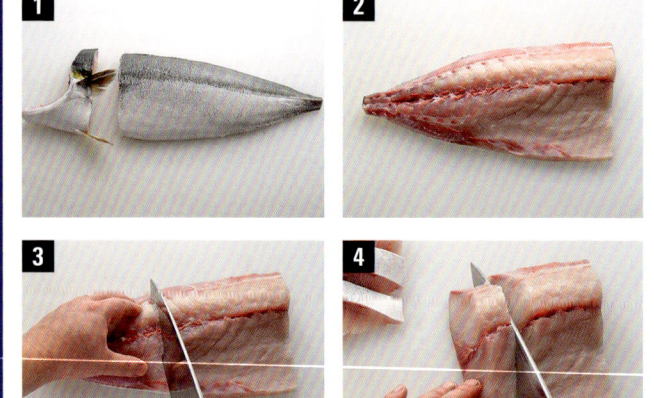

Removing the skin

1. Place the head end to the left and the skin-side down. The tail is full of sinew, so cut off the tail at its base.

2.
3. Place the fillet with the tail end away from you. Cut down the center, moving from the tail end toward the head end, and divide the fillet into two pieces, as shown.

4. Insert the knife at the tail end of the dorsal fillet and cut from the tail to the head end, leaving the bloodline bones (*chiaibone*) attached to the dark-meat flesh (*chiai*), slicing the dark-meat part off the fillet.

5. From top: dorsal fillet, dark meat, ventral fillet.

6. Change to a *yanagiba* knife. Place the ventral fillet with the tail end to the left and the skin-side down. Make an incision at the base of the tail. Insert the knife, blade facing right (*sakasabocho*), between the flesh and skin. While pulling the end of the skin with the left hand, slide the knife toward the head end, separating the flesh from the skin. At the head end, cut the final membranes connecting the flesh and skin.

fillet and removed skin

Cutting the fillet

Since the musculature of the fish is diagonal, it is easier to cut the fillet into equal-sized pieces by inserting the knife at an angle. Placing the fillet skin-side down makes it easier to cut pieces cleanly. The collar may be grilled or simmered.

1. Place fillet with the head end to the left, skin-side up. Cut off the collar along the line running from the base of the pectoral fin to the base of the ventral fin. (When using the collar for cooking, leave plenty of flesh on the collar side.)

2. Place the fillet with the head end (where the collar was cut off) to the right, skin-side down.

3. Cut off about one-third of the fillet on the tail end so that the other cuts will be of a uniform shape.

4. Steadying the flesh lightly with the left hand and holding the knife at a slight angle so the tip is lower than the hilt, cut the block into slices about 3 cm (1¼ in.) thick for pieces of about 50–60 g (about 2 oz.) per serving.

Kirikake-zukuri

This method of deeply scoring sashimi blocks a few times before cutting full slices is called *kirikake-zukuri* (notch-cutting) or *yae-zukuri* (multi-cutting). It is well suited to soft-fleshed fish with tough outer skin (like mackerel) or seafood such as squid that might have a resilient texture. For the fatty flesh of fish like yellowtail, this scoring allows soy sauce to better flavor the slices.

1 Cut into the fillet block fairly deeply at a point about 3 mm (⅛ in.) from the end.

2 Cut in notch at the same width as the first and the same depth.

3 After making three deep cuts, cut through the block to make a slice about 1 cm (½ in.) thick.

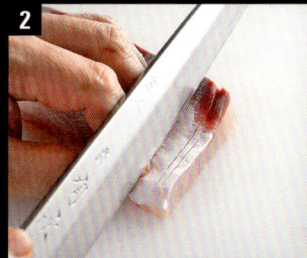

Notch-cut Yellowtail Sashimi

daikon curls	julienned *myoga*
cucumber curls	red *shiso* leaves
carrot curls	wasabi

Sashimi Garnishes

Garnishes (*ashirai*) used for sashimi include *ken*, *tsuma*, and condiments (*yakumi*), known generically under the term *tsuma*. Garnishes are vegetable-based and serve to cleanse the palate and enhance the taste of the sashimi.

Shoyu for dipping (*tsukejoyu*) sometimes accompanies sashimi, depending on the type of fish and how it is prepared.

Ken

Ken is made by peeling a vegetable in a continuous paper-thin strip (*katsuramuki*) and then cutting julienne-style, either with or against the grain. *Ken* cut with the grain (*tate ken*) is used for the mounded garnish sitting next to sashimi, while *ken* cut against the grain (*yoko ken*) is used as a bed on which the sashimi is laid. Vegetables like daikon, carrot, cucumber, *udo*, *myoga*, and others are used for *ken* and are called daikon *ken*, cucumber *ken*, and so forth. All *ken* is soaked in water after cutting and then drained thoroughly before serving.

Tsuma

Tsuma is often used for decorative purposes to add seasonal accent and color. Some *tsuma* including flowerets of *shiso* (perilla, Japanese basil), *shiso* buds, *benitade* (red water pepper), and so forth, are simply rinsed and used as garnish. Other *tsuma* that are soaked in water before using include *hamabofu* (glehnia, beach silvertop) and Suizenji nori freshwater algae. Some *tsuma* are formed into curls called *yori* by peeling a vegetable paper-thin, cutting it into fine strips at an angle, and placing the strips in cold water so that they curl up. Vegetables like carrot, *udo*, and cucumber often receive this treatment. Reminiscent of cresting waves, *yori* give an impression of freshness that make them a favorite garnish. Still other *tsuma* include *chishato* (stem lettuce) and *nanohana* (mustard greens), which are blanched in salted water before using; *kikuna/shungiku* edible chrysanthemum, parboiled in water with vinegar added; and cucumber or immature cucumber ("hanamaru kyuri") with blossom attached to provide color.

Condiments (*Yakumi/komi*)

Yakumi or *komi*, refreshingly stimulating or spicy, help enhance the flavor of sashimi. The best known among them is grated wasabi (Japanese horseradish). Wasabi, a Japanese native plant that has antiseptic properties and helps offset fishy odors, is an essential accompaniment to sashimi. Ginger in many forms, including grated (*oroshi shoga*) or finely slivered (*hari shoga*), or grated and squeezed into juice (*tsuyu shoga*), also goes well with seafood like bonito, squid, and horse mackerel (*aji*). Other condiments, depending on the type of fish, include grated daikon radish with chili powder (*aka oroshi*), thin-sliced green onions (*aonegi*) soaked in water to remove their mucous film and harsh smell (*arai-negi*), green onion shoots (*menegi*), and chives (*asatsuki*).

Tsukejoyu/Shoyu for Dipping

The taste of shoyu by itself is too assertive and can detract from the delicate flavor of fish, so shoyu is combined with other seasonings or condiments (*warijoyu*; see p. 245). Shoyu dipping sauces include *wasabijoyu* (shoyu with grated wasabi) or *tosajoyu* (a mixture of shoyu, *tamari* shoyu, and sake, to which katsuobushi bonito flakes have been added; see p. 245). Other dipping sauces may be flavored vinegars like *tosa-zu* (p. 245) or *pon-zu* (*tosa-zu* to which citrus juice has been added; see p. 245), which are served with *kobujime* (kombu-cured) or thin-sliced sashimi of white-fleshed fish.

Red Sea Bream and Tiger Prawn Sashimi

madai (red sea bream)
kuruma ebi (tiger prawns)
daikon *ken*
iris-cut daikon/iris-cut carrot
wasabi

Katsuo
BONITO
Katsuwonus pelamis

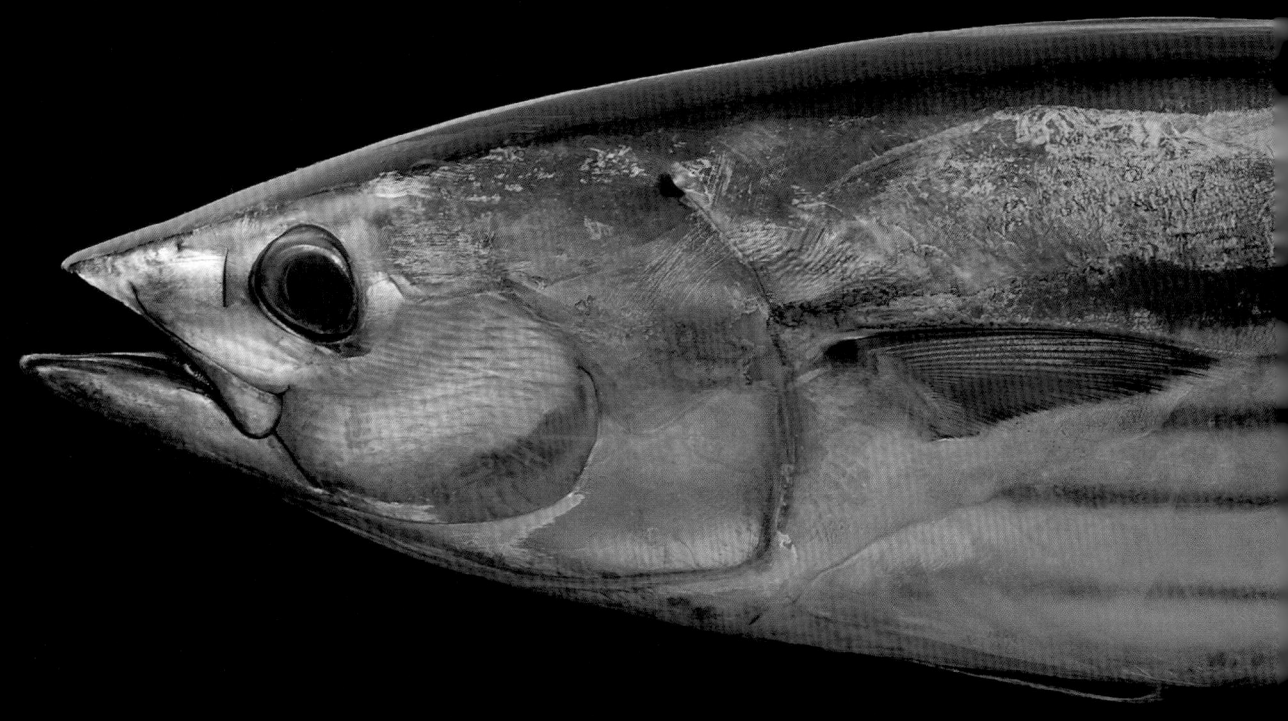

Bonito is in the family Scombridae of the order Perciformes. The fish are some forty to seventy centimeters in length with dark blue-purplish coloring on the back and dark blue stripes and silver gray on the belly. The clearer this striped pattern, the fresher the fish can be expected to be. The skin is covered from the dorsal fin to pectoral fin with hard scales, so preparation of *katsuo* begins with removing parts of the skin, scales and all.

Bonito are found widely in temperate and tropical waters, and they circulate the ocean seasonally. They move northward through the Pacific Ocean on the Japan Current, appearing in Japan's coastal waters in the spring, and then in autumn, after meeting the colder waters of the Okhotsk Current, turn back southward, appearing again.

Among the special pleasures of Japanese cuisine are the different ways that

the same ingredient may be prepared depending on the stage of the season when it is in its prime—whether early (*hashiri*), at the peak (*shun*), or late (*nagori*). A leading *hashiri* dish is *hatsu-gatsuo*, first bonito of the season. Bonito has been prized since the seventeenth century, when the appearance of this fish in coastal waters was considered to mark the advent of summer in Edo period (1603–1867) culture. The "early bonito" sold on the market from spring to early summer is lean and delicious served as *tataki* sashimi, with the surface lightly seared or grilled. Regular sashimi is the optimal dish for bonito caught after their "return" from the north—*modori-gatsuo*—when their flesh is sweet and succulent.

In addition to its vital role as the main source for katsuobushi fillets, bonito is an ingredient of *namari-bushi* (half-dried bonito) and *shiokara* (salted entrails).

CUTTING BONITO
INTO THREE PIECES

Removing the head and internal organs

1 Place the head to the left, belly facing you. Using a *deba* knife, slice into the base of the ventral fin and carve off the hard skin behind the fin as shown. (For sashimi this part is not very tasty.)

2 Lifting the gill cover with the left hand, insert the knife through the gill cavity and sever the tissue attaching the gill to the jaw.

3 Turn the fish so that the belly faces up and insert the knife through the gill cavity on the other side, connecting with the cut made in step **2**, and separate the gills from the jaw.

4 With the head to the left and belly facing
5 you, place the fish at an angle as shown. Insert the knife at the base of the anal fin and cut forward in the center of the belly toward the head up through the jaw. Use only the tip of the knife, taking care not to pierce the internal organs.

6 Place the head to the right, dorsal side facing you. Holding the gill cover open with the left hand, insert the knife under the gills at an angle.

7 With the head to the right, belly facing you, likewise insert the knife under the gills at an angle.

8 Place the head to the left, dorsal side facing you. Cut through where the cuts made in steps **6** and **7** meet and remove the head.

9 Shows the head removed and attached internal organs pulled out.

10 Place the head end to the right with the belly facing you. Opening the abdominal cavity with the left hand, cut the membranes around the blood pockets.

11 In running water, clean out the blood and debris using a *sasara* or other stiff brush.

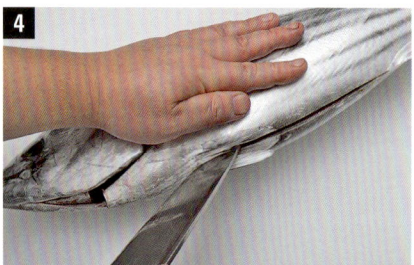

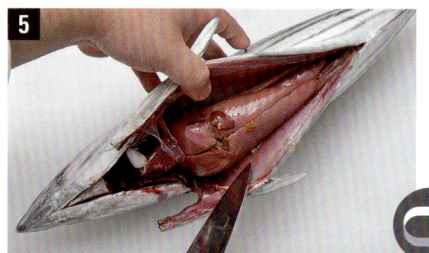

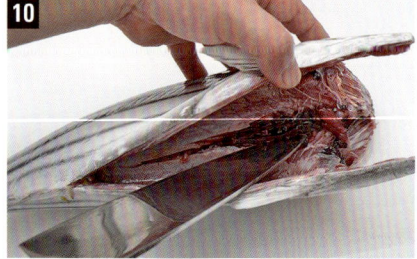

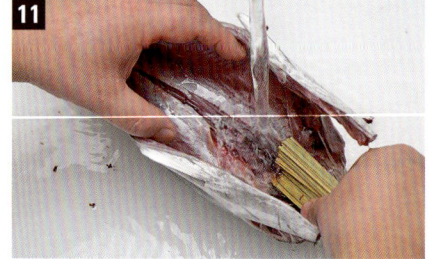

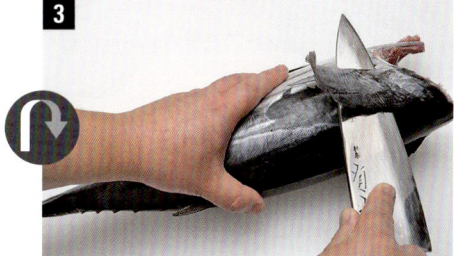

Removing the scales and cutting off the collar

1 Remove the scales from the hard areas around the fins. Steadying the fish with the left hand, make a shallow cut, blade facing right (*sakasabocho*) under the scales around the pectoral fin as shown.

2 With the blade facing the head end and moving up and down vertically, scrape off the scales.

3 Place the head end to the right and the dorsal side facing you. As in step **1**, slice under the hard part around the pectoral fin on the other side.

4 Place the head end to the left with the dorsal side away from you. Insert the knife at the base of the pectoral fin and, while steadying the collar with the left hand, cut at an angle to the dorsal side and remove the pectoral fin and collar. Remove the collar likewise on the opposite side of the fish.

5 Grip the fish by the tail end with the left hand, dorsal-side up. Turn the blade to face the head end (*sakasabocho*) and make a shallow slit cut through the skin along the side of the dorsal fin.

6 Following the line of the hard scales, make a slit along one side of the back.

7 On the other side of the dorsal fin, make a similar slit along the line of the hard scales.

8 Cut from the tail ends of the dorsal fin slits and remove the fin and scales.

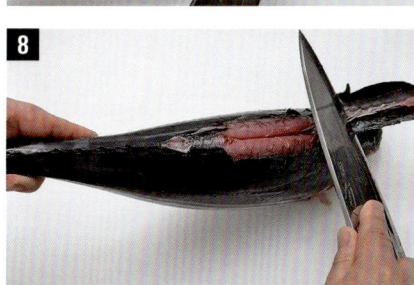

bonito showing the scales removed around the ventral fin, pectoral fin, and dorsal fin

Cutting the upper fillet

1 Place the tail to the left and the belly facing you, slanting upward to the right. Insert the knife in the slit in the belly.

2 Holding the fish as shown, slide the knife over the central bones and cut in the direction of the tail, separating the belly flesh from the central bones. Reinsert the knife and cut in further along the spine.

3 Roll the fish over so that the back is facing you. Make an incision along the crease where the dorsal fin was removed, sliding the knife over the central bones.

4 Reinsert the knife and cut in further, sliding the knife over the central bones and separating the flesh from the bones.

5 Holding the fish aloft by the tail (as shown), insert the knife into the incision made in steps **3** and **4** and cut downward, separating the flesh from the bones. Bonito may be filleted by the same procedure as for yellowtail (pp. 66–70), but the flesh is soft, and cutting in this way helps keep the knife from slicing into the flesh.

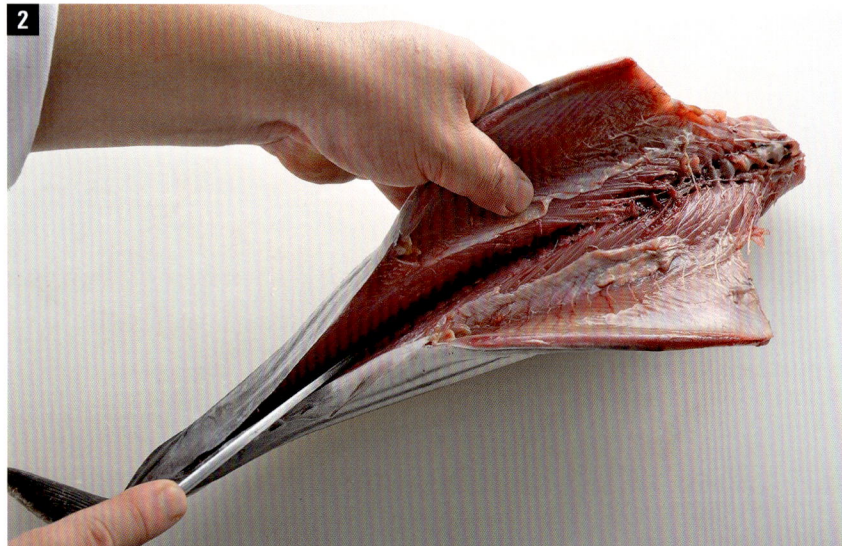

upper fillet removed

Cutting the lower fillet

1 Place the tail to the right and the dorsal side facing you. Make an incision starting just in front of the tail fin and continuing close along the line where the dorsal fin was removed, all the way to the head end. Reinsert the knife into the incision, and separate the fillet from the bones, sliding the blade over the central bones.

2 Making several passes with the knife, carefully cut the fillet away from the bones, taking care not to leave flesh on the center bones. Cut in deeply to the area of the spine.

3 Insert the tip of the knife, facing up (*sakasabocho*) just in front of the base of the tail.

4 Grip the fish just behind the tail with the left hand and, holding the fish aloft by the tail, slide the knife from the tail toward the head, as described in step **5** on the facing page.

5 Place the fish with the tail to the left, skin-side down. Holding the spine with the left hand, cut the fillet away from the tail.

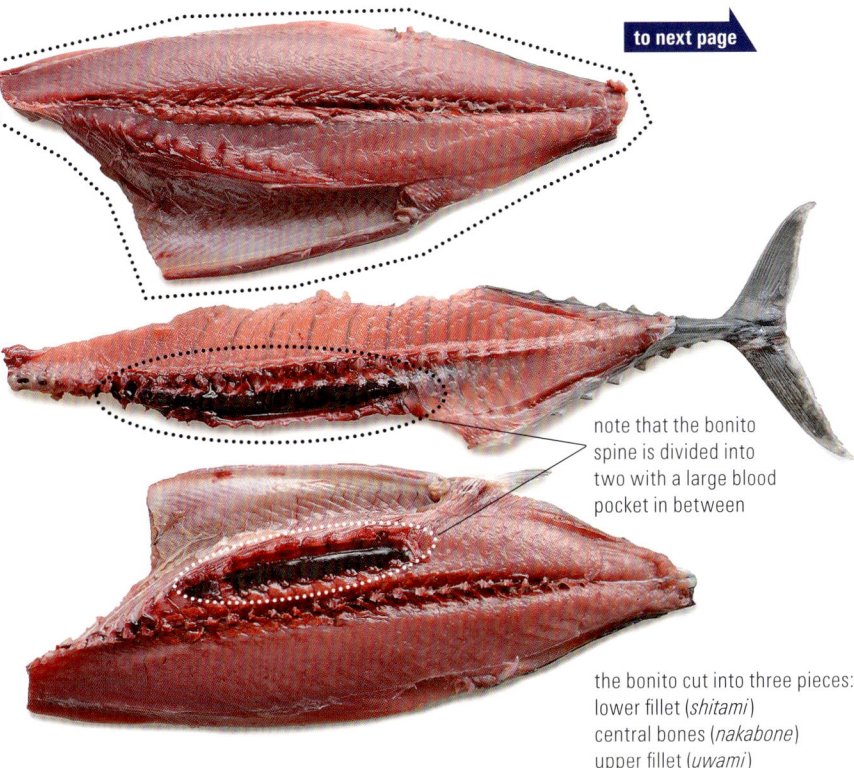

to next page

note that the bonito spine is divided into two with a large blood pocket in between

the bonito cut into three pieces:
lower fillet (*shitami*)
central bones (*nakabone*)
upper fillet (*uwami*)

from previous page

Removing the belly bones

1 Place the lower fillet with the head end facing away from you, skin-side down. With the cutting edge facing upward (*sakasabocho*), run the tip of the knife under the line where the belly bones are attached, making a shallow incision.

2 With the back of the knife, raise the belly bones along the incision cut in step **1**.

3 Turn the knife over and carefully cut along the flesh to the base of the bones.

4 Change to a *yanagiba* knife and cut off the belly bones (together with the thin membranes) at their base. Parasites (appearing like small white grains of rice) may be lodged under the thin membranes; remove if found.

Belly bones removed from the lower fillet (*shitami*). In the same way, remove the belly bones from the upper fillet (*uwami*).

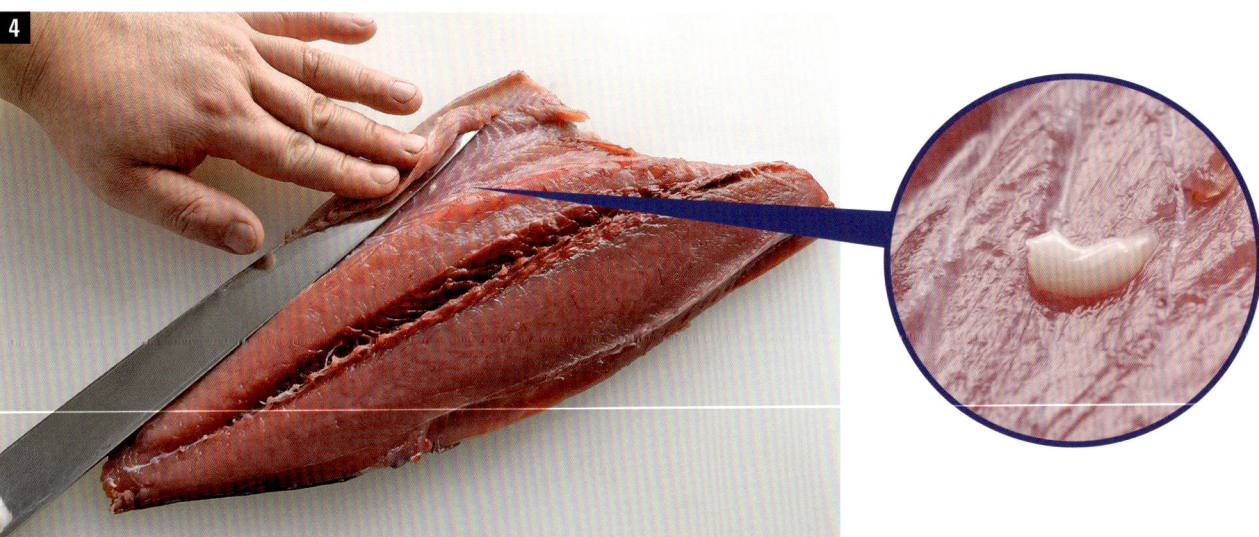

Preparing *saku* blocks

1 Place the lower fillet skin-side down with the tail end facing toward you. Insert the *deba* knife to one side of the path of the spine. Cut straight through to the base of the tail and separate the dorsal flesh block (right), leaving the dark-meat part (*chiai*) attached to the ventral flesh (left).

2
3 Turn the ventral fillet so that the belly side is to the right as shown. Cut along the side of the path of the spine, removing the dark meat together with the small bones remaining around the spine.

4 The fillet after the dark meat has been removed. The dark-meat part may be thick; it needs to be completely removed.

5 Any remaining dark meat on the ventral fillet (area in dotted line) may need to be removed.

6
7 Change to a *yanagiba* knife. Turn fillet so that the belly side is to the right and insert the blade at the divide between dark and light meat. Cut off the dark meat.

8
9 Remove any remaining membrane in the area of the belly bones. Insert the blade under the membrane, carefully skimming off the membrane only. Then cut it off clean (with blade pointed down). If any parasites remain, pick them out with tweezers.

The fillet with the belly membrane cut away. Perform the same procedure with the upper fillet (*uwami*), removing the dark meat (*chiai*) and bloodline bones and skimming off the belly membrane.

Tataki

The secret of good *katsuo-tataki* is the light grilling process. If grilled too much, the texture becomes dry, so the trick is to thoroughly sear the outside, leaving the flesh nicely rare. Note that *tataki* here means "seared," as contrasted with the chopping or dicing of fish such as seen in "chopped mackerel" (*aji tataki*). *Katsuo-tataki* is best served with a generous amount of grated daikon and chopped green onion and doused with *tosajoyu* (p. 245).

1 Use a *yanagiba* knife. Trim the ragged edge off of a fillet block from which the dark meat and belly membrane have been removed. Cut the remaining block into two pieces.

2
3 With the skin-side down, insert five skewers through the thick part of the flesh in a "fan-shaped" arrangement (as shown).

4 Turn the skewered block over and score the skin at about 3 mm (⅛ in.) intervals across the skewers (as shown) to counteract shrinkage of the skin during grilling.

5 Sprinkle a scant amount of salt on the skin. This adds flavor and promotes browning.

6 Grill the skin side first (the fish may be given a pleasant smoky aroma if a small amount of straw is placed on the coals while grilling).

7 Once the skin is nicely browned, turn over and roast the flesh side. Keep the roasting time short; the flesh should be rare.

8 Allow fish to cool, and then steady the block with the fingers while removing the skewers.

9 Cut the block into 1 cm (½ in.) widths. The meat is fragile, so slice through the skin in one forward stroke and then pull the knife toward you, for two strokes per cut.

10 Sprinkle with the juice of *sudachi* or *kabosu* citrus or the equivalent sour citrus (for germicidal effect).

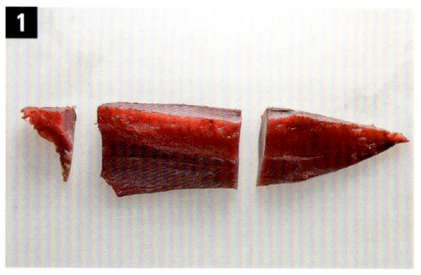

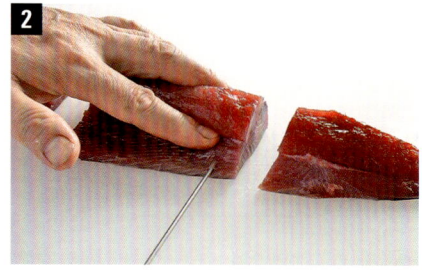

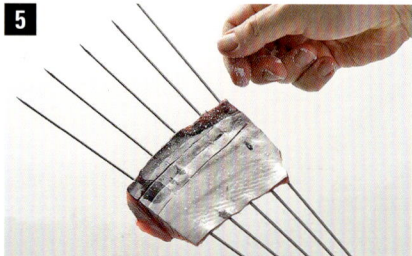

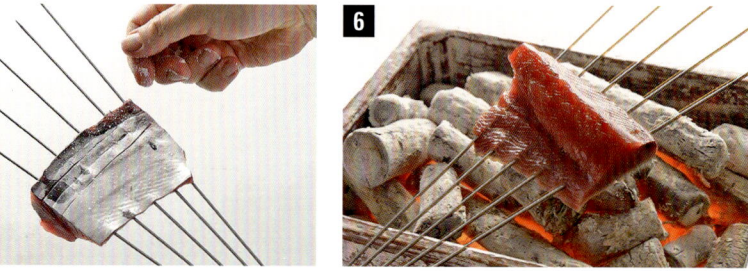

11 Pat the surface lightly to work in the flavor.

12 Cover the skin side with a layer of grated daikon mixed with chopped green spring onion.

Seared Bonito Sashimi with Garnishes

julienned daikon base layer

chopped green onion and grated daikon topping for fish

garlic chip aromatic

shiso floweret garnish

green *shiso* leaves

red *shiso* sprout leaf garnish

grated ginger

Managatsuo
BUTTERFISH

Pampas punctatissimus

Although this fish is commonly called *managatsuo* in Japanese, it is of a completely different branch of fish taxonomy from the Scombridae family, which includes bonitos (*katsuo*), mackerels, and tunas. Thirteen species in three genera of the family Stromateidae have been identified in the world, and three species of the genus *Pampus* inhabit the coastal waters of Japan. Since they are quite similar, they are all generally marketed in Japan as *managatsuo*.

Some fifty to sixty centimeters in length, the fish is flattish and diamond-shaped. It has no ventral fin. It has small eyes located close to the nose and a small mouth. The skin is a dark gray color with a golden sheen, and the scales are small and so easily removed that they have mostly come off in the course of being brought to market.

Managatsuo is a high-grade fish often served in fine Japanese cuisine. The flesh has a moderate amount of fat; it is a highly palatable, soft, white-meat fish that is particularly popular in the Kansai region of Japan. Its flavor is best in winter, but it is available all year round and is especially in ample supply from early to mid-summer, the butterfish fishing season. It is frequently grilled after being marinated in a miso (*misozuke*), teriyaki, or *yuan-yaki* sauce, but if sufficiently fresh is also excellent as sashimi.

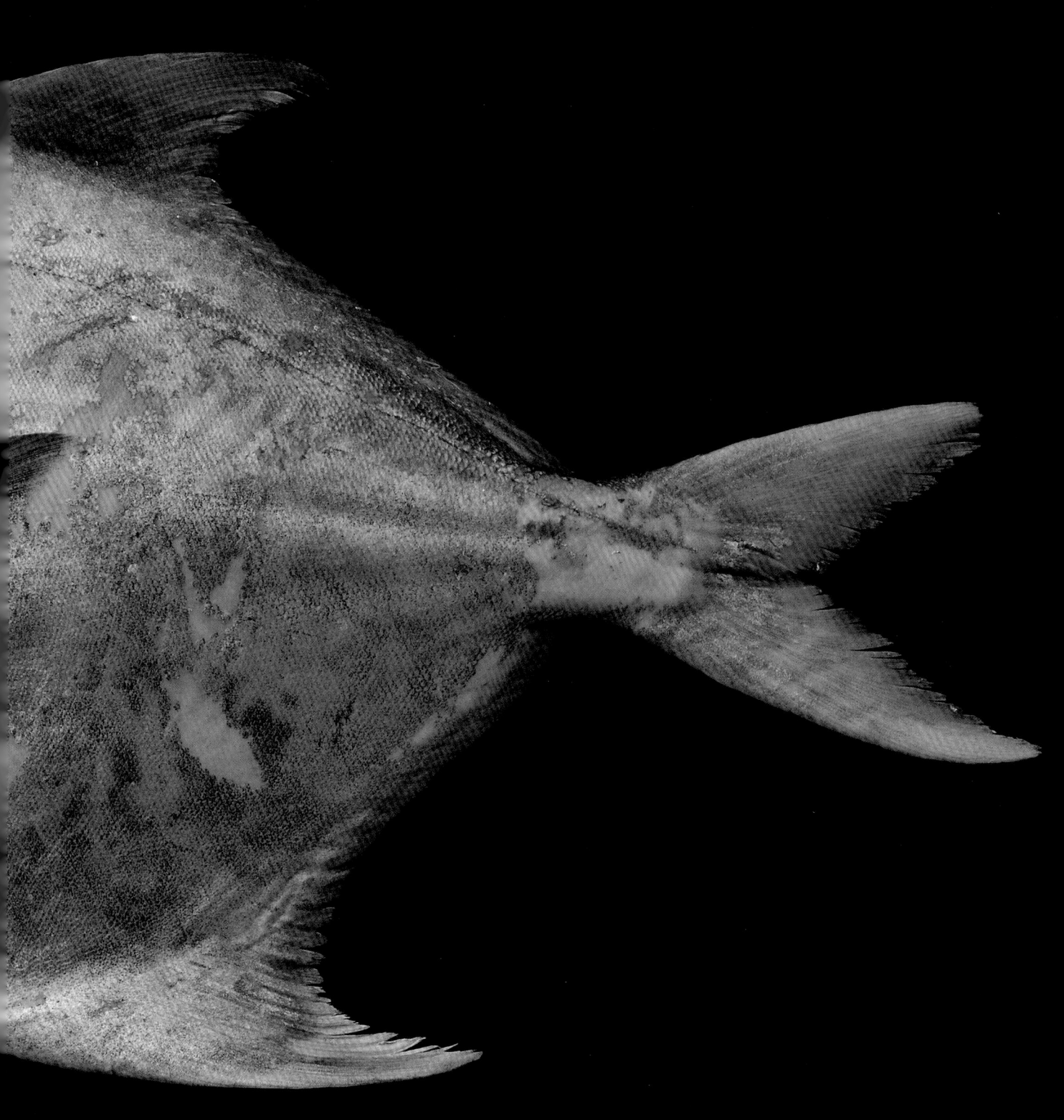

CUTTING BUTTERFISH INTO THREE PIECES

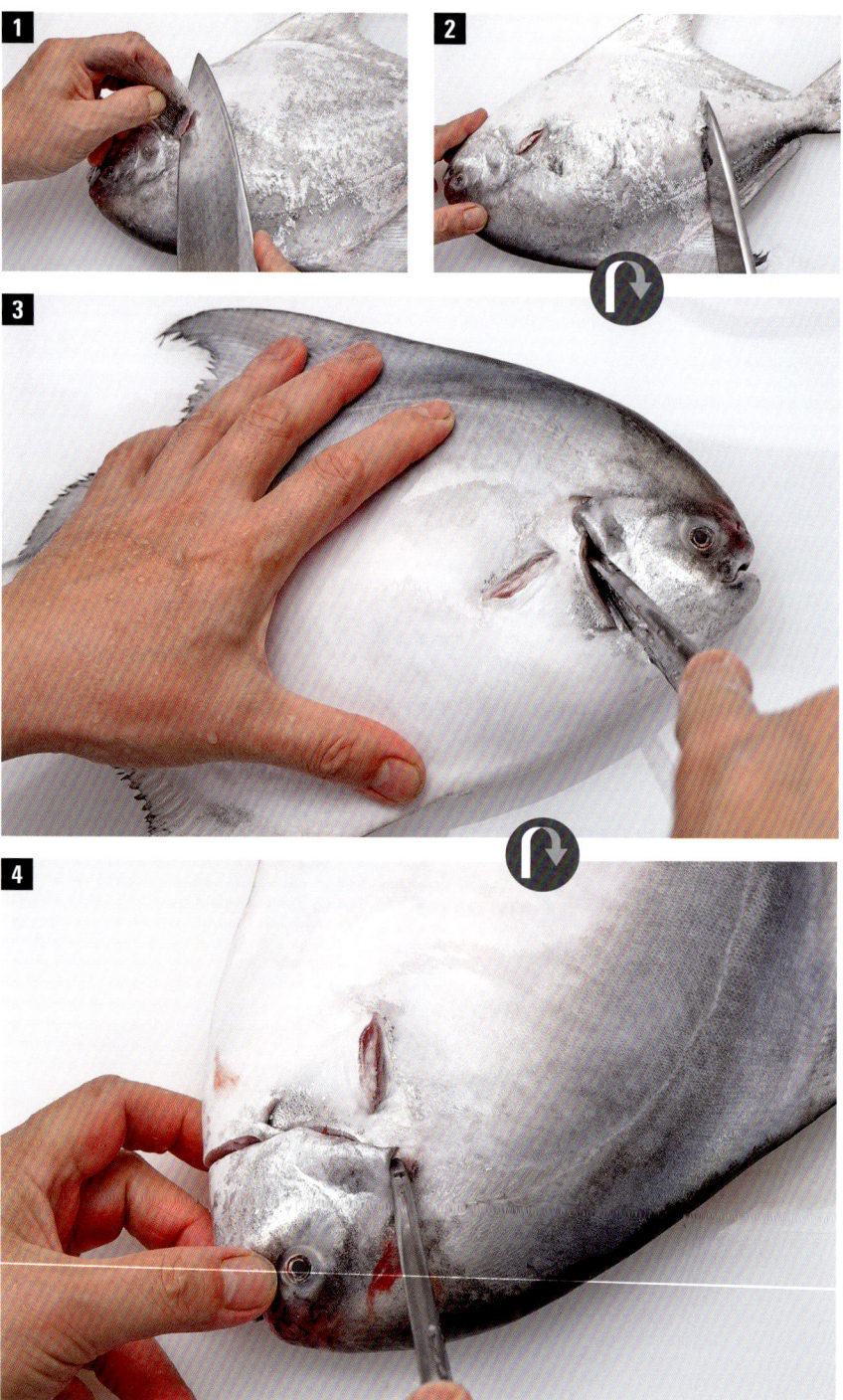

Preparation

1 Place the fish with the head facing left and the dorsal fin toward you. Using a *deba* knife, cut off the pectoral fin at its base.

2 Remove the scales by running the knife lightly over the fish from tail to head. Remove the pectoral fin and the scales on the opposite side as well. Wash well in running water and blot dry with a cloth.

3 Place the fish with the head facing right and the belly facing you. Insert the tip of the knife into the gill cover and cut through the jaw.

4 Turn the fish so the dorsal side of the head is facing you. Make an incision forming a V shape with the previous cut and then cut through to remove the head (see top photo, facing page).

body and head after removal

5 Place the fish with the tail to the left and the belly facing you. Make a shallow cut as shown (from where the head was) in the direction of the ventral fin.

6 **8** Reverse the knife so that the blade is facing the front of the fish (*sakasabocho*), insert the point just above the ventral fin, and cut in the anterior direction (where the head was). Connect the cut with the shallow cut in step **5**.

9 Pull the organs out of the inner cavity. Wash the cavity in running water and blot dry with a cloth (the flesh is soft, so do not use a *sasara* bamboo brush or other stiff brush).

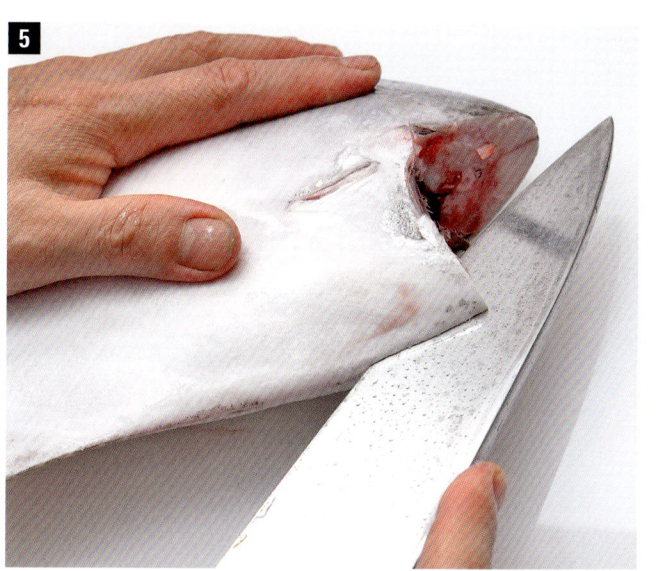

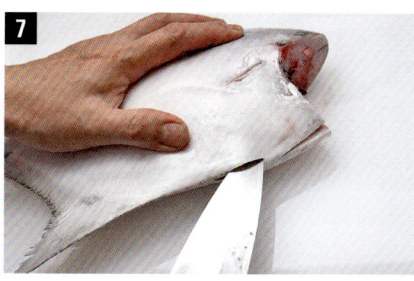

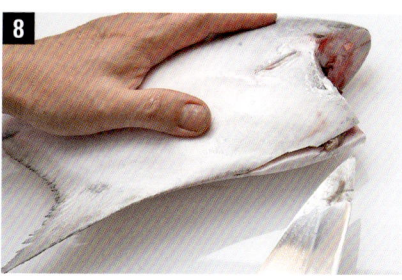

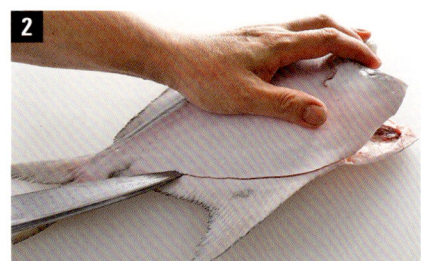

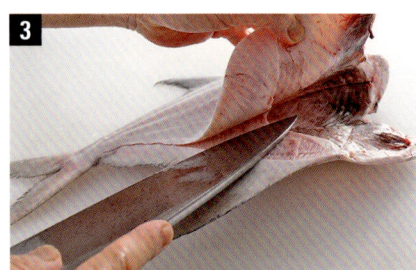

Cutting the lower fillet

1 Place the fish with the tail to the left and the ventral fin facing you. Insert the blade into the cut made in steps **6** – **8** on p. 87.

2 Make a shallow cut following a line passing just above the ventral fin, cutting just through the skin.

3 Lifting the fillet, place the knife with the tip visible along the shallow cut made in step **2** and, inserting the knife in several passes, cut the fillet away from the central bones.

4 Lifting the fillet with the left hand, place the knife at the edge of the belly bones and separate the fillet from the spine.

5 Cut further in, beyond the spine.

6 Sliding the knife carefully over the upper central bones beyond the spine, separate the flesh from the back of the fish. The bones are soft and the flesh is easily damaged, so be careful that the knife does not penetrate under the central bones.

7 Leaving the dorsal fin in place, cut the fillet free from the upper central bones.

8 Lift the fillet and cut it away from the spine at the base of the tail.

the lower fillet removed from the fish

to next page

from previous page

Cutting the upper fillet

1 Turn the fish over so the tail is to the left and the dorsal fin faces you. Grasping the ventral side of the anterior flesh with the left hand, insert the knife just in front of the dorsal fin.

2 Make a shallow cut passing over the side of the dorsal fin and over the upper central bones, cutting just through the skin.

3 Turn the fish over, with the tail to the right and the exposed spine web up. (Since the bones are quite soft, if the flesh is on top, the knife tends to stick into the bones. It is easier to cut closer to the bones with the flesh lying below.) Insert the knife into the shallow cut made in step **2** and slide under the upper central bones, cutting the flesh away from the bones.

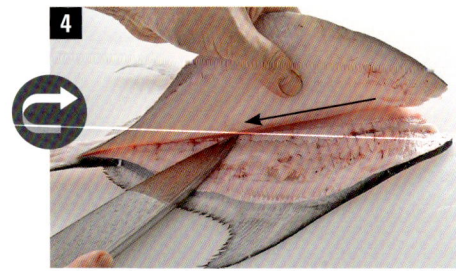

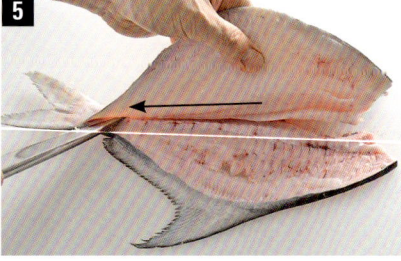

4 Turn the fish back over, so that the tail is to the left. Sliding the knife over the spine, cut the flesh away from the central bones, moving the knife right to left.

5 Insert the tip of the knife in a series of strokes, checking to make sure the cut is passing over the spine and beyond it.

6

6 Turn the fish so that the tail is to the right, head end to the left. Make a shallow cut starting at the base of the tail and along the belly of the fish, passing just above the ventral fin.

7

8 Reinsert the knife and cut inward, passing over the upper central bones, to start slicing off the ventral fillet.

9 Cut in, sliding the knife over the upper central bones, separating the fillet from the spine.

10 Steadying the fillet with the left hand, reverse grip on the knife and, with the blade up (*sakasabocho*), cut to the right to the base of the tail and through to free the fillet.

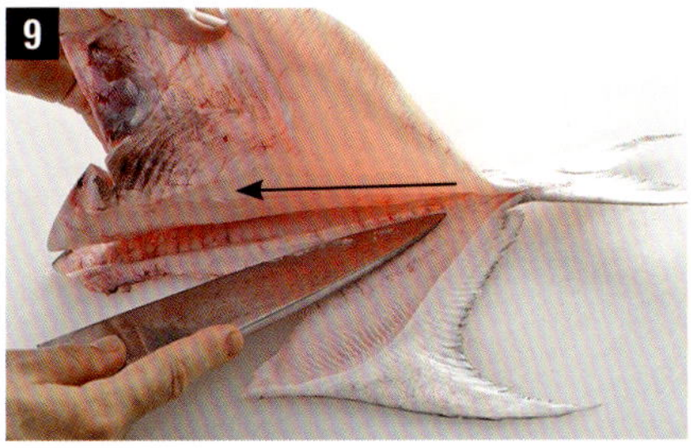

7

8

9

10

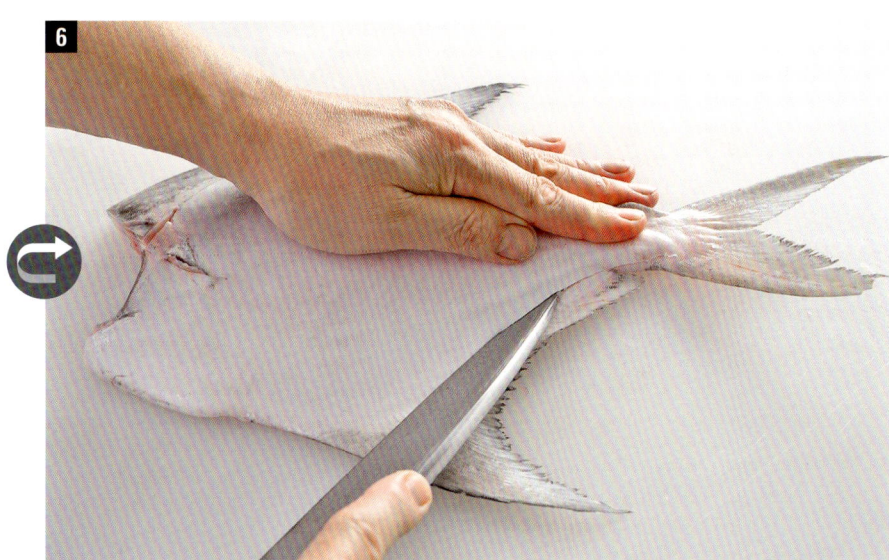

to next page

completed fillets, showing the upper fillet (*uwami*), the central bones (*nakabone*), and the lower fillet (*shitami*)

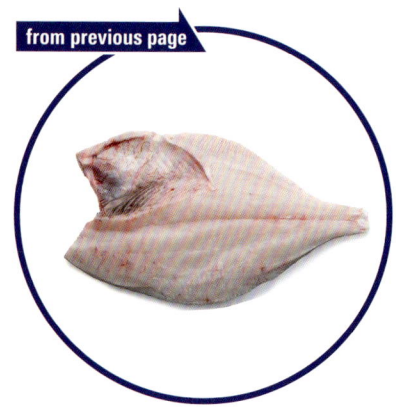

from previous page

Removing the belly bones, collar, and soft bones

1 Place the upper fillet with the head end toward you, skin-side down. Make an incision with a *deba* knife at the base of the belly bones.

2 Insert the knife at the base of the belly bones at a shallow angle, slicing off the bones with as little flesh as possible.

3
4 Cut along the center line of the fillet, slightly toward the dorsal side, and slice straight down along the length of the fish.

5 Separate the ventral and dorsal parts of the fillet.

6 To remove the row of small bones along the ventral side of the center line, cut off a thin strip along that side, as shown.

7 Reinsert the knife repeatedly, cutting away the strip and the small bones.

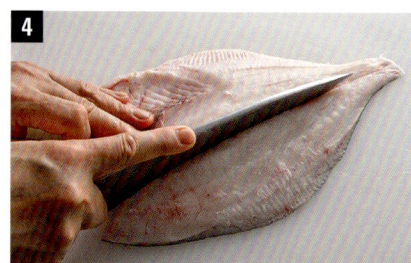

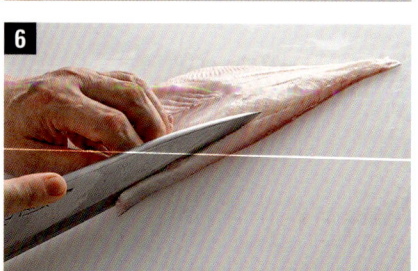

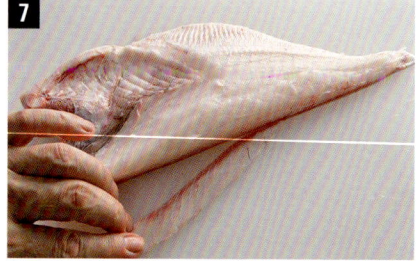

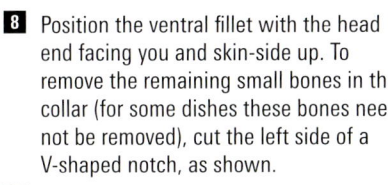

8 Position the ventral fillet with the head end facing you and skin-side up. To remove the remaining small bones in the collar (for some dishes these bones need not be removed), cut the left side of a V-shaped notch, as shown.

9 Cut the right side of the notch, removing the bones from the collar.

10 Use deboning tweezers to remove bones remaining in the collar.

11 Slice away the jaw cartilage.

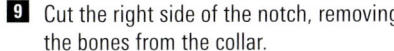

12

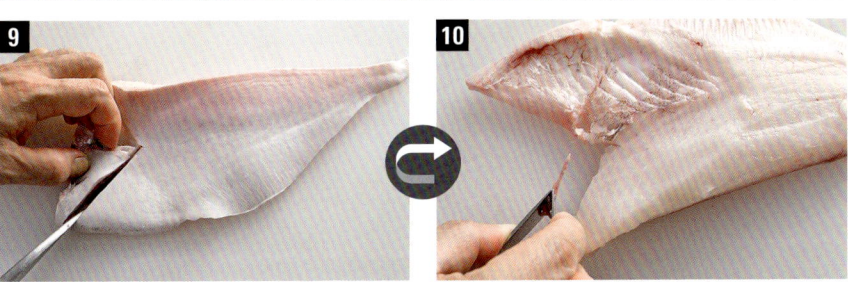

ventral fillet (top) and dorsal fillet (bottom)

Miso-marinated Butterfish

Managatsuo Misozuke

Marinating in miso is a leading way of preparing butterfish, with its moist, soft and moderately succulent flesh. Marinating in a sweet white miso brings depth to its flavor. This recipe is also well suited to *amadai* (tilefish), *buri* (yellowtail), *sawara* (Spanish mackerel), and similar fish.

Easy-to-use-quantity

A prepared butterfish fillet

Miso marinade

| 2.5 kg (5 ½ lbs.) coarse-grained white miso (*shiro ara miso*)

| 1 cup plus 1 Tbsp. mirin

1 Sprinkle a prepared fillet with salt (0.3–0.5 percent the weight of the meat) and let stand (this helps drain out excess water, so that the flavor of the miso is not diluted). After about an hour, blot the moisture off the fillets with a paper or cloth towel. Blend together the miso and mirin and spread half the mixture in a shallow pan. Spread a layer of gauze over the marinade and lay the fillet on the gauze.

2 Lay gauze over the fillet as well.

3 Spread remainder of miso marinade over the fillet and lightly smooth the surface. Keep refrigerated (40°F or 6°C is optimal) for 3 to 4 days.

4 Remove butterfish from the marinade and wipe off any miso clinging to the fish. Let fish rest until returned to room temperature.

5 Slice into strips of about 80 g (2⅔ oz.) each and thread onto skewers. Over a charcoal fire, grill both sides at medium heat, keeping sufficient distance from the fire to prevent scorching.

Miso-marinated Butterfish

Stem lettuce (*chishato*) pickled in salt koji

Sake
SALMON

Oncorhynchus keta

What is usually associated with the term "salmon" in Japan (order Salmoniformes, family Salmonidae, *sake* or *shake* in Japanese) is one of the species of Pacific salmon known as *shirozake* (*Oncorhynchus keta*, or chum salmon). Since ancient times it has been eaten raw and cooked and preserved by sun drying and salting; it is also used in offerings to the gods and is a standard for gift-giving on auspicious occasions such as New Year's.

The fish is fifty to eighty centimeters long with dark blue-gray coloring on the back and a silvery white belly coat. During the spawning season, the males' appearance undergoes various changes, their snouts growing into a hook and black, yellow, and pink mottling appearing on the skin.

Most salmon fry migrate out to sea after a certain point in their growth and return to the river or stream where they were born after three or four years.

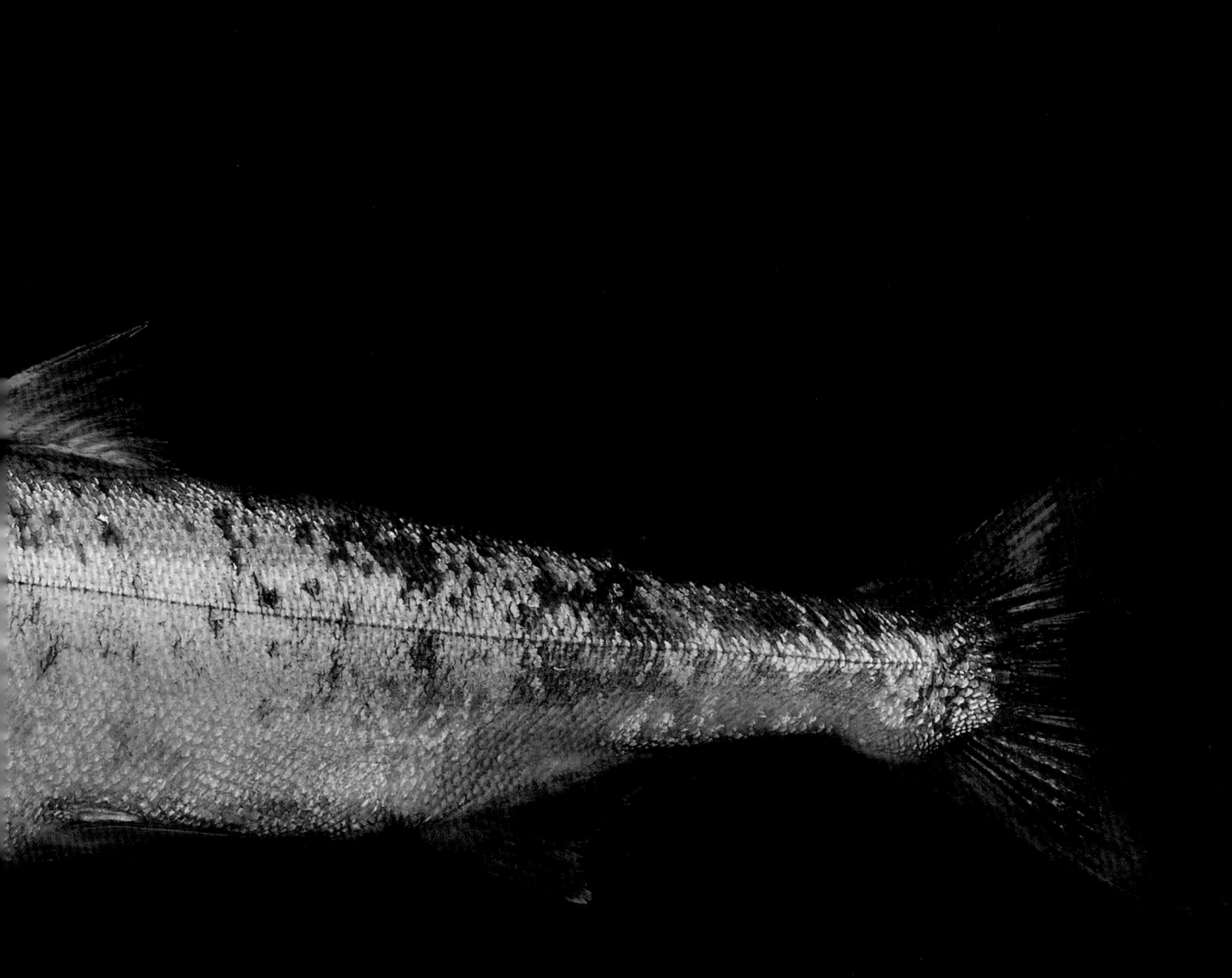

The eggs of *shirozake* salmon hatch in the autumn and the grown fish that have traveled long distances in the ocean return in the autumn, so the fish is often called *akizake* (autumn salmon) and commonly caught and consumed then in Japan. Salmon caught from spring to early summer before spawning begins are distinguished from autumn salmon with the name *tokishirazu* (off-season). Spring salmon do not carry egg or sperm sacs yet are well fleshed out and have ample fat. Quantity is limited, so the price is sometimes on the high side.

Fresh salmon is enjoyed in all kinds of dishes—grilled, in soups, smoked, and so forth—and also used for canned and other types of preserved foods. *Sujiko*, or salmon roe preserved in salt in the sac, and *ikura*, the eggs freed from the sac and pickled with salt, also frequent the Japanese table.

CUTTING SALMON INTO THREE PIECES

Preparation

1. Place the fish with the head to the left and belly facing you. With the *deba* knife, scrape from the tail toward the head as shown to remove scales and mucous coat, wash in running water, and pat dry with a towel.

2. Turn so that the head is to the right and the belly is facing up. Insert the knife under the gill cover with the back of the blade to the left (*sakasabocho*).

3. Holding the gill cover in place with the left hand, cut between the jaw and the gills to detach the gills.

4. With blade facing down, as shown, re-insert into the gill cover to cut the other attachment.

5. Pull the gills out from under the gill cover.

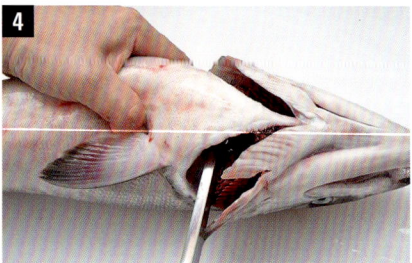

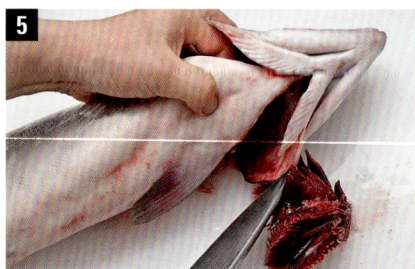

6. Place the head to the right and the belly facing you. Make a cut under the jaw to between the pectoral fins as shown.

7. Reverse direction of the blade (*sakasa-bocho*) and insert the tip of the knife into the vent opening.

8. Continue cutting along the underside of the belly toward the head to join with the cut made in step **6**.

9. Open the belly and remove the internal organs.

10. After the internal organs have been removed, a white membrane will be visible.

11. Make an incision into the bloodline (*chiai*) sac.

12. Continue cutting to the back of the fish, removing the bloodline sac.

13. Wash the inside of the belly and pat dry with a cloth. Be careful to clean out all remaining bits of blood and membrane.

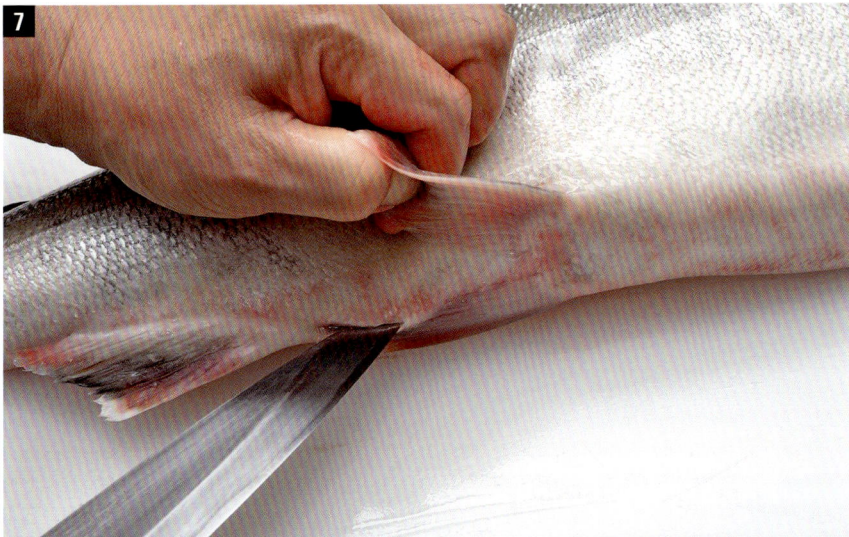

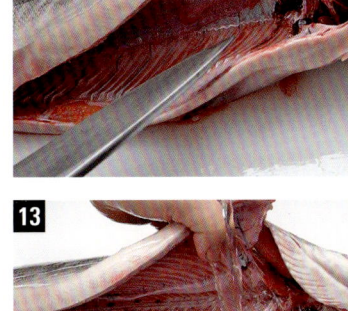

Removing the head

1 Place the head to the left with the belly toward you. Insert the knife on a diagonal from next to the gill slit to just below the pectoral fin, as shown, and slice down until the knife meets the spine.

2 Bend the head away and cut the part under the jaw.

3 Turn the fish over (head to the left and the back facing you). Cut into the neck on the diagonal from the top of the head toward the area behind the pectoral fin.

4 Press down hard with the tip of the knife and cut off the head.

Cutting the lower fillet

1 Place the head end to the right and the belly facing you. Insert the knife into the incision in the belly.

2 Cut in the direction of the tail, sliding the knife over the central bones.

3 Make several passes with the knife, checking the position and cutting further back to gradually separate the flesh from the upper central bones.

4 Inserting the knife at the base of the rib bones, separate the bones from the spine.

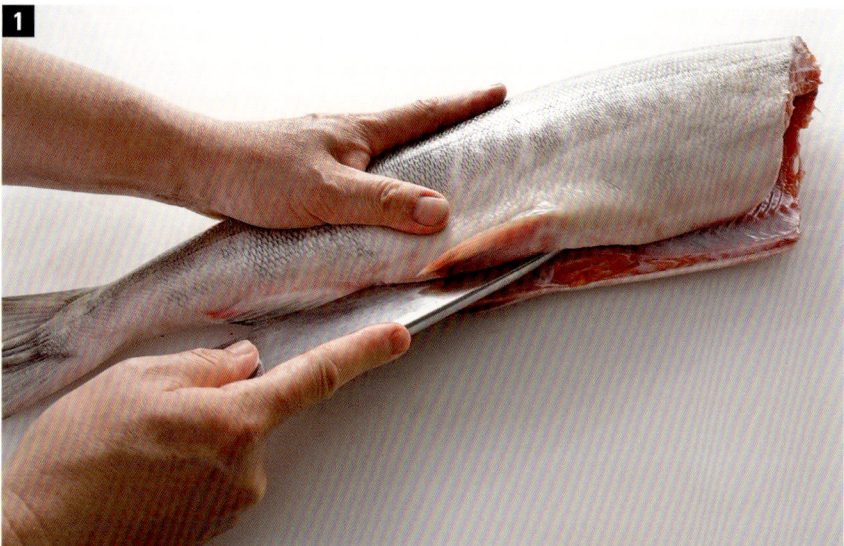

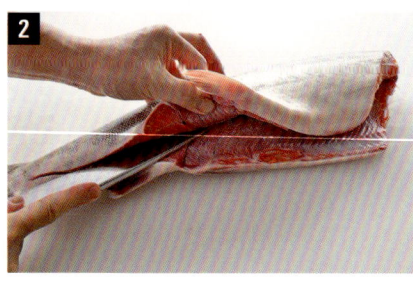

5
6 Continue in the direction of the tail, running the knife along the crease between the spine and the flesh, completely separating the flesh from the spine.

7 Lifting the side of the fish, insert the tip of the knife deeper beyond the spine.

8 Sliding the knife over the upper central bones, continue cutting just above the dorsal fin toward the tail.

9 Continue cutting toward the tail.

10 Cut the fillet off at the base of the tail.

lower fillet after removal and remaining side of fish

to next page

from previous page

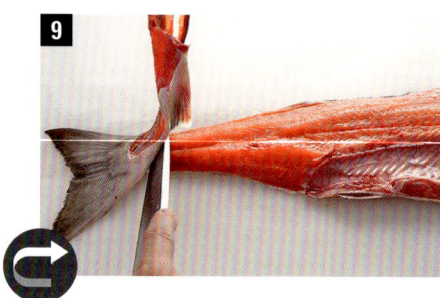

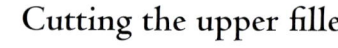

Cutting the upper fillet

1 Place the head side to the right with the back of the fish facing you. Make an incision just above the upper central bones along the back of the fish.

2 Steadying the fish with the left hand, cut in with the knife over the upper central bones.

3 Turn the fish over, with the skin-side down, back side toward you. Insert the knife into the incision made over the upper central bones.

4 Lifting the dorsal fin with the left hand, carefully cut so no flesh remains on the bones, separating the fillet (both bones and flesh are very soft, so it may be necessary to lift the edge of the blade slightly to keep from cutting into the flesh).

5 Turn the fish so that the skin side is up, belly toward you. Make an incision just above the anal fin.

6 Reinsert the knife into the incision made in step **5** and cut the flesh away from the central bones and spine starting from the tail.

7 Insert the knife between the spine and the belly bones.

8 Cut through the base of the belly bones and separate them from the spine.

9 Place the fish with the skin-side down and the belly toward you. Lift the spine and cut it away from the fillet at the base of the tail.

to facing page

the fish cut into three pieces, from top: upper fillet (*uwami*), central bones (*nakabone*), lower fillet (*shitami*)

from facing page

Removing the belly bones, ventral fin, and belly membrane

1 Place the upper fillet with the head end to the left, the skin-side down. Insert the knife under the base of the belly bones.

2 Making a shallow cut along the base of the belly bones, skim them away from the flesh.

the belly bones removed and the clean fillet

3 Make repeated passes of the knife to separate the belly bones from the flesh.

4 Pull out the ventral fin with the left hand.

5 Cut the ventral fin off at the base.

6 Remove the bones remaining in the dorsal fillet with deboning tweezers.

7 Change to a *yanagiba* knife and remove the white bits of membrane remaining around the edges.

SALMON　103

Yuan-style Grilled Salmon

Sake Yuan-yaki

Marinating salmon in a mixture of shoyu, sake, and mirin and then grilling is known as *yuan-yaki* and is one of the leading preparations of salmon. The refreshing aroma of yuzu brings out the flavor of the fish. Garnishing with chestnut and a maple leaf further accentuates the sense of the autumn season when salmon is at its best.

Serves 4

4 pieces salmon, each weighing 80 g (2⅔ oz.) salmon fillet

Yuan marinade

| ¾ cup de-alcoholized sake

| ¾ cup mirin

| 100 ml (scant ½ cup) *usukuchi* shoyu

| 3 thin (5 mm or ¼ in.) slices of yuzu

| Cool down de-alcoholized sake (use 360 ml or 1½ cups to obtain 180 ml or ¾ cup after burning off alcohol). Place liquid ingredients in a bowl. Add yuzu slices.

1 Prepare the fish. Cut a salmon fillet into slices of about 80 g (2⅔ oz.) each.

2 Marinate the slices for about 12 hours.

3 Remove salmon from marinade and pat dry. Pierce each of the pieces with two skewers, as shown. Over charcoal embers, first grill the top side of the slices at medium heat an appropriate distance away (to avoid scorching). Turn over and grill the bottom side (aim to cook top about two-thirds done and the bottom about one-third done).

Yuan-style Grilled Salmon

simmered chestnut
chrysanthemum-cut turnip
chrysanthemum leaf

Chapter 3

Special Techniques

This chapter introduces cutting techniques that diverge from standard three-piece filleting (*sanmai-oroshi*) as presented in chapter 2 or that are tailored to the anatomy of particular fish. These techniques include five-piece filleting (*gomai-oroshi*) for fish with thin or large bodies, involving cutting the fish in three parts and then subdividing the upper and lower fillets into dorsal and ventral parts. Another technique, called *sebiraki* ("butterfly cut"), calls for the fish to be spread out from the head and along the back in butterfly fashion. Also introduced are techniques for cutting blocks of flesh needed for making *maguro* sashimi and various kinds of sushi.

Hirame
FLOUNDER
Paralichthys olivaceus

A member of the family Paralichthyidae (the large-tooth flounders), the order Pleuronectiformes, *hirame* flounder is an oval-shaped flatfish very similar to *karei* flounder in its outward appearance, although the eyes are on the left side when placed with the dark skin-side up and the ventral fin facing you, as contrasted to *karei*, one of the righteye flounders (family Pleuronectidae). *Hirame* may grow to a little less than a meter in length. The fish's coloring is normally brown on its dark side and pure white on the opposite side, but the coloring of its dark side changes subtly in accordance with the habitat of the sea floor.

Wild *hirame* have a clear contrast of colors between the dark and white sides, but farmed *hirame* may have dark spots on the white side and white spots on the dark side. A clarity of color on the dark side and bright redness of the gills are marks of freshness. Choice *hirame* are well fleshed out and firm over the entire body.

Among the various species of the order Pleuronectiformes, *hirame* is the highest-quality fish, prized for its succulent white-meat flesh. It is fished all year long, but carries the most fat and umami in the late fall to winter season. The flesh on the dark side of the fish is white with a brownish cast and that on the white side has a pink cast; the white-side flesh is thought to be better for sashimi, although the umami of the dark side is stronger.

Hirame features in *usu-zukuri* and *kombujime* sashimi and is also often served in simmered, steamed, and grilled dishes. The muscle at the base of the dorsal and anal fins is called the *engawa* and is rich in cushiony fat, but the amount of this part on one fish is relatively small, so the *engawa* is a luxury in sashimi and sushi.

CUTTING FLOUNDER INTO FIVE PIECES

Removing the scales, gills, and head

1 Place the head to the right with the dark side up. The scales are small and thin and are overlapping, so they are removed by scraping or slicing them off with the *yanagiba* knife (*sukibiki* technique). With the blade facing right (*sakasabocho*), remove the scales from the tail end.

2 Slice the scales away as you move the blade back and forth toward the head. Be careful not to cut into the skin.

3 Raise the tail and twist the body to better scrape off the scales in the areas near the fins and other spots.

4 Scrape off the scales from the underside (white side) as well. The head is not used in sashimi, so it need not be scaled on either side.

5 Change to a *deba* knife. Place the dark side up and head to the left. Insert the knife at the base of the pectoral fin and cut the tissue where the gills and internal organs are attached.

6 Place the head facing away from you and cut a V shape along the edge of the gill cover.

7 On the underside, with the head facing to the right, open the gills with the knife and cut through the base of the gills.

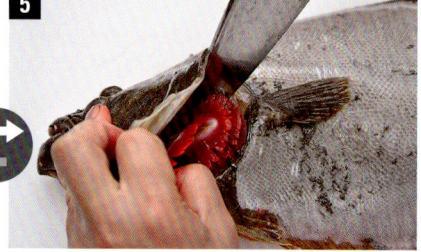

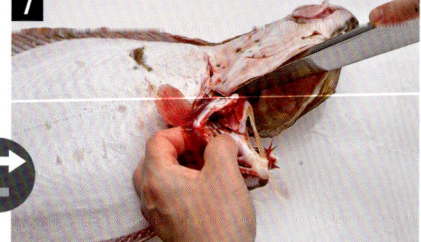

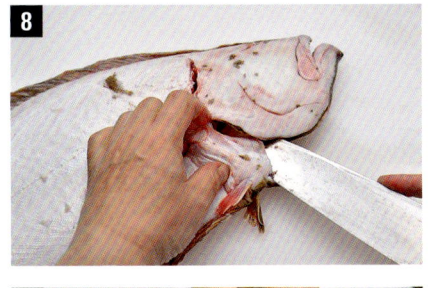

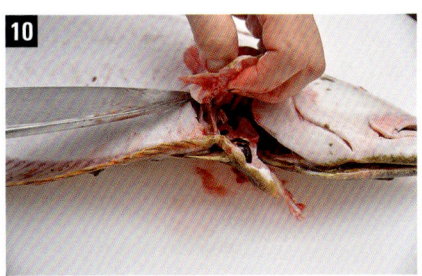

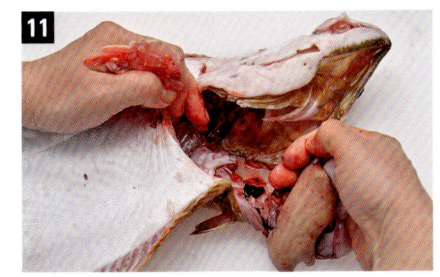

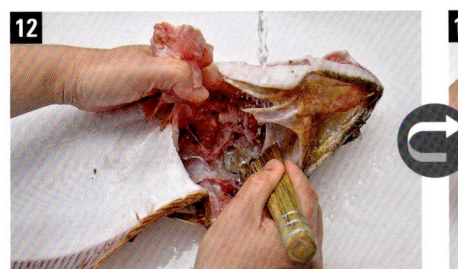

8 Steadying the gill cover with the left hand, make a cut into the edge of the collar.

9 Cut the tissue at the point where the head and the collar join.

10 Cut the connection between the gills and the collar.

11 Lifting the edge of the body with the left hand, pull out the gills and the internal organs attached to them with the right hand.

12 In running water, clean out the inside of the belly with a *sasara* or similar brush and wash thoroughly. Blot off excess moisture with a cloth.

13 Place the dark side up with the head to
14 the left. Lift up the pectoral fin together with the gill cover and cut along the edge of the gill cover. Cut through along the edge of the gill cover to the other side.

15 Turn the fish over and insert the knife to match the cut made in step **14**.

16 Cut the head away from the body.

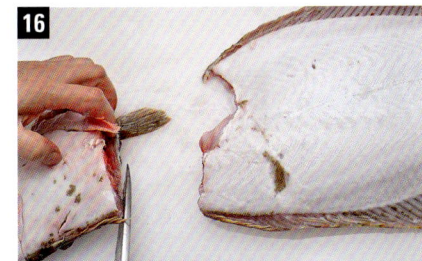

Head detached from the body. The head will not be served but may be salted and used for making dashi.

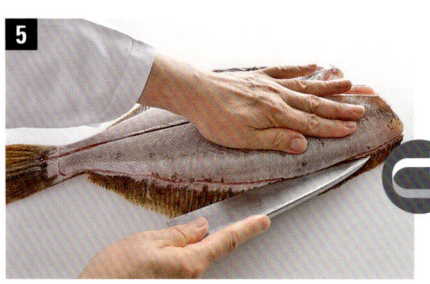

Cutting the fish into five pieces

1 Place the top (dark) side up and the tail to the left. Make an incision from the head end all the way to the base of the tail along the crease marking the spine.

2 Turn the knife to face right (*sakasabocho*) and insert the tip at the base of the tail as shown.

3 Make a shallow incision moving toward the head along the outer edge of the dorsal fin muscle (*engawa*) up to the midpoint.

4 Shift your grip on the knife and make a shallow cut along the outer edge of the *engawa* starting from the head end.

5 Cut up to the midpoint, joining the cut made in step **3**. Pivot the fish and perform the same steps for the other side, so that the outer edge of the flesh is cut from the fins all around the fish.

6 Place the fish with the head end facing toward you. Insert the knife in the incision made in step **1**.

7 Opening up the flesh with the left hand, cut through to the bone of the spine all the way to the tail.

8 Pulling up on the flesh with the left hand, cut in under the flesh over the central bones toward the head and separate the flesh (including the *engawa*) from the bones.

9 Shows one side of the dark-side flesh cut away; the *engawa* remains attached to the flesh.

10 Place the fish with the head end facing away from you and insert the knife from the head end at the incision made in step **1**.

11 Cut the other side of the flesh, including the *engawa*, away from the central bones as in step **8**.

to page 114

Shows the ventral fillet of the upper flesh (*uwami*)

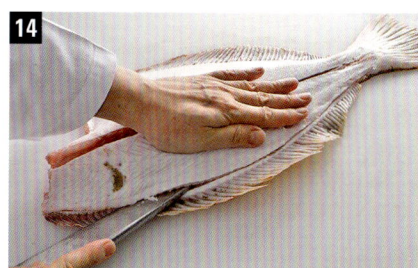

12 For the underside of the fish, follow the same procedure described in step **1** and make an incision along the crease of the spine.

13 Place the head end facing toward you. As in step **3** above, make a slit along the *engawa* from the tail end toward the head end.

14 Continue the slit all the way to the head end. Pivot the fish and perform the same steps for the other side, so that the outer edge of the flesh is cut from the fins all around the fish.

15 Place the head end away from you. Opening up the flesh with the left hand, cut along the incision made in step **12** through to the bone of the spine all the way to the tail.

16 As in step **8** above, pull up on the flesh
17 with the left hand and cut in over the central bones to separate the flesh from the bones. Cut through to the base of the tail.

18 The flesh cut away from one half of the underside. The flesh is thin on the underside, but the *engawa* muscle is fairly thick.

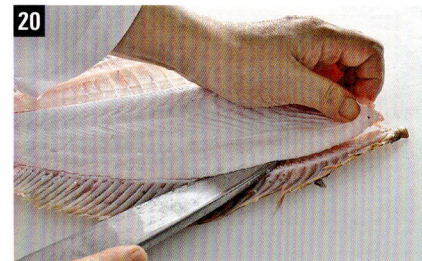

19 Cut the flesh away from the other side, as in step 13, by making a slit along the edge of the *engawa* from the head to the base of the tail.

20 Cut from the slit made in step 19 to the midpoint.

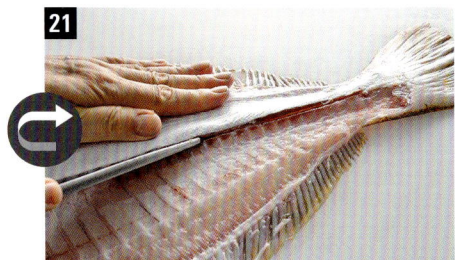

21 Place the head end facing toward you. Slice in from the base of the tail over the central bones.

22 As in step 8, cut in under the flesh and separate the flesh from the central bones.

Shows the ventral fillet of the lower flesh removed. This completes the division of the fish into five parts: two fillets for each side of the fish, and the central bones.

from page 112

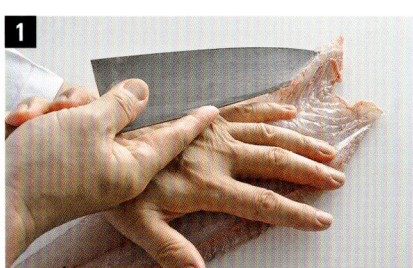

Trimming the *saku* blocks and preparing the *engawa*

1 Place one of the ventral fillets with the head end away from you. Lightly steady the belly bones with the left hand, as shown. Holding the knife blade-up (*sakasabocho*), insert the point as shown and cut along the base of the belly bones.

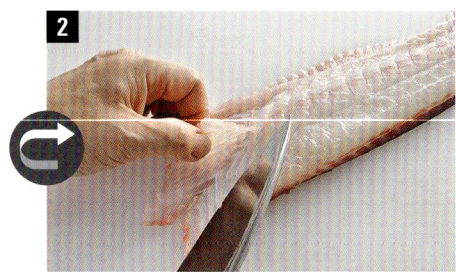

2 Turn the fillet so that the head end is facing you. Slide the knife into the incision and cut the belly bones away from the fillet. Follow the same procedure to remove the bones from the other ventral fillet.

3 The belly bones after cutting from the fillet.

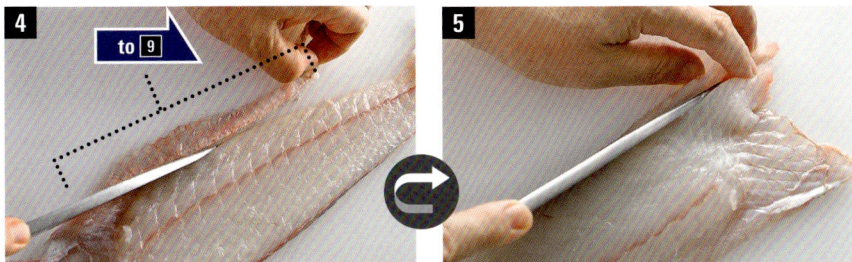
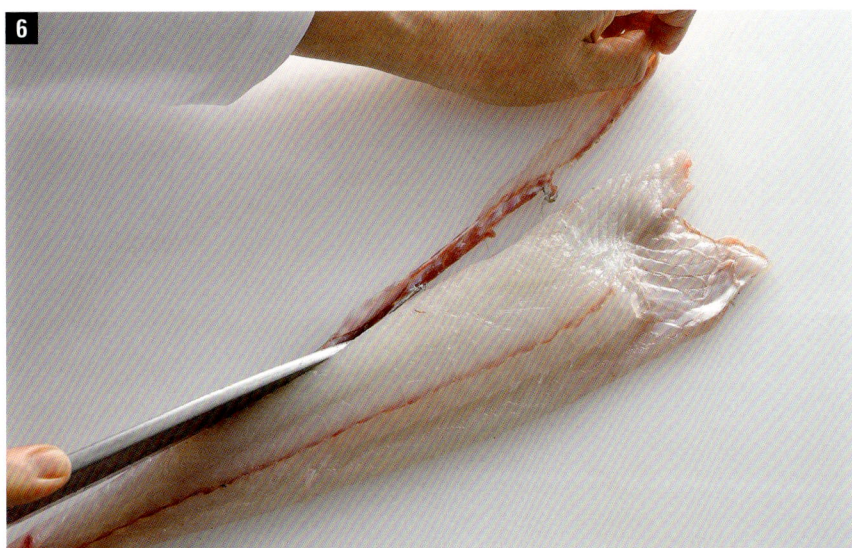

4 Taking care not to damage the flesh of the fillet, cut away the *engawa* from the edge of the fillet. It is easier to remove the skin from the *engawa* after it has been cut off (see step 9).

5 Place the head end facing away from you and insert the knife into the strip of dark meat (*chiai*) on the outer edge.

6 Cutting toward the tail, trim along the edge along the line between the dark-meat part (*chiai*) and the rest of the flesh.

7 Change to a *yanagiba* knife. Insert the knife, blade facing right (*sakasabocho*), between the skin and the flesh at the tail end.

8 While pulling on the skin with the left hand, draw the knife between the skin and the flesh.

9 Skin the *engawa* following the same procedure, pulling on the skin with the left hand while drawing the knife between the skin and the muscle.

skin removed from the fillet

skin removed from the *engawa*

Hegi-zukuri

Sashimi made by inserting the knife into the block at an angle and slicing in a shaving motion is called *hegi-zukuri*. This cutting method is used for sea bream, flounder, and other white-flesh fish that are firm in texture. This recipe is for *hegi-zukuri* wrapped in blanched purple and yellow chrysanthemum petals and decorated with a chrysanthemum leaf and auspicious red and white "pine-needle" (*ore-matsuba*) garnishes.

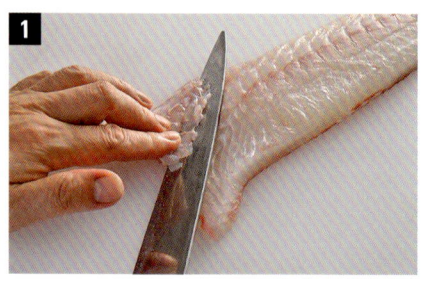 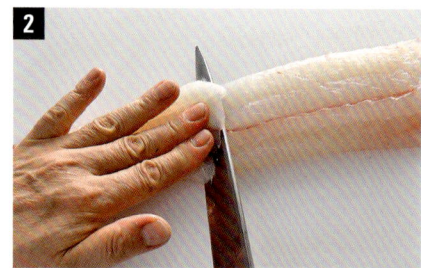

1 Steadying the tip of the fillet lightly with the left hand, insert the knife lying almost flat.

2 Cut in at a thickness of 5 to 6 cm (about
3 2 in.), drawing the knife toward you.

4 Grasp the piece with the fingertips of the left hand and cut the final attachment to the fillet.

Cutting the *engawa*

1 Score the skin side of the *engawa* strip with vertical strokes. The vertical scoring allows you to check and remove small bones that may remain and also enables the shoyu to permeate more easily.

2 Cut the *engawa* into easy-to-eat pieces about 2 cm (about 1 in.) long.

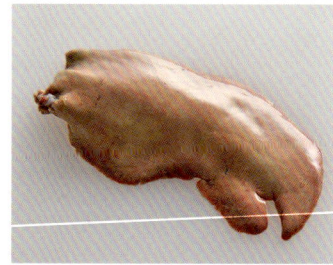

The flounder liver. Of the internal organs, only the liver and ovaries (*mako*) are used in cooking. The liver should be plunged in boiling water. The ovaries are seasoned and simmered.

Thin Sliced Flounder Sashimi

ore-matsuba daikon and carrot

blanched purple and yellow chrysanthemum petals

chrysanthemum petals

chrysanthemum leaf

red *shiso* leaf buds

wasabi

Kochi
BARTAIL FLATHEAD
Platycephalus sp. 2

Among the members of the Platycephalus—"flathead"—family, the bartail (*Platycephalus sp.2*) can be recognized by eyes small in relation to the head and the wide space between them. *Magochi* is commonly called simply *kochi*. The back of the fish is tan and brown covered with a fine spotty or blotchy pattern, but while alive the color of the fish actually changes to blend in with its habitat on the sea floor. The pectoral fins have sharp spines, so care must be taken in handling this fish. The bartail flathead lives in relatively sandy-bottomed shallow seas of up to about thirty meters deep, and some grow to as much as one meter in length. Flatheads of about thirty to forty centimeters are thought to have the best flavor and firmest texture. The fish is hermaphroditic, changing from male to female; males are generally smaller, up to about thirty-five centimeters long, while females are forty centimeters or longer. The spawning season is from spring to summer, and the fish is best fleshed out in summer. Bartail flathead is a luxury white-meat fish. The flesh has a firm, chewy texture and a refined flavor, and when served in thin slices (*usu-zukuri*) is on a par with *fugu* (pufferfish) as a delicacy. It is served not only as sashimi but grilled with salt, deep-fried as tempura, and in hot-pot and other dishes.

CUTTING BARTAIL FLATHEAD INTO THREE PIECES
(*Daimyo-oroshi*)

Daimyo-oroshi is a variant of filleting into three pieces. Cutting in from the dorsal side at the head end and slicing back over the backbone toward the tail, this filleting technique leaves more flesh on the bones. It is used for fish with soft or easily damaged flesh or when the flesh is thin on the bones.

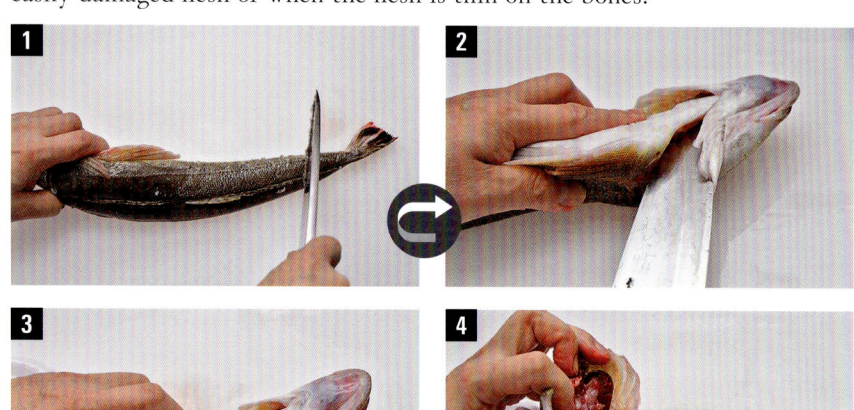

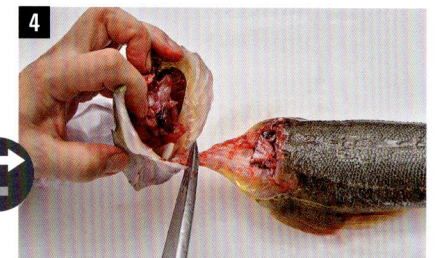

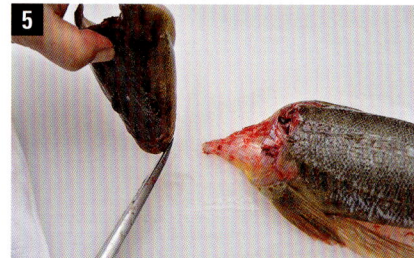

Removing the scales, head, and internal organs

1 Place the head to the left, dorsal side up. With the *deba* knife, scrape off the scales in strokes moving from tail to head. Turn the fish over and scrape off the scales on the ventral side.

2 With the ventral side up, place the head to the right. With the blade facing up (*sakasabocho*) and to the right, open the gill cover with the tip, insert the tip, and cut away the gills where they are attached under the jaw.

3 With the knife vertical and blade down, cut the membrane that attaches the gills to the collar.

4 Cut the membrane along the edge of the collar and remove the head.

5 Shows the head (left), which contains the gills, and the body (right).

6 Make an incision in the center of the jaw, as shown.

7 Turning the fish so the head end is away from you, insert the knife in the vent with the blade facing up (*sakasabocho*) and cut through the center of the belly toward the head end to meet the cut made in step **6**.

8 When the belly is cut through to the vent, open out with the fingers.

9 Open the belly with the left hand and, with the knife, steady the underpart of the collar; then pull out the internal organs.

10 Cut the membranes containing bloody parts with the tip of the knife.

11 Under running water, use a *sasara* or other stiff brush to clean away the blood and debris remaining in the cavity. Blot with a cloth.

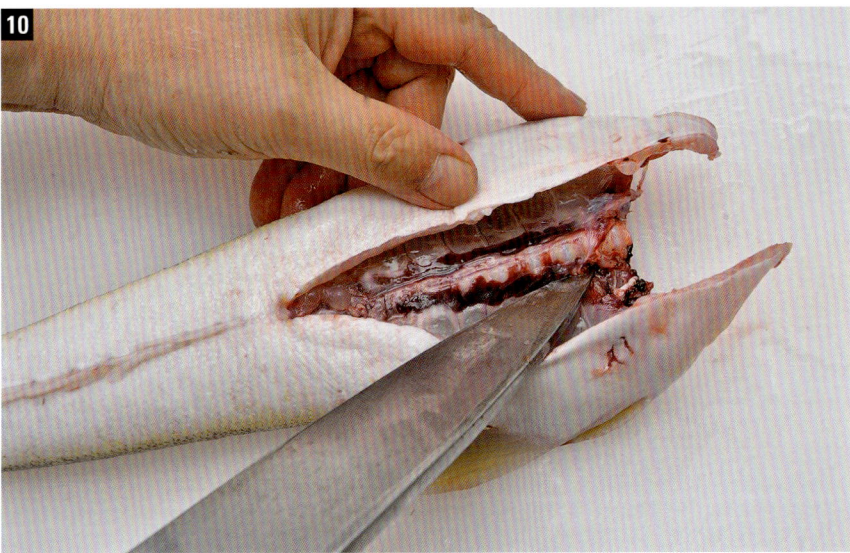

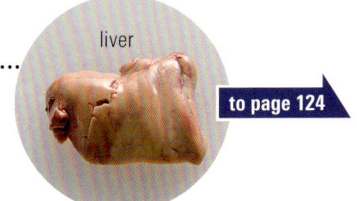

liver

to page 124

Daimyo-oroshi filleting

1 Place the head end facing away from you and the tail toward you. Insert the knife on the left side of the dorsal fin.

2 Cut along the spine from the incision at the head end, straight through toward the tail.

3 Holding the cut open with the left hand makes cutting easier.

4 Cut through to the tail, removing the fillet.

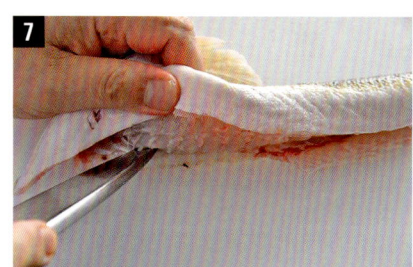

5 Place the remaining part of the fish with the head end and belly side toward you. Insert the knife at the side of the anal fin.

6 Steadying the fish with the left hand and holding the knife horizontally, cut in the direction of the head, sliding the blade over the central bones.

7 With the tip of the knife, cut the tissue connecting the central bones and the belly bones.

8 Place the fish with the head end away from you and the tail facing you. Insert the knife alongside the dorsal fin.

9 Lifting the flesh with the left hand, slide the knife, blade held flat, along the central bones, moving toward the tail.

10 Cut through the flesh between the fillet and the central bones.

11 Place the fish with the head end to the left, belly side facing you. With the blade facing away from the head end (*sakasabocho*), cut off the fillet at the base of the tail.

to facing page

lower fillet (*shitami*)

central bones (*nakabone*)

upper fillet (*uwami*)

from facing page

Removing the collar and the belly bones

1. Place the lower fillet with the head end to the left. Lift the ventral fin with the knife and insert the blade behind it.

2. Remove the collar, cutting through at an angle. Remove the collar from the other fillet in the same way.

3. Place the fillet with the head end away from you. With the knife horizontal and facing right (*sakasabocho*) as shown, insert the tip at the base of the belly bones.

4. Pressing on the belly bones from above with the fingers of the left hand, slip the knife between the belly bones and the flesh. The belly bones are curved and sink into the flesh, so the bones should be cut off along with a small amount of flesh.

5. Cut away the belly bones at the edge of the fillet.

6. With deboning tweezers, remove any remaining small bones.

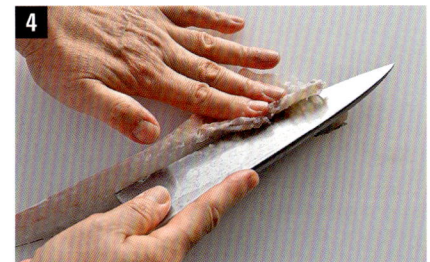

belly bones

Removing the skin

1 Change to a *yanagiba* knife. Place the fillet with the tail end to the left. Insert the knife, blade facing right (*sakasabocho*), between the skin and the flesh at the tail end.

2 While pulling on the tip of the skin with the left hand, slide the knife between the skin and flesh toward the head end and remove the skin.

fillet with the skin removed

Usu-zukuri

Because the flesh of the bartail flathead is quite dense, the best way to serve it as sashimi is in paper-thin slices (*usu-zukuri*), which allow enjoyment of the chewy yet soft texture.

1 Lightly pressing the flesh with the left hand, begin slicing thinly from the heel of the knife, drawing the blade toward you in a single motion.

2 Slices should be 2 to 3 mm (about ⅛ in.) thick.

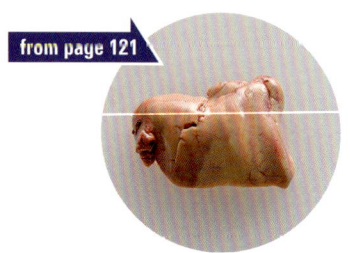

from page 121

Bartail flathead liver may be enjoyed as *kimojoyu* (liver shoyu) to accompany *usu-zukuri* sashimi, simmered or in various other ways.

Kimojoyu: First cut the veins on the surface of the liver and draw out the blood by soaking in a 3 percent salt solution for half a day. Start cooking the liver from cold water, removing it 1½ minutes after water comes to a boil over high heat. Blot away moisture and put through a fine sieve. Soften the sieved liver with a mixture of equal amounts of de-alcoholized sake and shoyu, for a delicacy distinguished by the rich flavor of the liver itself.

Thin-sliced Bartail Flathead Sashimi

skin, after blanching in boiling water

shiso leaves

carrot curls

aka-oroshi

sudachi

Okoze
DEVIL STINGER

Inimicus japonicus

Inimicus is the genus of venomous fishes of the order Scorpaeniformes, the only edible species of which is the devil stinger, *I. japonicus*. The fish, called *okoze* in Japanese, has a large, flattish head, no scales, and a rugged, rock-like appearance that is rather grotesque. It is nevertheless considered a delicacy, and its white flesh has a refined taste on a par with the much-prized *fugu* (see pp. 152–153). Endowed with protective coloration, it turns various colors in accordance with the hues of its habitat on the sandy, rocky bottom of the sea and can be blackish brown, reddish brown, and other colors.

The spines of its dorsal fin are connected with poison glands. The sting of these spines causes severe and long-lasting pain, so care is needed in touching the live fish, since it may attempt to strike when removed from water or handled.

Devil stinger is thought to taste the best from early spring to early summer, but it is available on the market all year long. The flesh is firm as well as refined in taste. It is served as sashimi and *kara-age* deep-fry and produces a tasty broth, so is well suited to soups and hot pot.

CUTTING DEVIL STINGER INTO THREE PIECES
(*Daimyo-oroshi*)

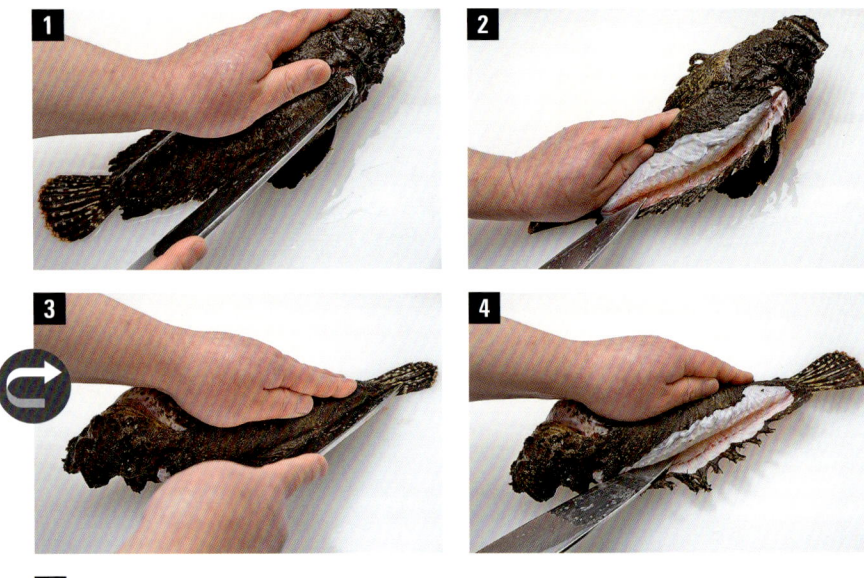

Removing the dorsal fin and preparation of the internal organs

1 Insert the *deba* knife at the crown of the head to paralyze and kill the fish by the *ikejime* technique described on page 43. Remove the poison-containing dorsal fin (steps **1** through **6**). Place the fish with the head facing away from you, back-side up. Taking care not to touch the spines, sink the knife in deeply along the side of the dorsal fin.

2 Cut along the dorsal fin where it attaches to the spine and open up the flesh all the way to the tail.

3 Now place the head facing left and cut in deeply from the tail along the base of the dorsal fin.

4 Open the fish along the base of the dorsal fin all the way to the base of the head.

5 Holding up the flesh with the left hand, use the knife to press the dorsal fin at the tail end against the cutting board, and pull it out of the body.

6 In order to avoid touching the poisonous dorsal fin, hold the fin down firmly with the knife and pull the body away, separating them. (Because of the poison in the spines, special care should be taken in disposing of this part of the fish, by burning or other safe means.)

7 Place the head to the right and the belly facing up. Press down the tip of the head with the knife. Insert the fingers into the gill cover and pull up firmly on the body.

8 Insert the knife at the base of the lower jaw.

9 Slice in the joint between the base of the jaw and the spine and cut off the head.

10 The head removed. The gills remain on the head side.

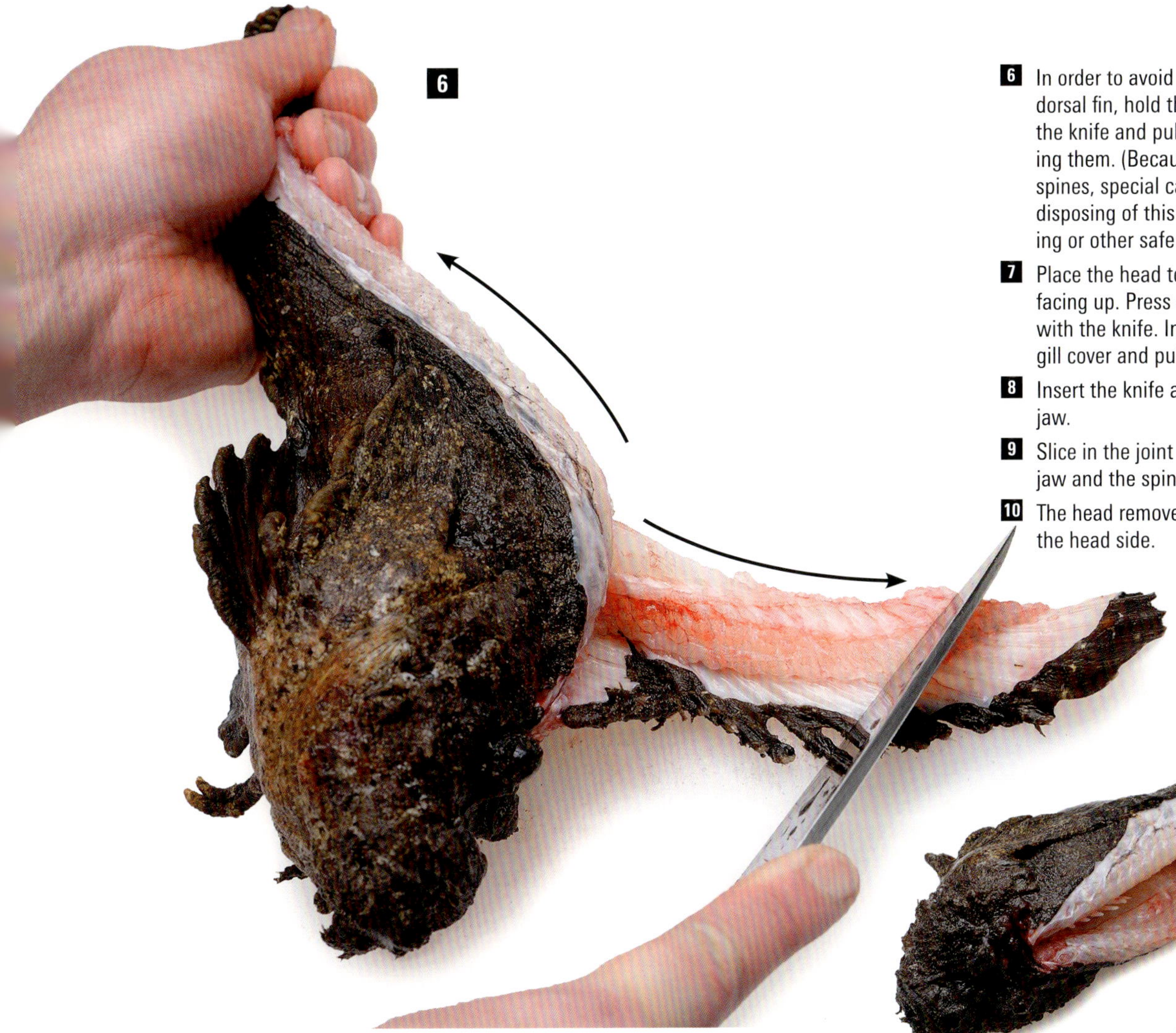

dorsal fin removed

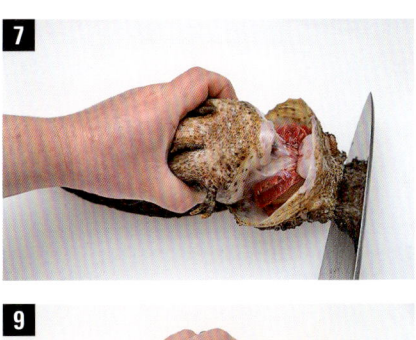

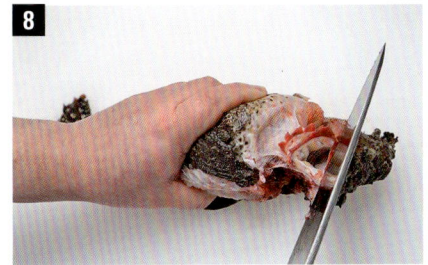

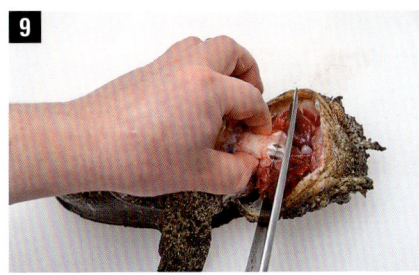

11 Place the fish dorsal side up with the head end facing you. Holding up the tail with the left hand (the body is soft and slippery, so it is helpful to hold it by the tail), make an incision in the center of the base of the collar, as shown.

12 Hold the fish with the head end facing to the right and the belly side facing you. Insert the knife at the incision made in step **11** and cut the center of the belly in the direction of the tail, as shown.

13 Cut all the way to the vent (the internal organs will now be clearly visible).

14 Holding down the lower part of the collar with the knife, pull out the internal organs with the left hand.

15 Cut off the organs where they are attached to the body.

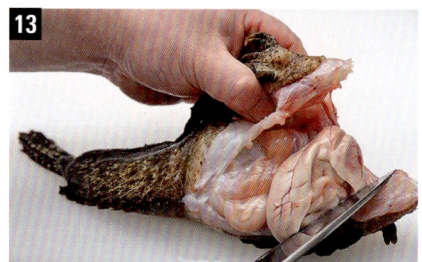

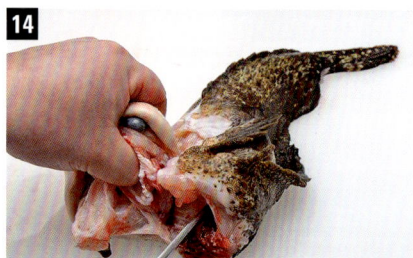

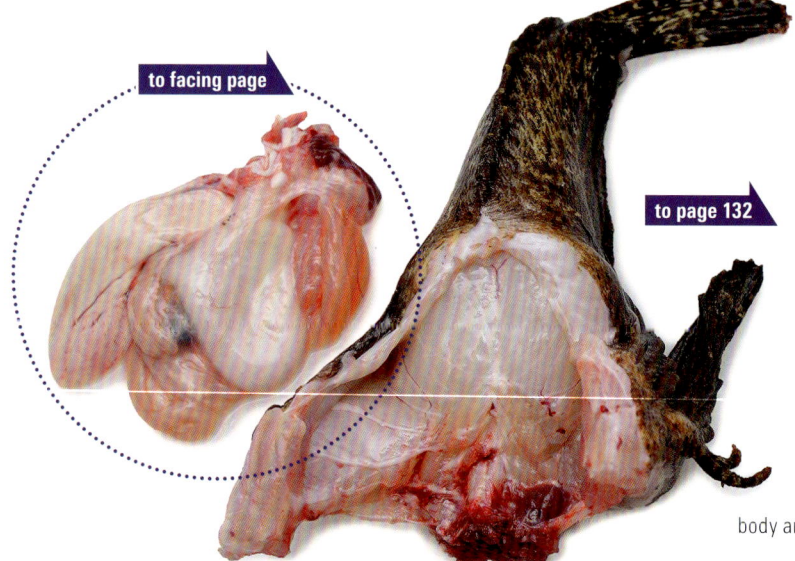

to facing page

to page 132

body and removed internal organs

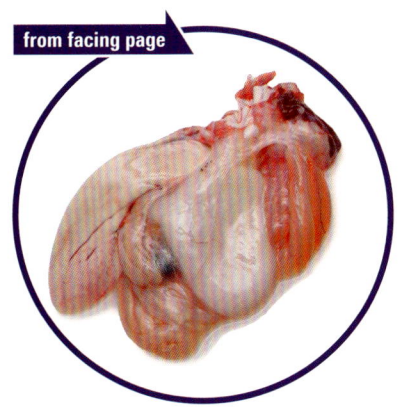
from facing page

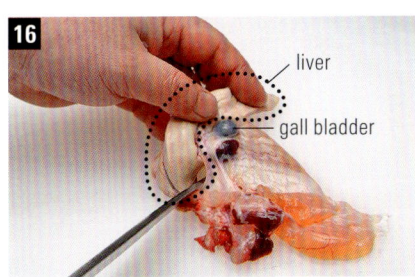

liver
gall bladder

16 Cut the attachments to the stomach and liver. Be careful not to puncture the gall bladder (green in the photo), causing its bitterness to flavor other parts of the flesh.

17 Remove the liver.

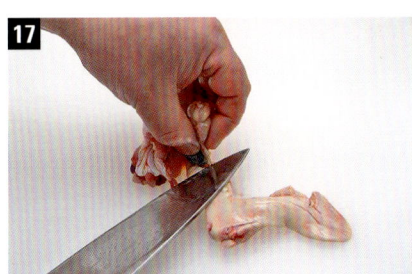

18 Shows the liver cut away.

19 Cut the ovary sac from the intestines.

20 Separate the intestines from the stomach.

21 Scrape off the surface membrane of the stomach with the knife.

22 Cut the edge of the stomach (to open up the stomach sac).

23 Open the stomach sac and scrape it inside to remove extraneous membranes.

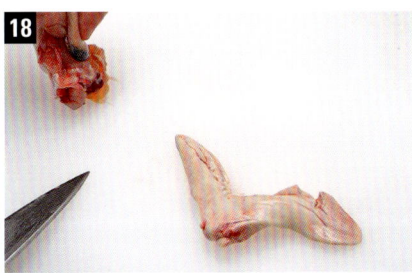

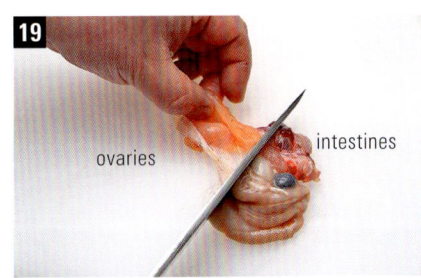
ovaries   intestines

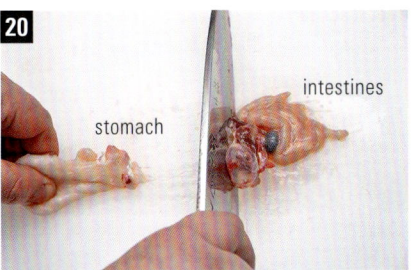
stomach   intestines

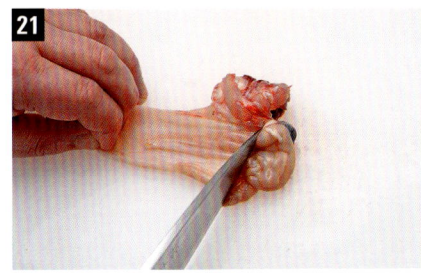

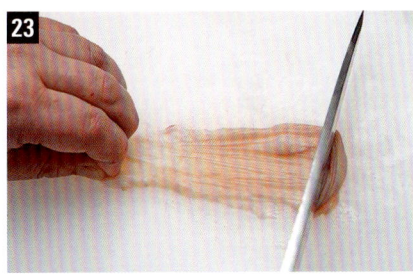

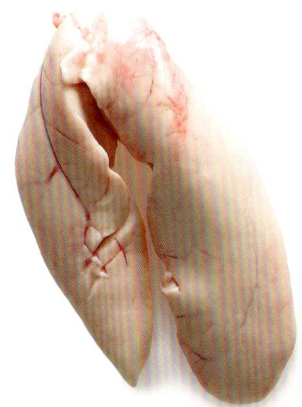

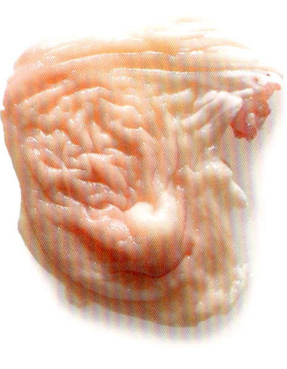

From left: ovaries, liver, stomach.
The intestines, gall bladder, and heart are not eaten and may be discarded.

from page 130

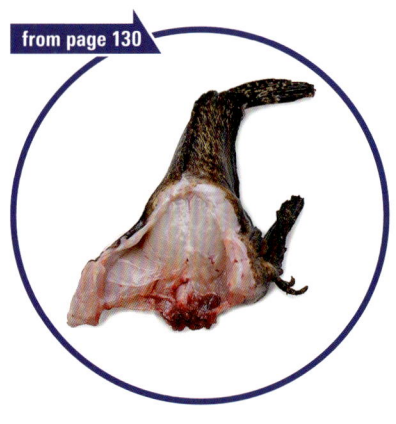

Daimyo-oroshi filleting

1 In running water, clean the fish carefully using a *sasara* or other stiff-bristled brush to remove bits of blood and debris. Blot dry with a cloth.

2 Place the back of the fish facing you. Insert the knife along the line of the dorsal fin and cut in and along toward the tail, sliding the knife over the central bones.

3 Shift the head end to the left. Cut in as far as the spine.

4 Shift the head end to the right. Lifting the flesh with the left hand, cut along and over the spine toward the tail.

5 At the tail, cut to detach the fillet.

6 Cut the attachment of the belly bones from the spine.

7 Place the remaining parts of the fish with the head end to the left, belly-bone side facing you. Insert the knife in the center of the belly from the tail end. Cut away the flesh, with the knife following the central bones.

8 Shift the head end to the right. Pulling the flesh up with the left hand, cut over the spine.

9 Lifting the flesh up, cut away from the central bones all the way to the tail.

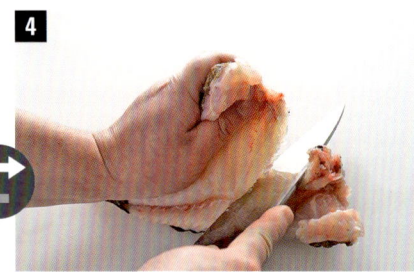

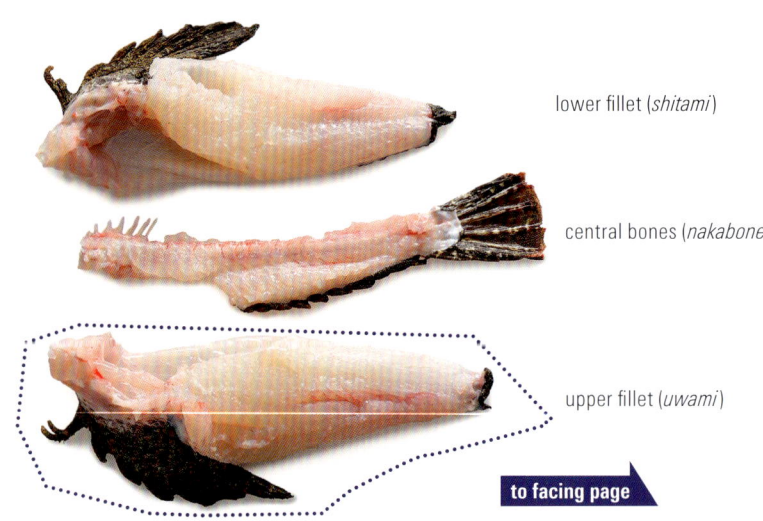

lower fillet (*shitami*)

central bones (*nakabone*)

upper fillet (*uwami*)

to facing page

completed *daimyo-oroshi* fillets

Cutting off the collar, removing the skin
Removing the belly bones

1 Place the upper fillet (*uwami*) head end to the left, skin-side down. Insert the knife at the edge of the belly bones.

2
3 Pulling the area around the belly bones with the left hand, insert the knife vertically on the side with the flesh, then pull the skin off while pushing with the knife as if to scrape off the flesh.

4 Cut the skin off at the base of the belly bones.

5 Turn the knife blade to face up (*sakasa-bocho*) and insert the tip under the base of the belly bones remaining on the fillet to separate them from the flesh.

6 Cut away the belly bones.

7 Pull out remaining small bones with deboning tweezers. Perform the same procedure for the lower fillet.

the collar, upper fillet, and skin, separated

Kuzu-dredged Devil Stinger Hot Pot

Okoze Usukuzu-jitate Nabe

To keep umami from escaping, pieces of fish are covered carefully with kuzu powder. This dish allows enjoyment of the soft and smooth texture of this type of fish.

Serves 4

1 devil stinger of about 400 to 450 g (about 1 lb.)

kuzu powder, as needed

2 sheets *hikiage yuba* (about 30 cm x 12 cm or about 12 in. x 5 in. fresh *yuba*, each cut in half)

4 stems *mitsuba* (honewort/trefoil), blanched

100 g (3⅓ oz.) *mibuna* (a type of wild mustard, cut to 7 cm or about 2½ in.)

150 g (5 oz.) tofu, cut into 8 equal parts

2 Tbsp. sake

½ Tbsp. juice of grated ginger

Devil stinger dashi

  bones of 1 devil stinger

  1 L (about 4 cups) *ichiban* dashi (p. 245)

  5 g kombu (sheet about 15 cm x 7 cm or 6 in. x 3 in.)

  ½ tsp. salt

  1 tsp. *usukuchi* shoyu

  2 Tbsp. sake

  dissolved kuzu powder (20 g or ⅔ oz. kuzu dissolved in 4 Tbsp. water)

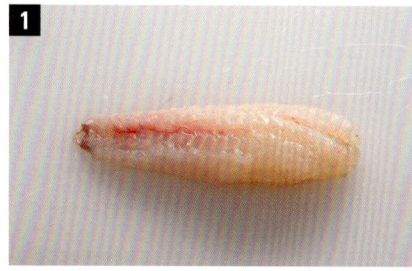

Kuzu-dredged devil stinger morsels

1 Use the upper fillet of devil stinger prepared as above.

2 Score the fillet at 5 mm (¼ in.) intervals and cut into four equal pieces.

3 Sprinkle lightly with salt (about 1 percent by weight of the fillet).

4 Dust kuzu powder over the devil stinger pieces, applying the powder carefully with a brush so that it entirely covers all surfaces. Plunge the dusted pieces in boiling water for 30 seconds so that they are about halfway cooked through. Transfer to ice water for about 5 seconds to remove most of the heat, then remove and drain.

Make the hot pot

1 Sprinkle salt over the head (cut in two), collar, central bones, belly bones, liver, ovaries, and stomach sac (3 percent by their total weight) and let stand for about 30 minutes. Plunge into boiling water briefly and transfer to cold water (*shimofuri*); remove any debris.

2 Place the collar, bones, and organs in a pot, add the *ichiban* dashi and kombu, and place over high heat. Reduce heat to low just before it boils and skim off foam while it simmers for 10 minutes. Season with salt and *usukuchi* shoyu, and add a slight viscosity using dissolved kuzu.

3 Transfer devil stinger dashi and the collar, liver, stomach sac, and ovaries to a clay hot pot. Add the *yuba* pieces (tied up with the *mitsuba* stems), tofu, and kuzu-dredged morsels and place the pot over medium heat. When the broth comes to a boil, add the *mibuna* leaves, and lastly the sake and ginger juice. Adding the sake at the end brings the whole together and unites the flavors into one.

Amadai
TILEFISH

Branchiostegus japonicus

Tilefish is a general term for members of the family Malacanthidae (order Perciformes). Three species of tilefish are fished in Japan's coastal waters—red tilefish (*aka amadai*), yellow tilefish (*ki amadai*), and white tilefish (*shiro amadai*).

The species most commonly found in markets in Japan is the red tilefish. The fish is widely known in the Kansai region as *guji*, a word that is also often used to refer to lightly-salted tilefish.

Recognizable for its large head with pronounced forehead, the tilefish is between thirty and fifty centimeters in length and reddish in color. It is in season between autumn and spring and is considered tastiest in winter, when it carries the most fat. Since ancient times *amadai* has been an especially prized

fish for the umami and sweetness of its flavor.

While the flesh is heavy with water and is thus soft and easily crushed, the scales and bones are extremely hard, so skillful carving takes some practice. Before carving, the fish is usually salted lightly in order to remove excess water. Tilefish is well suited to a wide variety of dishes—grilled Wakasa-style with scales attached, served raw (as is or cured in kombu), cured in miso, steamed, and cooked in soup. The skin has a distinctively sweet aroma when roasted, so the skin, scales not removed, is left for grilling. Preparation of the fish differs depending on the dish. Two methods are presented here, one for filleting after removing the scales, and the other for splitting the fish, head and all, through the center line in a butterfly cut (*sebiraki*) without removing the scales.

CUTTING TILEFISH INTO THREE PIECES
(*Harabiraki*)

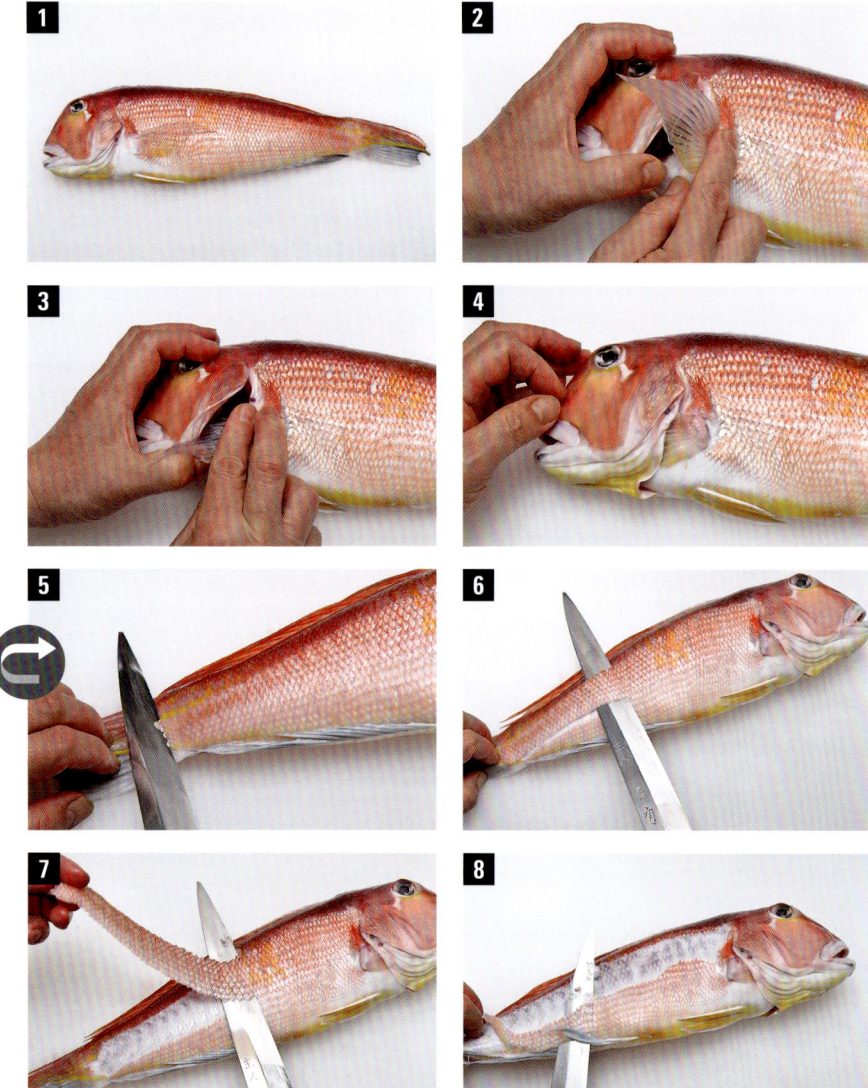

Preparation

1 Wipe away the mucous film from the surface of the fish with a cloth and place it with the head to the left, belly facing you.

2 Pull open the gill cover with the left hand and with the right hand lift the pectoral fin at its base.

3 On both sides of the fish, insert the pectoral fin into the gill cover.
4

5 Place the head to the right and the belly facing you. Holding the tail firmly with the left hand, place a *yanagiba* knife at the base of the tail, blade facing up (*sakasabocho*) and to the right.

6 Moving the knife up and down, slice off the thin outer layer of skin with the scales (*sukibiki* technique) as shown. *Sukibiki* is performed most often when opening the fish from the belly, but sometimes in the case of *sebiraki* (opening from the back of the fish). Cut off the layer up to the edge of the gill cover. In slicing away the scales, be careful not to cut into the skin itself.
7

8 Use the same technique to slice off the thin layer with the scales from the entire body.

scales removed from the entire
fish by the *sukibiki* technique

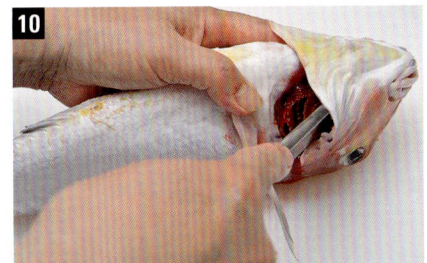

9 Pull out the pectoral fins from the gill cover and place the head to the right with the belly facing up. Now using a *deba* knife, open the gill cover with the left hand and, with the blade facing upward, insert the tip into the gill cover to cut the gills off on one side where they are attached.

10 Cut the attachment of the gills on the other side.

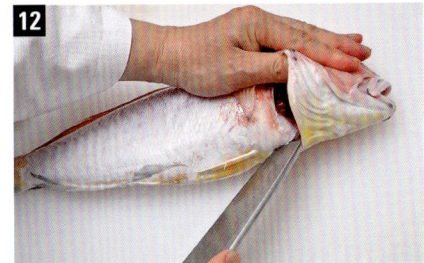

11 Remove the detached gills from the gill cover.

12 With the head to the right and belly facing you, insert the knife, blade facing the tail, at the underside of the jaw.

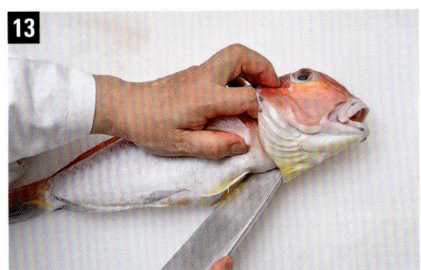

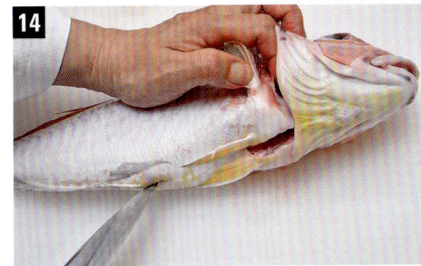

13 Steadying the fish with the left hand, cut along the belly to the area by the base of the ventral fins.

14 Turn the knife to the right (*sakasabocho*) and insert the tip at the base of the anal fins.

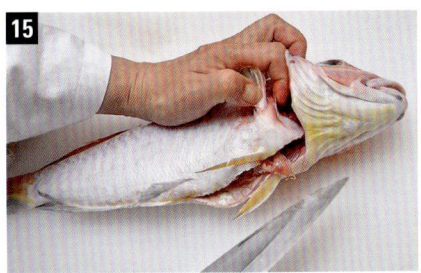

15 Continue cutting in the direction of the head, connecting with the opening made in step **13**.

16 Remove the internal organs from the abdominal cavity.

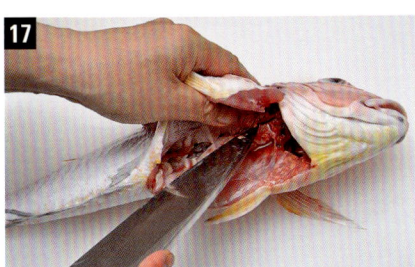

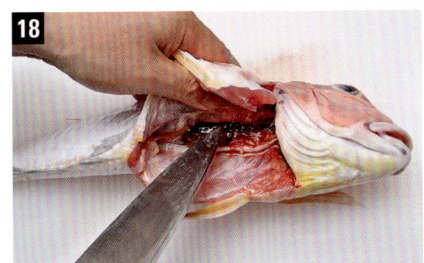

17 Insert the knife tip into the membranes
18 visible at the back of the abdominal cavity and cut them open.

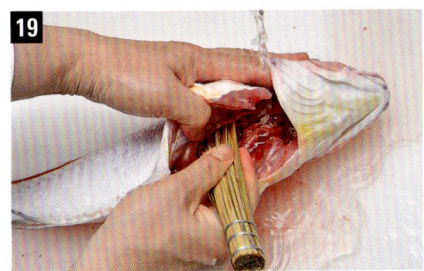

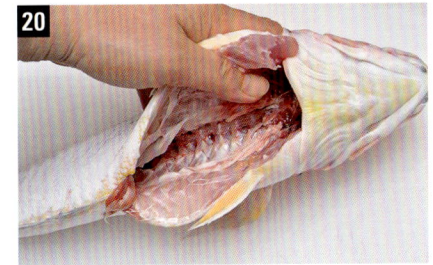

19 In running water, clean out the blood, tissue, and other debris using a *sasara* or other stiff brush.

20 The abdominal cavity cleaned out.

Removing the head

1 Place the head to the left and the belly facing you. Insert the knife at an angle under the pectoral fin as shown.

2 Grip the head with the left hand and cut in until the knife meets the spine.

3 Turn the fish over so that the belly faces away from you and place the knife at an angle (matching the angle in step **1**) under the pectoral fin.

4 Cut in until the knife meets the spine.

5 Press with the knife and cut through the spine where it connects to the head, cutting away the head.

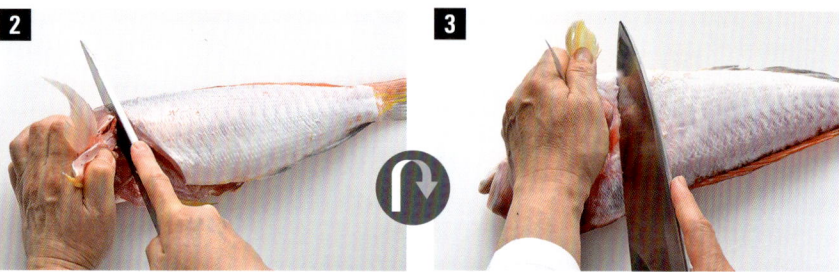

the head cut away, leaving as little flesh on it as possible

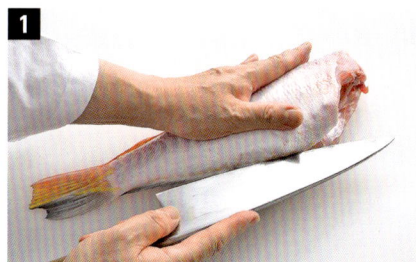

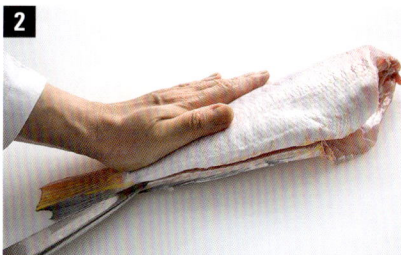

Cutting the upper fillet

The tilefish flesh is soft and the bones hard, making it difficult to separate the flesh from the bones, so the first three steps are performed in preparation for filleting the lower side later on.

1 Place the fish with the tail to the left and the belly facing you. Position the knife at the cut in the belly of the fish.

2 Cut straight along the belly, passing just to the side of the anal fin.

3 Make another pass with the knife, running the blade over the central bones. Cut in further, sliding the blade over the central bones and separating the ventral flesh from the bones.

4 Place the fish with the tail to the left and the back of the fish facing you. Steadying the fish with the left hand, position the knife just above the dorsal fin.

5 Cut in at an angle, sliding the blade over the central bones and toward the tail.

6 Reinsert the knife, lifting the flesh while cutting further in.

7 Make another pass with the knife, cutting in deeper and separating the dorsal flesh from the bones.

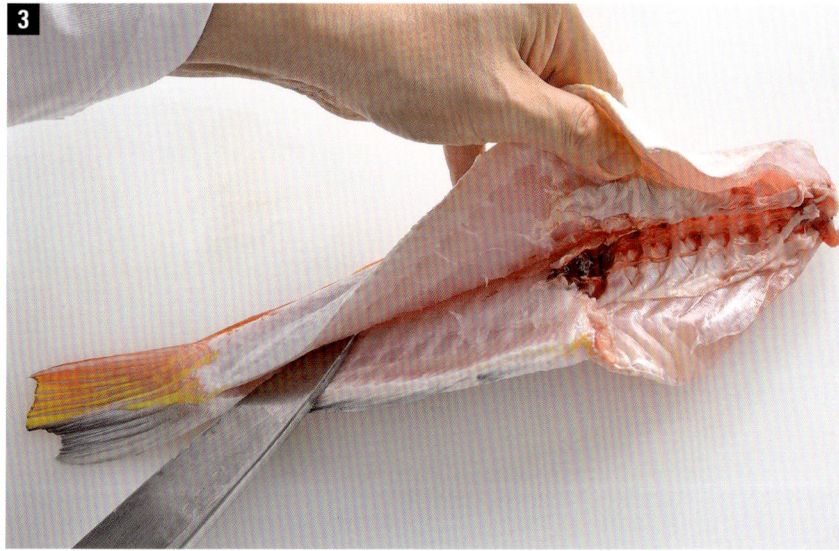

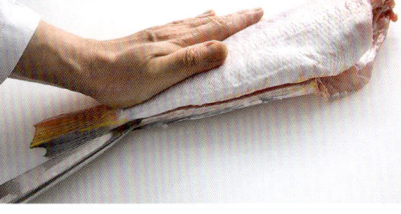

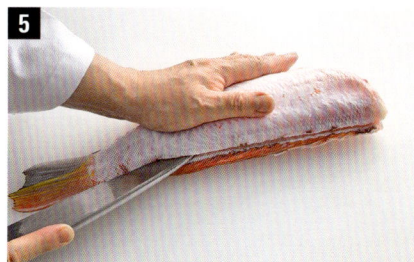

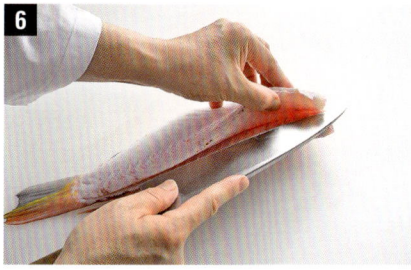

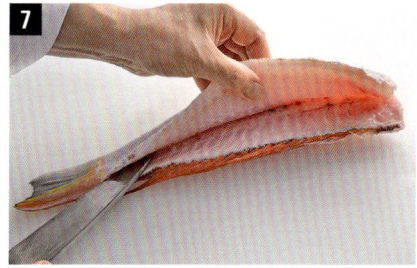

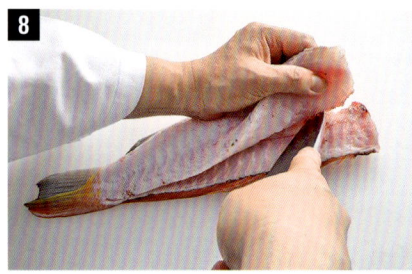

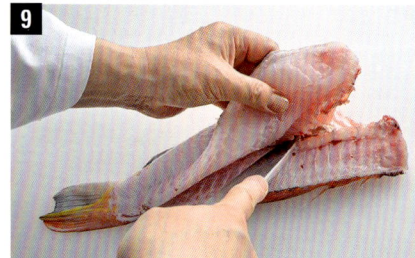

8 Position the knife on the belly bones where they are connected to the spine. Apply extra pressure to cut the belly bones from the spine, sliding the blade over the spine.

9 Continue cutting to about midway along the spine.

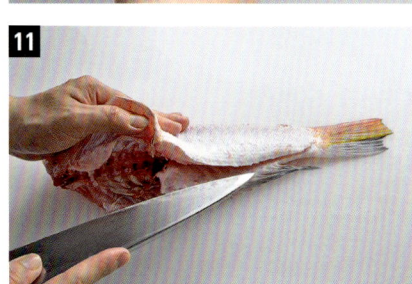

10 Turn over the fish so that the tail is to the right, belly side facing you, and position the knife just above the anal fin. Cut while sliding the knife over the central bones.

11 Lifting the ventral flesh with the left hand, check to see that the knife has penetrated all the way across the lower central bones.

12 Place the tip of the knife, blade facing to the right (*sakasabocho*), into the incision made in step 9 and separate the flesh from the spine.

13 Cut up to the tail. With the knife tip at the
14 base of the tail, cut the fillet free using the knife blade slightly raised, as shown.

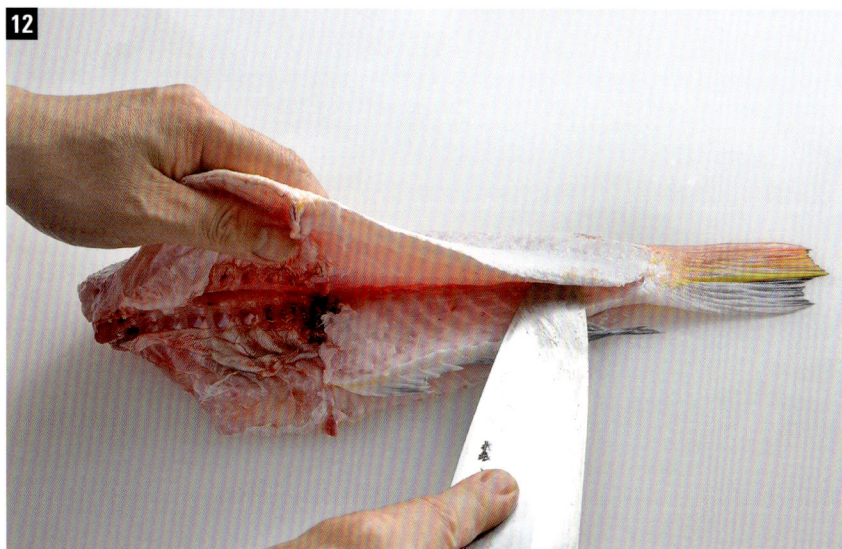

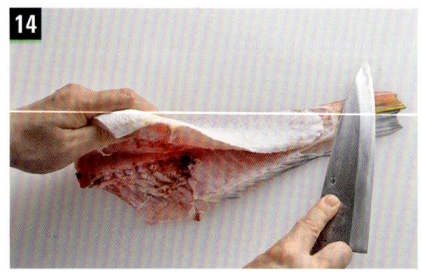

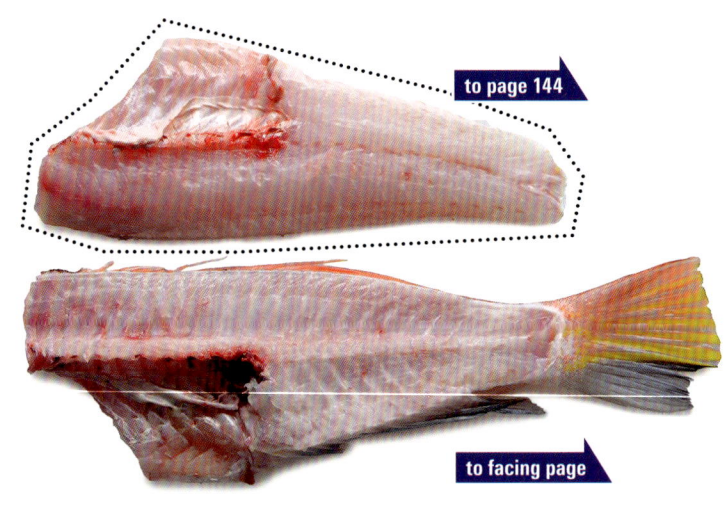

to page 144

to facing page

the lower fillet (*shitami*) cut away

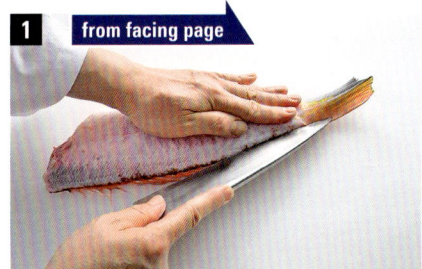

from facing page

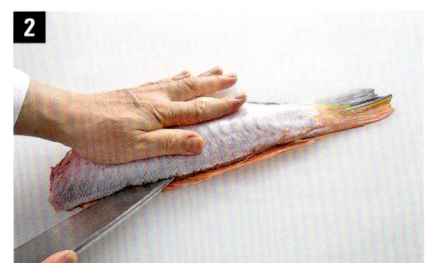

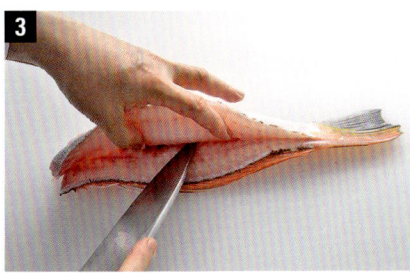

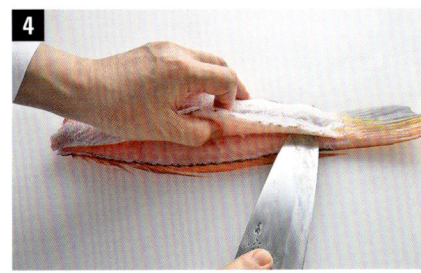

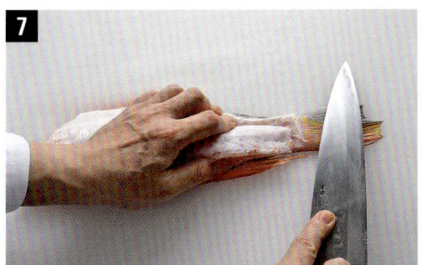

Cutting the lower fillet

1 With the tail to the right, skin-side up (dorsal side facing you), place the knife blade just over the dorsal fin.

2 Steadying the fish with the left hand, cut in firmly over the central bones. Reinsert the knife in another pass and, sliding the blade over the central bones, separate the dorsal flesh from the bones.

3 With repeated passes, cut deeper.

4 Face the knife blade to the right (*sakasa-bocho*) and cut over the central bones and spine to just before the tail, separating the fillet from the bones.

5 Turn the knife over (facing left) and insert it into the slit.

6 Continue cutting, separating the flesh from the central bones and spine.

7 With the blade facing right (*sakasa-bocho*), cut through the flesh at the base of the tail, separating the fillet from the tail.

the completed fillets (from top):
upper fillet (*uwami*)
central bones (*nakabone*)
lower fillet (*shitami*)

from page 142

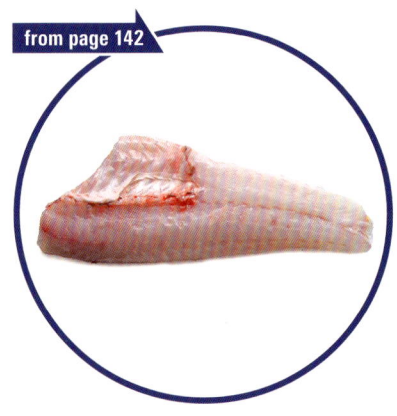

Removing the belly bones
Removing the skin

1 Steadying the fillet with the left hand (dorsal side facing you), use the tip of the knife to cut the base of the belly bones from the flesh.

2 Turn the fillet around so that the head end is facing you, insert the knife where the base of the belly bones was cut from the flesh and cut shallowly to peel off the belly bones.

3 Reinsert the knife and slice off the belly bones. Cut off at the edge.

4 Remove remaining bones using deboning tweezers.

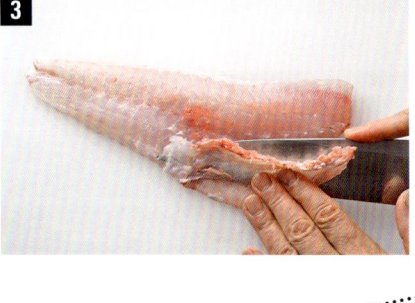

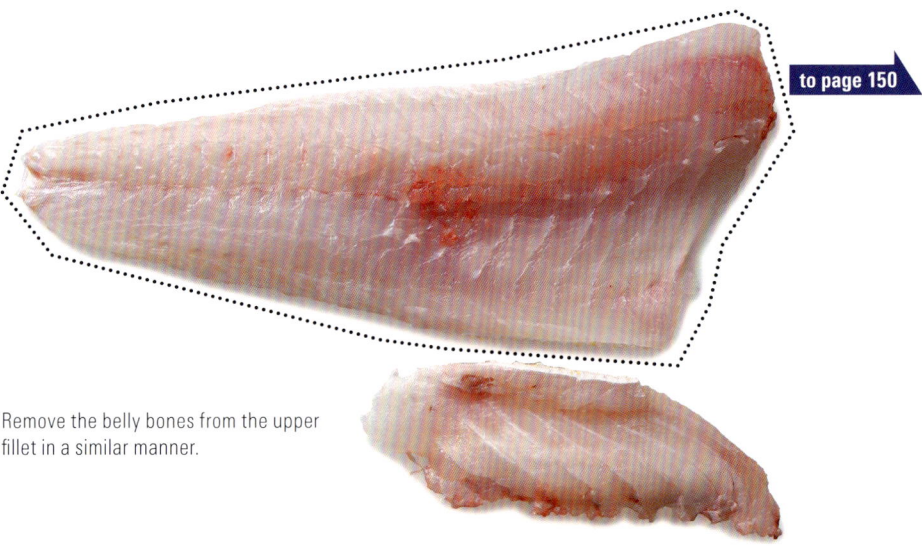

to page 150

Remove the belly bones from the upper fillet in a similar manner.

BUTTERFLY CUT (*Sebiraki*)

One of the leading preparations of tilefish (*amadai*) is by salting and grilling in the aromatic *wakasa-yaki* style, without descaling. Tilefish's soft flesh spoils easily, so it is generally salted down immediately after catch. The following shows how to open the fish from the back in the butterfly cut, the scales left on.

Leave the scales on.
Wipe the mucous film from the fish with a cloth.

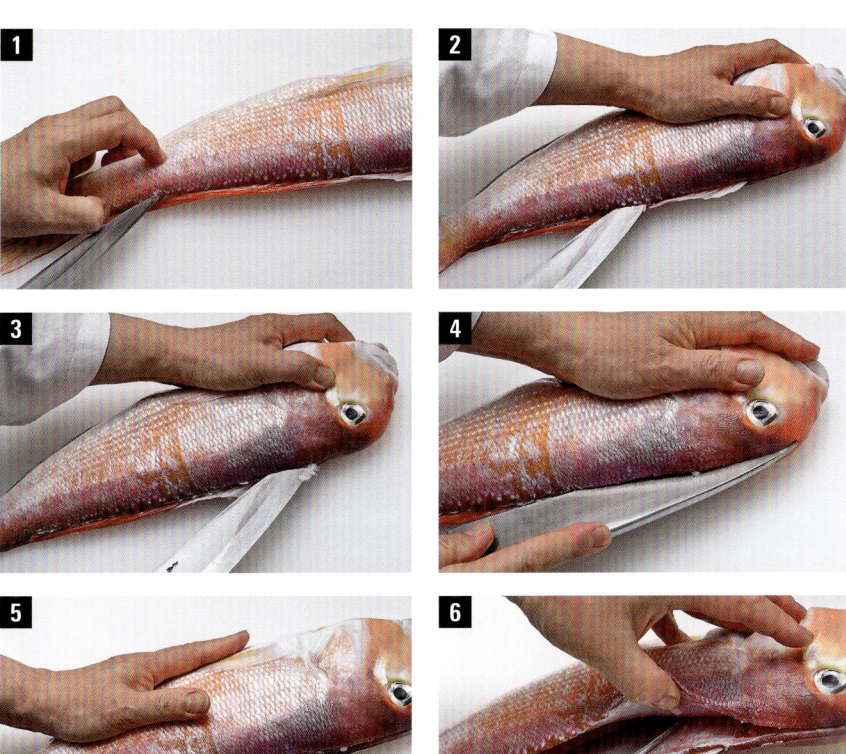

1 Place the fish with the tail to the left, dorsal side facing you. Using a *deba* knife with blade facing right (*sakasabocho*), insert the tip of the knife at the tail just above the dorsal fin.

2 Make a shallow cut along the dorsal fin, continuing onward toward the head.

3 Making this cut against the grain of the scales helps to prevent the scales from falling into the cut. Continue to just above the eyes.

4 Turn the knife over with the blade now facing left and reinsert in the cut made in step **3**.

5 Holding the body with the left hand, cut toward the tail, sliding the blade over the central bones.

6 In repeated passes of the knife, cut the dorsal flesh away from the central bones.

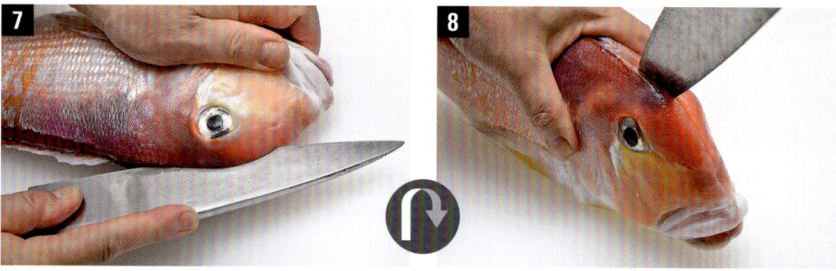

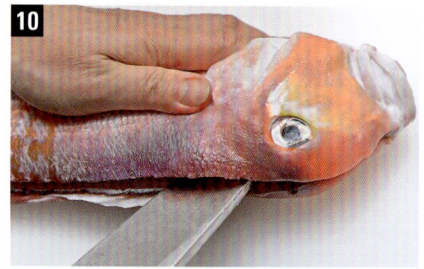

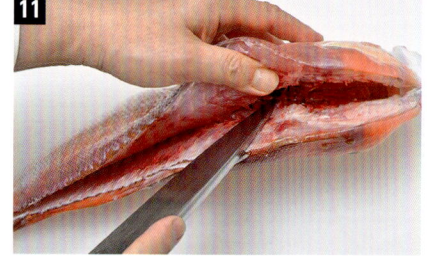

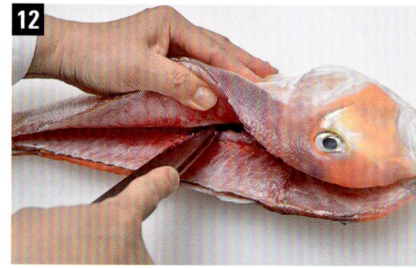

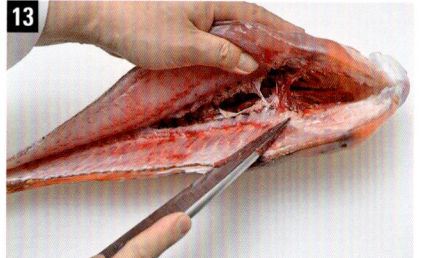

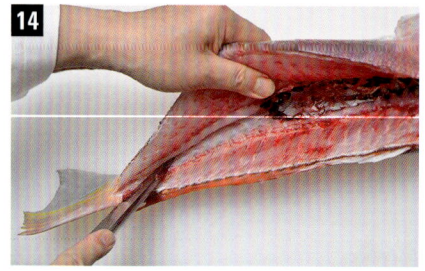

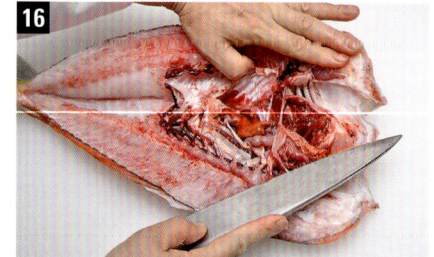

7 In preparation for splitting the head in half, make an incision along the center line between the eyes. Continue the incision down to the upper jaw.

8 Place the fish belly down and grip the body firmly with the left hand. Insert the knife vertically into the crown of the head.

9 Push the knife in and down firmly so that it splits the head cleanly in half to just above the jaw.

10 With the dorsal side facing you, reinsert the knife, blade facing left, in the cut made in the head.

11 Position the knife at the base of the belly bones, where they connect to the spine.

12 While cutting the belly bones away from the spine, slide the knife over the spine in the direction of the tail.

13 When the belly bones are cut loose, the internal organs beyond them will be visible.

14 Insert the knife further beyond the spine toward the tail, separating the ventral flesh from the central bones.

15 Place the fish on its belly and insert the knife vertically in the cut in the head, as shown. Cut down firmly, splitting the upper jaw in half.

16 Press down firmly on both halves of the fish to spread it open.

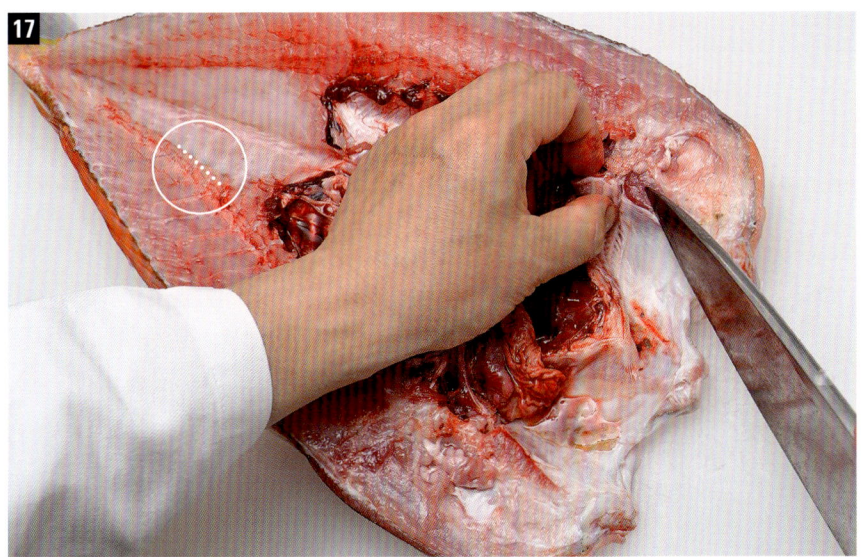

17 Pull out the gills and cut them away at the base. Make a 5 cm (about 2 in.) incision at the edge of the central bones (see dotted line). The incision allows the salt to more easily permeate the flesh as a whole.

18 Cut the base of the gills on the other side and remove.

19 Cut away the tissues holding the internal organs to the head end.

20 Cut away the other tissues holding the organs in place.

21 Remove the organs and wash fish in running water.

22 Wash carefully, using a *sasara* or other stiff brush to remove the blood and debris among the bones. Blot dry with a cloth.

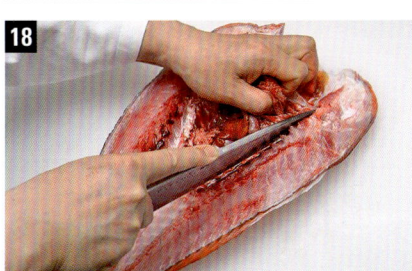

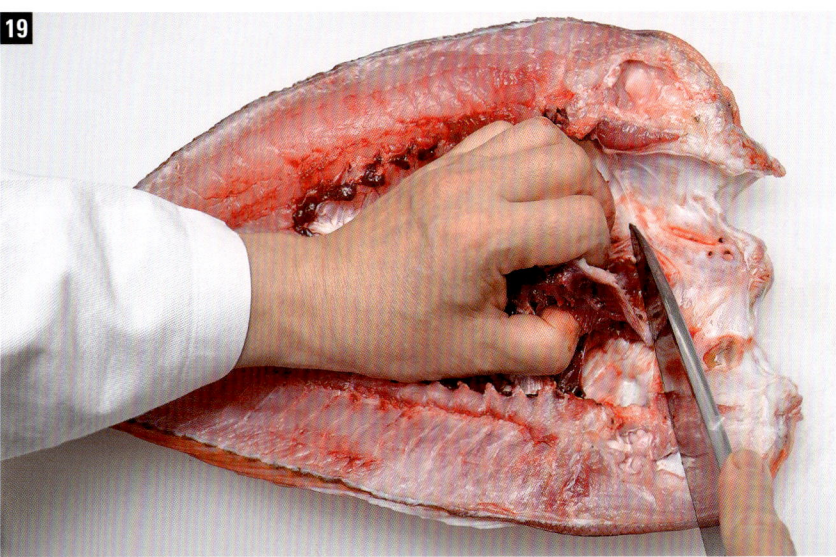

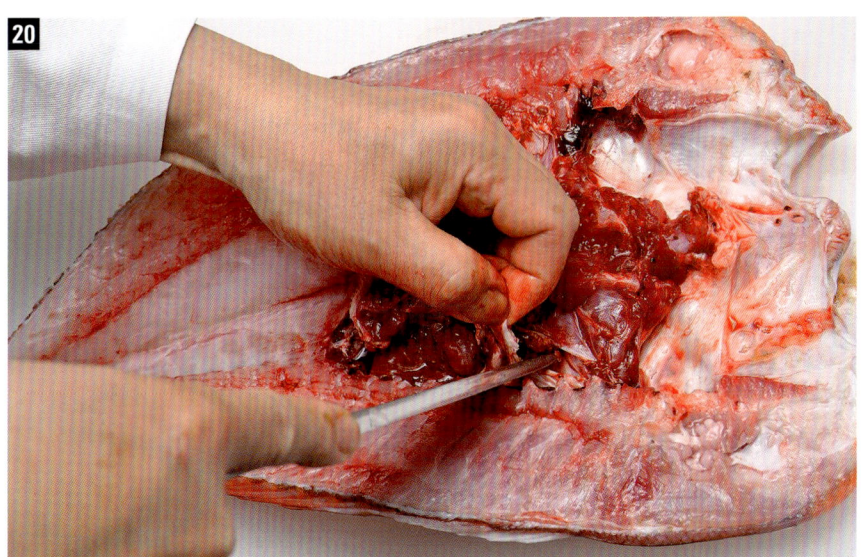

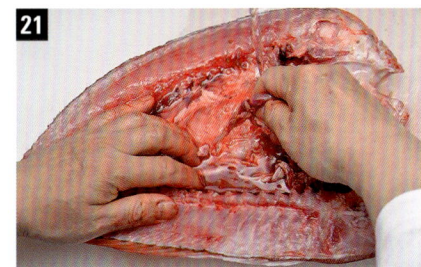

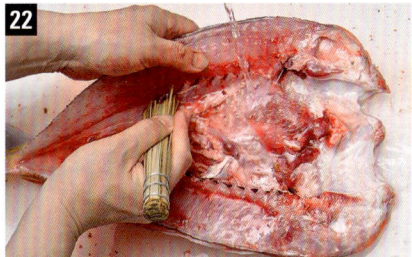

Light salting

1 Place the opened fish skin-side down on a cutting board lightly sprinkled with salt.

2 Sprinkle salt (2 percent by weight) by hand lightly over the entire fish. Sprinkle liberally where the flesh is thickest, more scantly for the area around the tail and more thinly fleshed places, and let stand in the refrigerator for at least 6 hours. (An alternative is to soak the fish in a 3 percent salt solution.)

Cutting the fish in two pieces

1 After an hour, use a cloth to blot up the moisture that has collected on the fish.

2 Place the tail to the left, skin-side down. With the *deba* knife positioned at the lower jaw as shown, make a vertical cut.

3 The bone just beyond step **2** is quite hard; bear down firmly on the knife to divide that part.

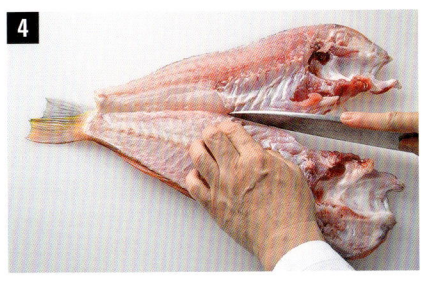 

4 Insert the knife along the center line of the belly and cut back to just beyond the belly bones.

5 Turn the knife to face left, lying flat on the bones. Lay the upper half of the fish on top of the knife so that the dorsal side is facing you.

6 Cross the left hand over to steady the fish and, with the knife remaining flat, cut toward the tail.

7 Cut through the flesh at the tail and separate the two pieces.

butterfly cut, in two pieces

Hoso-zukuri

Since tilefish flesh is high in water content, the *kobujime* curing technique (see p. 57) is well suited to the task of drawing out excess moisture and enhancing the concentration of umami. The flesh is soft and easily fragmented, so slices for *hoso-zukuri* should not be made too thin.

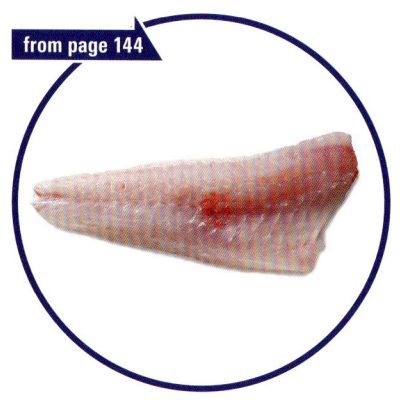

from page 144

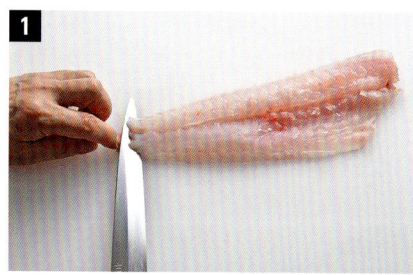

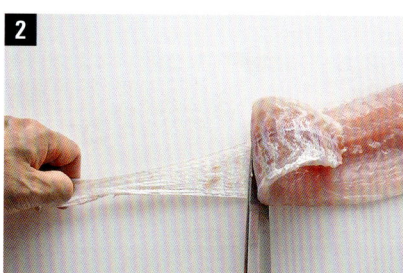

Removing the skin

1 For *hoso-zukuri* (fine-cut) sashimi, select either upper (*uwami*) or lower (*shitami*) fillet meat. Place horizontally with the head end facing away from you, skin-side down. Using a *yanagiba* knife with the blade facing to the right (*sakabocho*), insert at the tip of the tail end.

2 Pulling on the skin with the left hand, cut the flesh away from the skin, moving the knife in up and down strokes toward the head.

For cutting *hoso-zukuri* sashimi, see p. 56.

fillet with the skin removed

Fine Cut Tilefish Sashimi

kamogawa freshwater algae
hamabofu leaves
wasabi
warijoyu (p. 245)

Torafugu
TIGER PUFFER
Takifugu rubripes

Order Tetraodontiformes, suborder Tetraodontoidei, family Tetraodontidae. Tiger puffer (*torafugu*) is considered the most flavorful of pufferfish, and wild catches, especially, are classified in the top tier of all offerings on the fish market. Measuring from seventy to eighty centimeters long with a football-shaped body and no ventral fin, the fish has dense, small prickles growing on the back and abdomen. The skin is grayish black along the back and upper body, and a large white-rimmed black splotch marks the area behind each pectoral fin.

Like other pufferfish, tiger puffer contains the deadly nerve poison tetrodotoxin, and in Japan a license is required for its preparation. Toxicity varies by species, body part, and season of catch, but is known to be especially high in the liver and ovaries.

Edible portions include the flesh, skin, and milt (*shirako*). Because the milt, unlike the poisonous ovaries, is prized for its richness, male puffers generally command higher prices. The fishing season for pufferfish lasts from September to the following May, with winter as the peak. The translucent white flesh, delicate in flavor and firm and springy in texture, is variously served as sashimi (called *fugusashi* or *tessa*), grilled, deep-fried, or in a hot pot. The skin is blanched and offered raw or jellied; the milt may be grilled or simmered in a hot pot. The fins are dried, toasted over an open flame, and enjoyed for the faint flavor they impart when steeped in warmed sake.

A license is required for preparation of *fugu* in Japan. For details, see p. 154.

Handling Pufferfish

There are about one hundred species of pufferfish, and of the forty or so species that inhabit the seas around Japan, more than twenty are deemed edible. Although pufferfish stands at the pinnacle of luxury dining for its delicate and umami-rich white flesh, its liver and several other organs are lethal; some species carry a poison so powerful that even their flesh cannot be eaten. Japan has "pufferfish ordinances" (*fugu jorei*) based on the country's Food Sanitation Act, which are enforced on the local government level. They prohibit the sale of the fish's poisonous parts and are designed to prevent accidents from eating pufferfish.

It should be noted that the ordinances regarding the licensing of chefs (*chorishi*) and other *fugu*-related activities in Japan differ from one prefecture to another. For example, the ordinance on pufferfish in places like Tokyo and Kyoto defines the "handling of *fugu*" as applying to "those species of pufferfish that are edible" and as constituting the "removal, preservation in salt (*enzo*), or other processing of ovaries, livers, and other parts that may be damaging to human health." Such ordinances limit the culinary preparation of pufferfish for cooking to those who have passed official examinations. They also give detailed provisions concerning the issuing and revocation of licenses, restrictions on products processed from pufferfish, and penalties for violation.

The species of pufferfish that may be used for eating as well as the areas where they may be fished are clearly specified by law. The seventeen species so defined may be caught only in the coastal waters of Japan, the Japan Sea, the Bohai Sea, the Yellow Sea, and the East China Sea. The tiger puffer, served at exclusive restaurants, is considered the "king" of pufferfish as far as flavor, price, and quality are concerned. Pufferfish are marketed in both live and spiked (p. 40) condition and also sold after removing the poisonous parts as *migaki*, or dressed pufferfish.

Pufferfish Poison

Pufferfish in the family Tetraodontidae, the order Tetraodontiformes, carry the deadly nerve poison tetrodotoxin. The toxicity of the poison varies according to species and body part. Generally, the liver, kidneys, digestive organs, and ovaries are highly toxic. As the poisonous parts differ by species, so the edible parts differ as well. Taking the tiger puffer for example, its milt, skin, and flesh are edible, while its liver, ovaries, and digestive organs are poisonous. Ingestion of a poisonous part prompts symptoms such as vomiting, paralysis, and difficulty in breathing, which can lead to death. Recent research has shown that tetrodotoxin is not produced by pufferfish themselves but is the accumulation in their bodies of poison derived from what they feed on.

The toxicity of pufferfish is very high. The poisonous parts of a single wild tiger puffer could kill thirty adults. No effective antidote is available, and mortality is high among those who are poisoned. Amateur cooks should avoid handling pufferfish alone or without instruction and appropriate oversight.

CUTTING TIGER PUFFER

Removing the fins

1 Wash the entire fish with a stiff brush to remove the mucous film.

2 Wash carefully, especially around the fins, where parasites sometimes cluster.

3 Turn over and wash the belly side. Rinse all over once more to assure that no part has been missed. Blot dry with a cloth.

4 Wear cloth gloves to prevent injury from the rough skin. Place the head to the left. Pull out on the dorsal fin; inserting the *deba* knife at an angle, cut the fin off at the base.

5 Pull out on the pectoral fin and sever while pushing the flat surface of the knife close against the fish to make the cutting easier.

6 Turn the fish over and cut off the anal fin with knife in the manner shown in step **4** above.

7 Leaving the fish belly up, cut off the other pectoral fin as described in step **5**.

to page 177

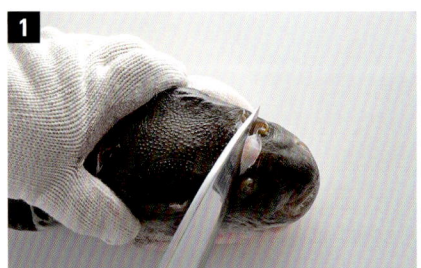

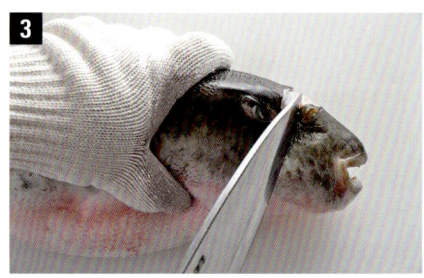

Treatment of the beak

1 Insert the knife just above the nostrils.

2 Tip the head toward you and insert the knife at an angle.

3 Tip the head away from you and insert the knife at an angle.

4 Pressing the beak against the cutting board with the knife, grip the body firmly with the left hand.

5 Position the knife under the projecting part of the collar and pry the beak part open (downward).

6 Holding the body firmly, pull out the beak part with the knife and cut it off (minimize the area of rough skin included with the beak part).

6

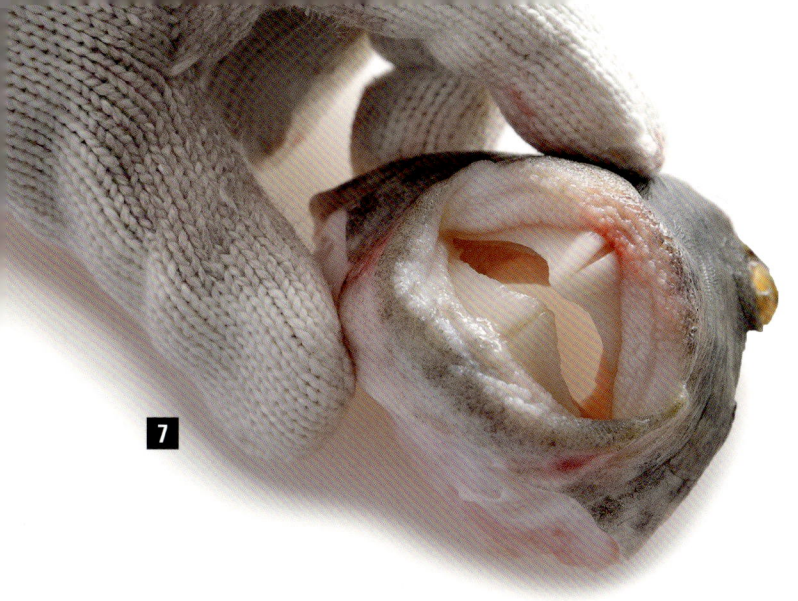

7 The beak removed. Note the two teeth in the upper and lower jaws.

8 Place the heel of the knife at the center of the upper jaw.

9 Cut down, slicing the beak in two.

10 Flatten the halves with the side of the knife.

11 Turn over the beak, grasp the tissue forming a ring around the mouth, and insert the knife at its base.

12 With the knife flat, pull the tissue around the mouth against it and cut it off.

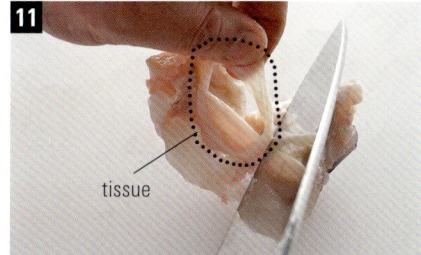

tissue

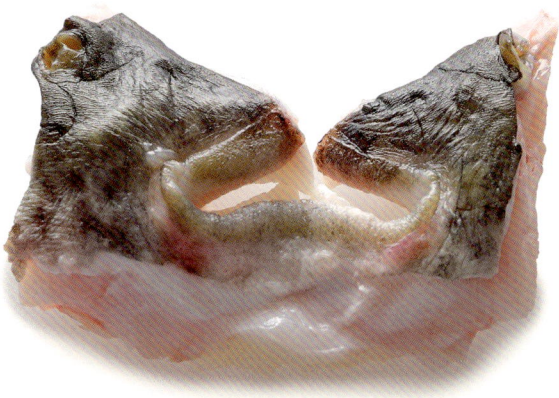

Outer side of the beak part. The skin is left on, since this piece is served after plunging in boiling water to remove the mucous film.

Removing the skin

1 Place the fish with the head end toward you.

2 While pulling on the white ventral skin with the left hand, cut through the skin from just below the aperture left after removal of the pectoral fin to the edge at the head end. Be careful not to cut into the flesh or internal organs. Leaving the inner skin (*totoumi*) beneath the white ventral skin intact (see more on p. 176), insert the knife to separate these layers from the flesh.

3 With the knife facing right (*sakasabocho*), insert the tip into the pectoral fin aperture.

4 Holding the white ventral skin up with the left hand and keeping the blade flat (to avoid cutting into the fish and damaging the flesh), cut through the skin above the pectoral fin all the way to the base of the tail.

5 Turn the fish over and cut the skin between the pectoral fin and head end on the other side as shown in step **2**.

6 Place the head end facing you and, as in step **3**, cut over the pectoral fin toward the tail with the knife facing right (*sakasabocho*).

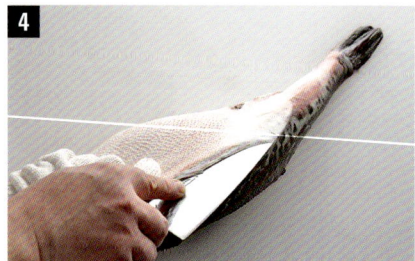

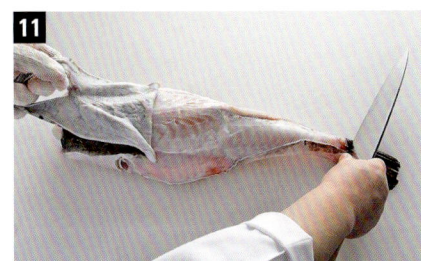

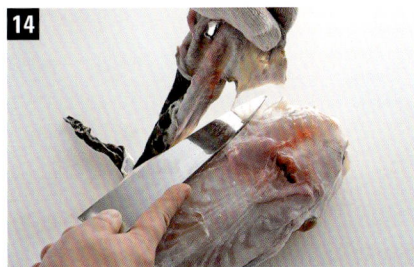

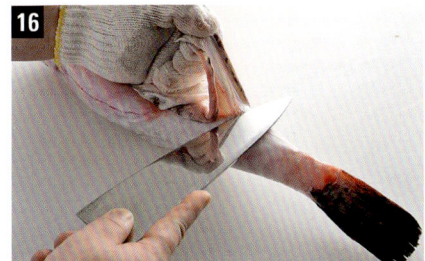

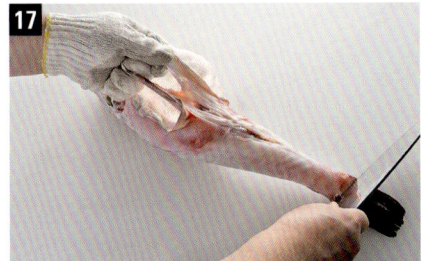

7
8 As in step **4**, cut up to the base of the tail.

9 Insert fingers under the skin at a point near the tail of the fish, raise the skin, and cut the black skin part at the base of the tail.

10 Insert fingers into the hole where the dorsal fin was removed and lift the black skin. Taking care that the inner skin does not separate from the outer, rough skin, pull both layers off toward the head.

11 After cutting the skin away up to the base of the dorsal fin, press down on the tail with the blade of the knife and, with the left hand, pull back the black skin (with inner skin attached) in one movement.

12 When the skin has been pulled back as far as the head, insert the tip of the knife between the flesh and the skin until the point is visible.

13 Then strip away the black skin together with the inner skin down toward the end where the beak was removed.

14 Sever the black skin at the lower part of the cheeks of the fish.

15 Place the fish belly-side up with the head to the left. Cut the white skin at the base of the tail.

16 Holding up the white skin, insert fingers into the hole where the anal fin was removed and lift off the white skin, cutting it away from the flesh as done in step **10**.

17 Once the white skin has been cut away to the base of the anal fin, use the knife to hold down the tail, and with the left hand draw the white skin toward the head end, pulling it off in one movement.

to page 174

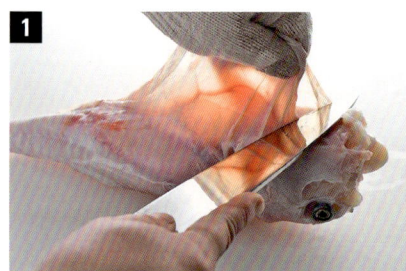

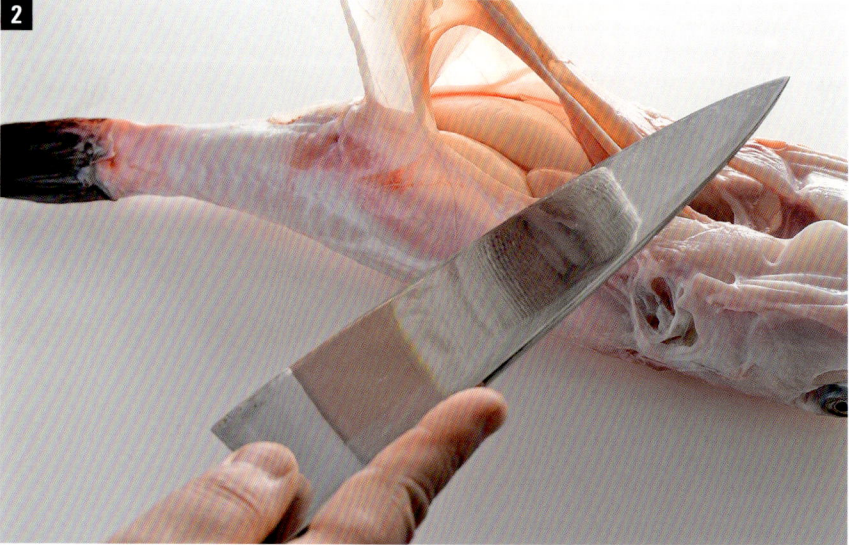

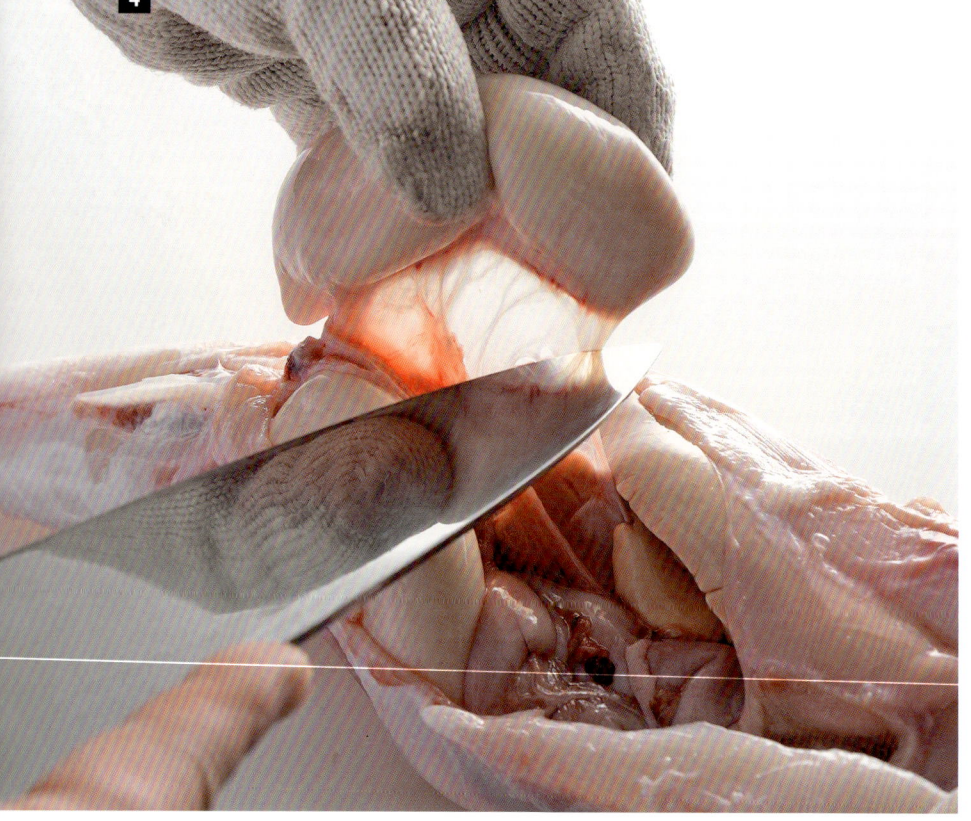

Removing the belly membrane

1 Pull up the membrane covering the internal organs with the left hand and cut through it from the back of the beak to the edge of the jaw with the knife.

2 Pulling on the membrane with the left hand, cut it away toward the tail (be careful not to damage the flesh or internal organs).

3 Cut the membrane away at the end of the belly. The belly membrane is inedible.

4 Once the belly membrane has been removed, the internal organs will be visible. If there is a pair of sperm sacs (milt, *shirako*) located near the base of the anal fin, pull them up and cut the membrane attaching them to the rest of the organs.

5 Cut the membrane carefully so as not to damage the milt, and remove it. Ovaries (which are inedible) are easily distinguishable from the milt, since they have a hollow inside.

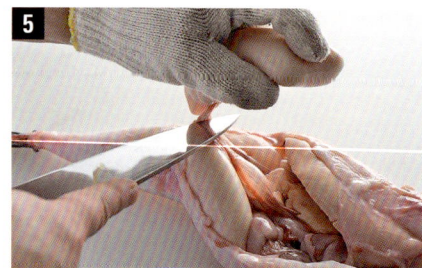

Removing the collar

1 With the head to the left, place the dorsal side down on the cutting board. While pulling the collar (also called *kaerubone*, or "frog bone" for its shape after removal) outward, insert the tip of the knife, blade facing up (*sakasabocho*), at the base where the pectoral fin was cut off.

2 Cut away from the pectoral fin area and cut off the edge of the ventral flesh.

3 Pull up the ventral flesh (collar), and place the knife angled down at the connection between the collar and the body.

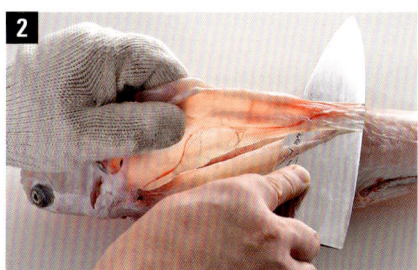

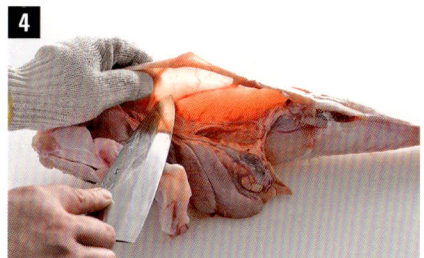

4 For the other side of the fish, go back to step **1**, placing the fish in the same position, and insert the knife as in step **1**.

5 Cut away from the pectoral fin area as in step **2**.

6 Lift the collar up and cut at an angle to remove it from the body.

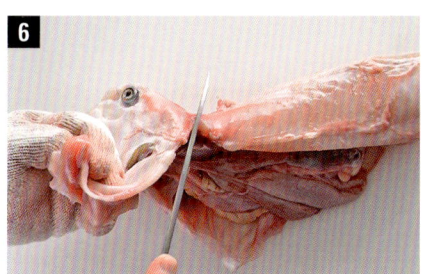

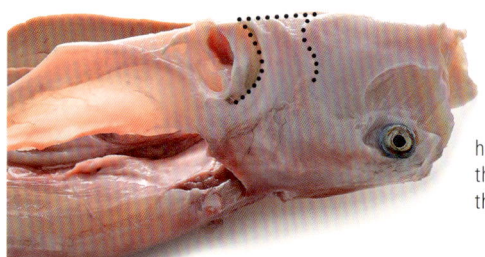

head end before removal of the collar (dotted line shows the operculum)

7 With the head facing toward you, place the dorsal side down on the cutting board. Insert the knife in the underside of the small, flattish operculum, located close to the belly.

8 Now place the knife behind the larger jawbone closer to the mouth side than the smaller, flattish bone.

9 Cut in and down to the base of the bones at the spine.

10 Cut the connection between the gill cover and the flesh.

11 Lift up the collar and position the knife at its base.

12 Cut through the connection (*wakibone*) between the gills and the collar.

13 Lift up the lower jaw part with the left hand.

14 Cut off the part connecting the lower jaw to the head bone.

15 Holding the head bone against the cutting board with the knife, with the left hand pull up on the collar until it comes off.

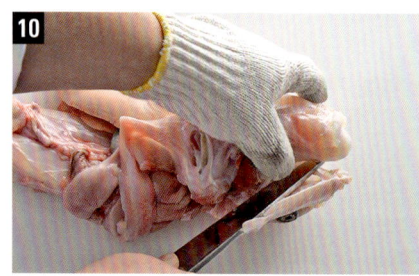

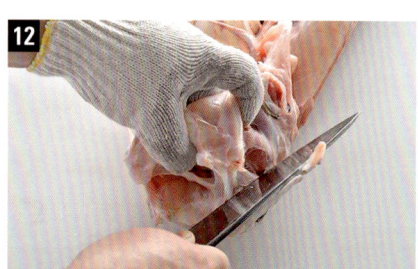

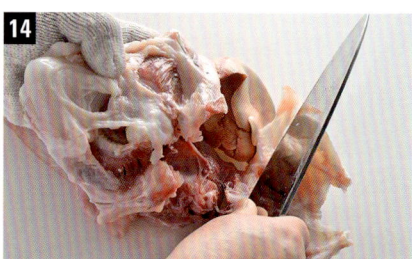

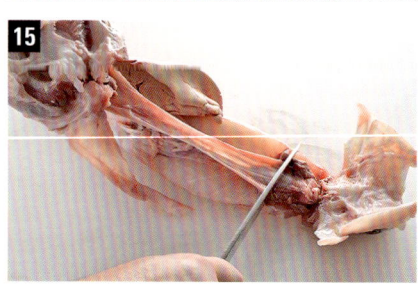

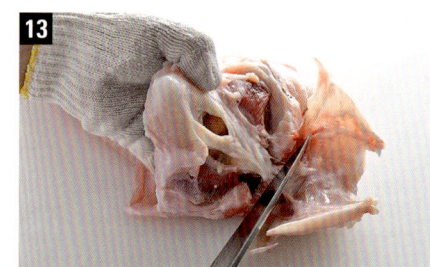

flesh attached to the head bone

to page 164

internal organs attached to the collar

to facing page

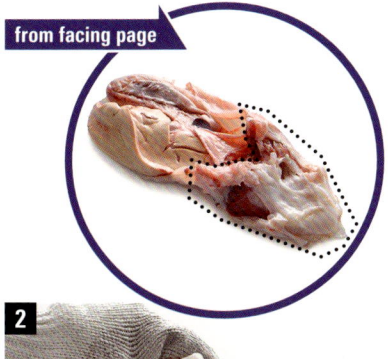

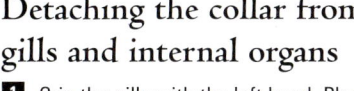

from facing page

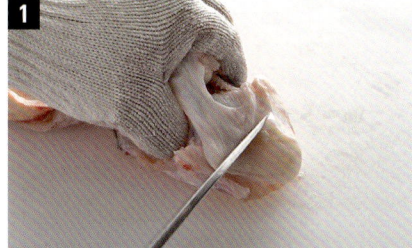

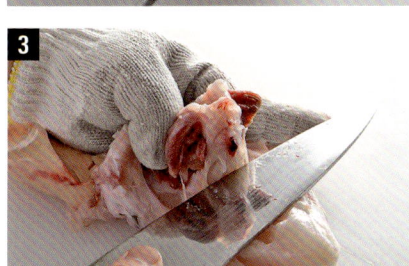

Detaching the collar from gills and internal organs

1 Grip the gills with the left hand. Place the knife at the base of the gills directly above the heart (take care not to cut into the heart).

2 Cut around the base of the gills.

3 Cut carefully around the gills so that they will come out cleanly.

4 Holding the collar down with the flat of the knife, put your fingers through the hole of the gills and pull them up, cut the tissue attaching them to the base, and remove.

5 Carefully remove the kidney attached to the collar without allowing it to touch the other organs, which will be discarded.

6 Detach the kidney on the other side.

7 While pressing down with the flat of the knife over the heart (so that the internal organs will not come into contact with the collar bone), pull out the collar bone.

8 Disconnect the collar bone.

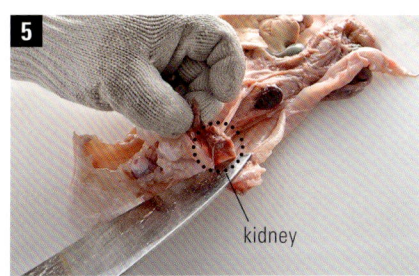

kidney

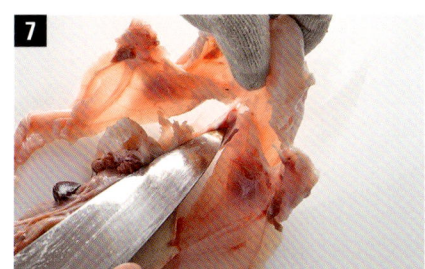

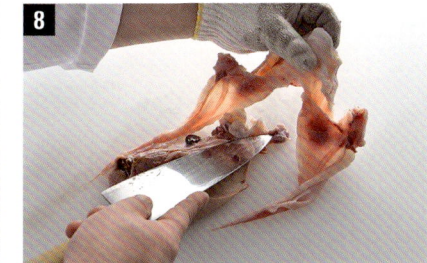

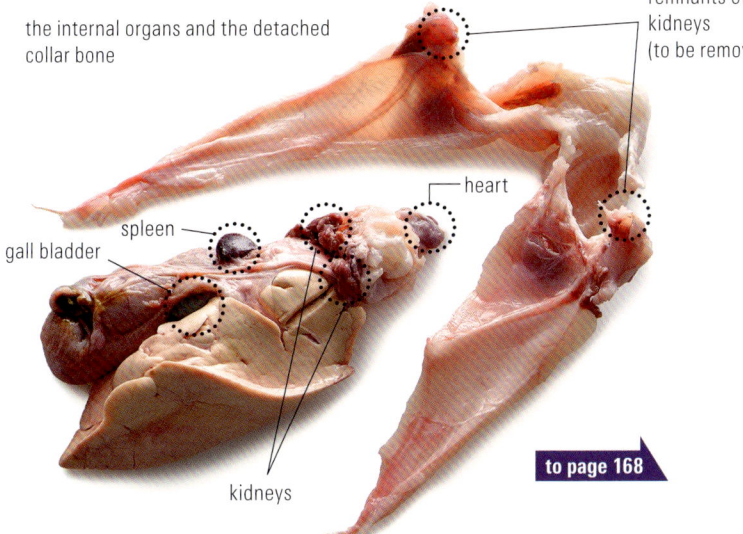

the internal organs and the detached collar bone

remnants of the kidneys (to be removed)

heart

spleen

gall bladder

kidneys

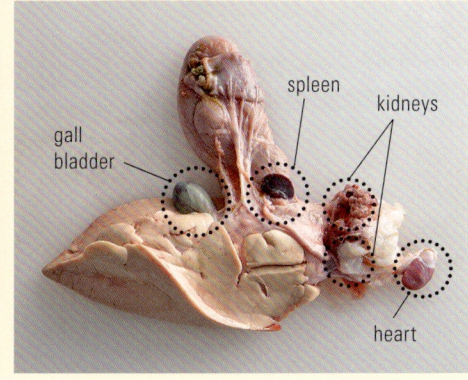

Internal organs removed; to be discarded since all but the milt are inedible.

gall bladder

spleen

kidneys

heart

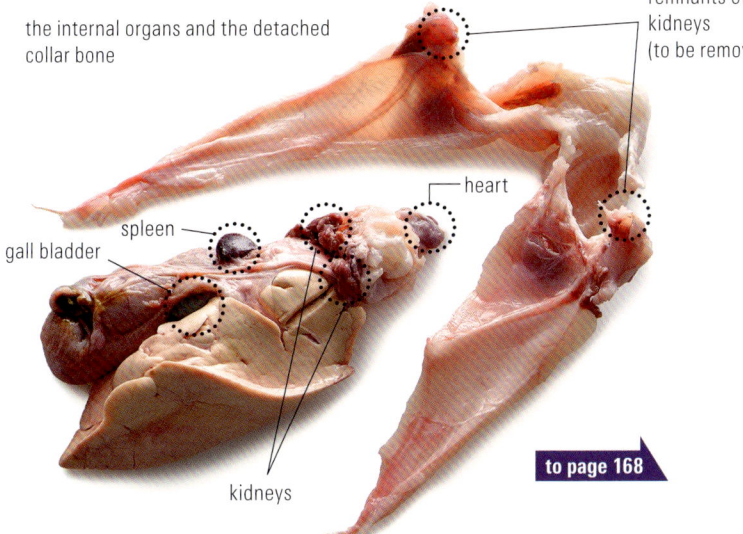

to page 168

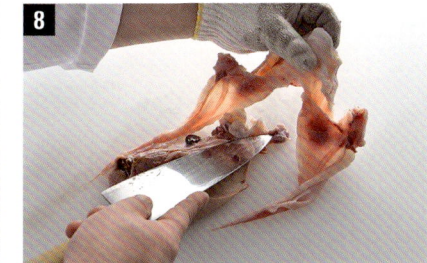

from page 162

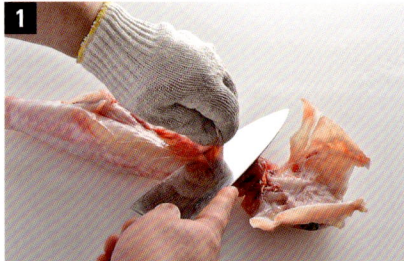

Removing the head bone and remnants of the kidneys

1 Place the head end to the right. Insert the knife in the vicinity of the removed anal fin.

2 Pull out on the ventral membrane and cut it away.

3 Insert the knife where the head bone is attached to the body.

4 Cut the head bone away from the body.

5 Insert the knife along the part adjacent
6 to the red kidney at the side of the spine and dislodge the kidney with the tip of the knife.

7 Perform the same steps on the other side of the spine.

8 Remove remnants of the kidneys from both sides.

9 The flesh and the kidneys after removal.

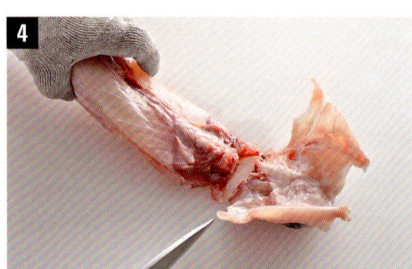

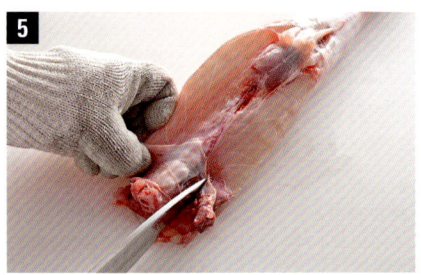

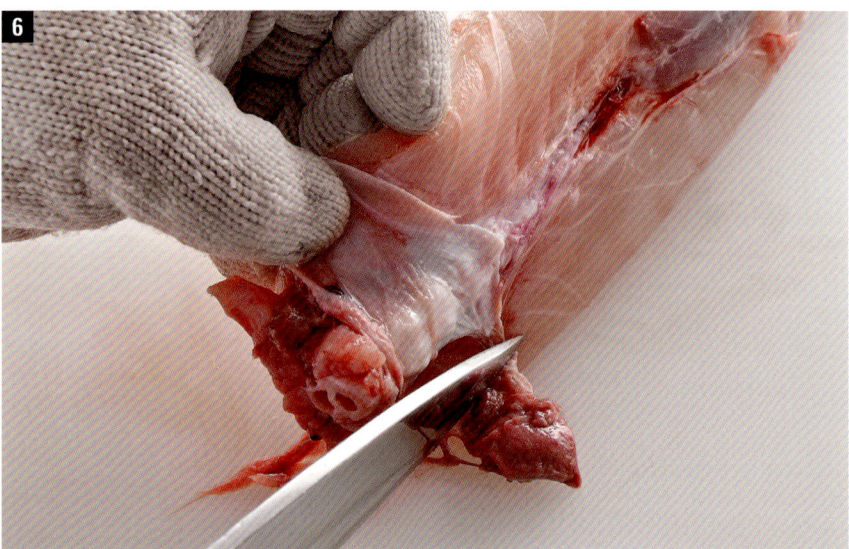

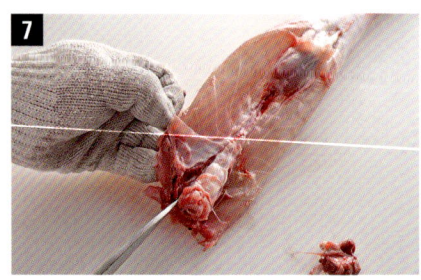

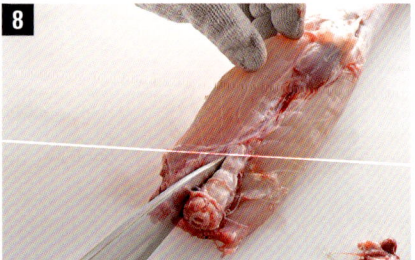

to page 166

head bone as removed in step **4**

10. Hold the head bone against the cutting board with the eyeball part down.
11. Cut away the projecting eyeball. (Cut away the eyeball on the other side as well.)
12. Turn the head bone back side up and insert the knife in the center.
13. Chop through the bone to divide the head in half.
14. Cut off the base part of the head bone (in order to remove the remnants of the kidney).
15. The head bone with the base part cut away.
16. Stand up the cut head bone and use the tip of the knife to clear the brain out of the bone cavity.
17. Clean out the cavity carefully and be sure that no brain tissue remains.

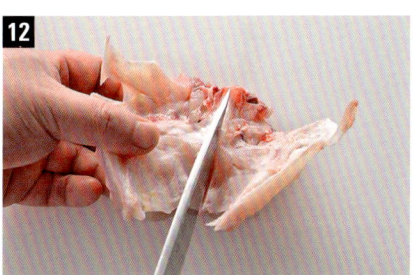

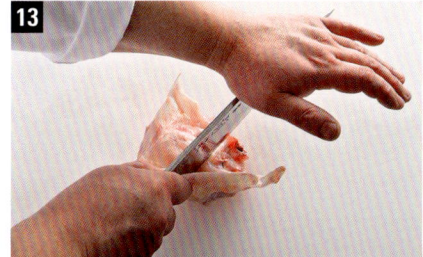

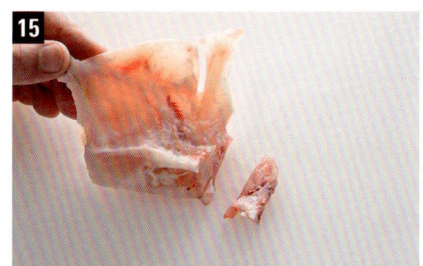

to page 169

from page 164

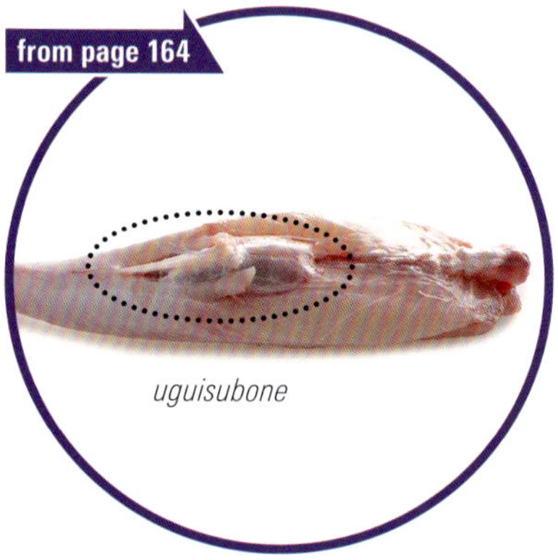

uguisubone

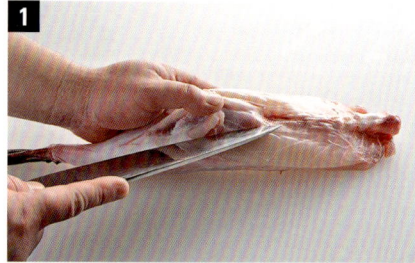

Removing the *uguisubone**
Removing the membrane

1 With the head end to the right and the dorsal side down, pull the *uguisubone* muscle to the side and insert the knife at its base.

2 Continuing to hold the muscle aside to the left (to make it easier to cut), cut in all the way to the spine.

3
4 Turn the fish with the head facing to the left. On this side of the fish, cut likewise under the *uguisubone* from the spine all the way to the base of the throat.

5 Turn the head end to face right again and pull out the *uguisubone*.

*dark muscle at the base of the anal fin

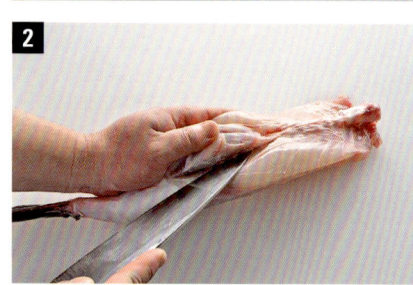

the *uguisubone* removed

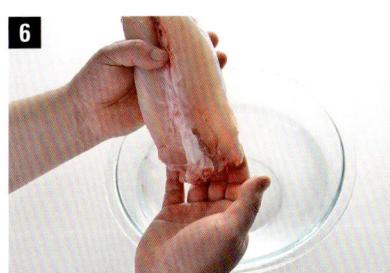

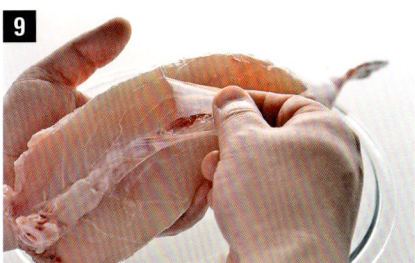

6 Wash the flesh. Fill a bowl with water and put the flesh into the water head-side first (this makes it easier to grasp and peel off membranes).

7 With fingers, remove remnants of the kidneys clinging to the spine.

8 Grasp the membrane around the spine with the hand and pull it back toward the head (pull off as much as can be grasped by hand).

9 Peel off the membrane, grasping it and pulling it toward the tail. Pull off on both sides of the spine. There may be clots of blood between the spine and the membranes on both sides of the spine; wash in the bowl of water. Dispose of the debris with inedible parts.

to page 171

from page 163

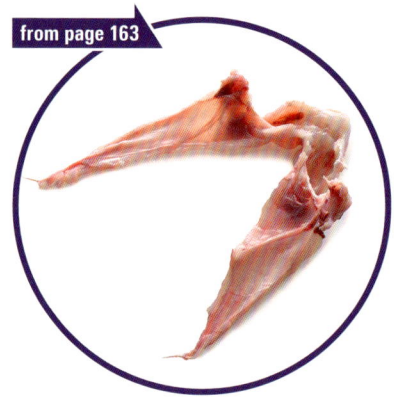

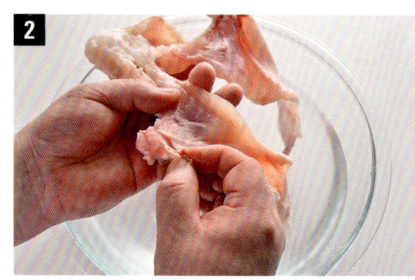

Cleaning the collar

1 Prepare a bowl of water for washing the collar.

2 Check to make sure there are no fragments of the kidneys remaining on the collar's underside.

3 If any kidney fragments remain, remove with the fingers.

4 Wash carefully, taking care to remove any trace of the kidneys.

5 Peel away all of the membrane clinging to the collar.

6 Pull out the membranes on the inner side and peel away.

7 Peel off all remaining membrane from the inner side.

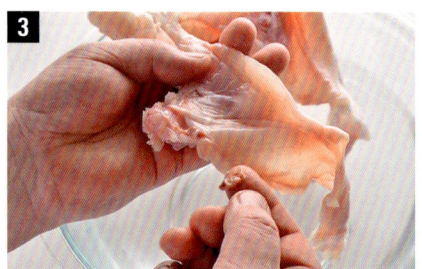

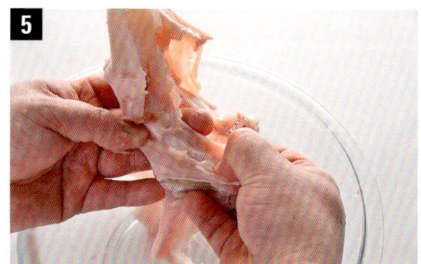

the collar after cleaning

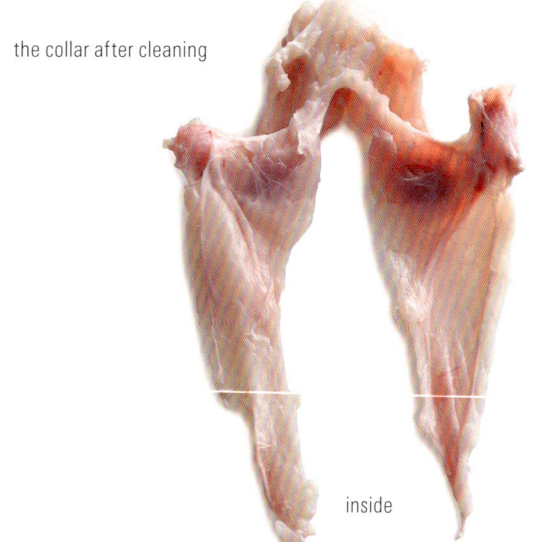

inside

outside

to page 170

from page 165

Cleaning the head bones

1 Prepare a bowl of water for the cleaning. Remove by hand any small bones remaining on the underside of the head bone.

2 The bones are held in place with a membrane; remove both bones and membrane.

3 Pull out the small bones.

4 After removing the bones and membrane, wash.

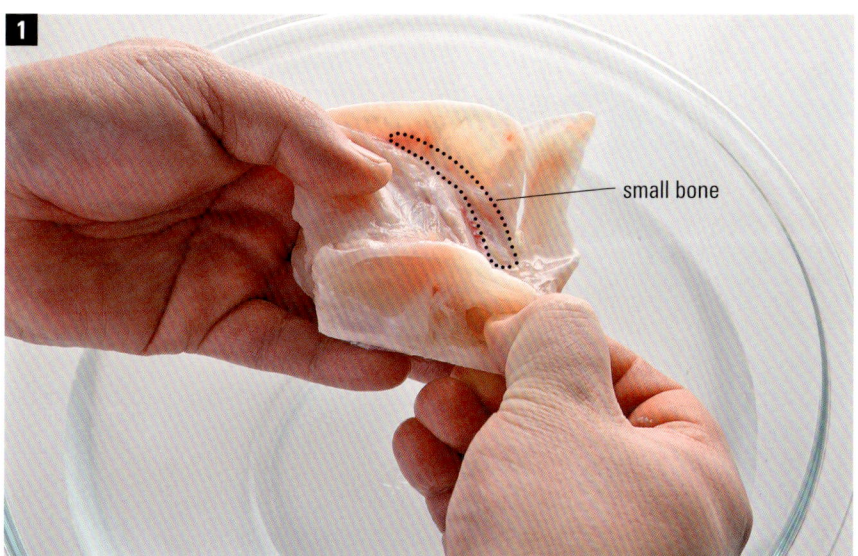

small bone

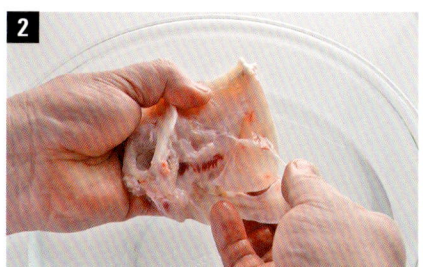

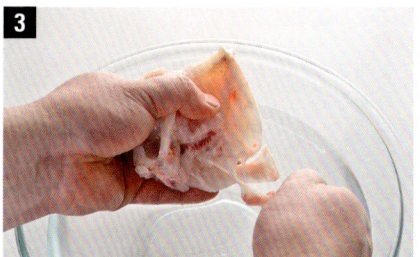

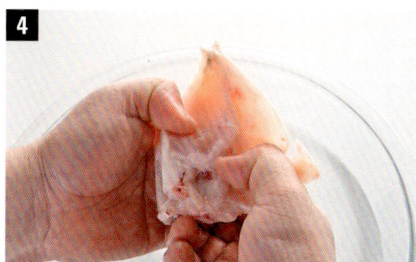

from page 168

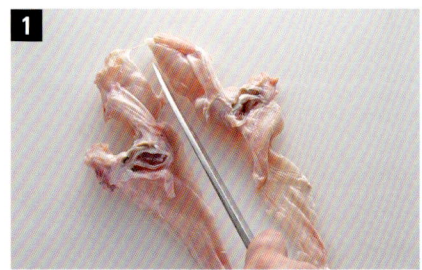

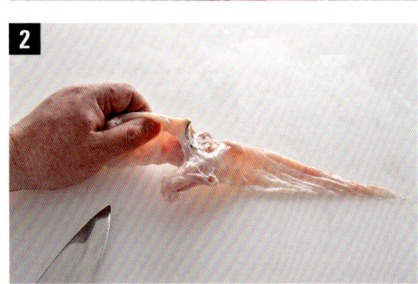

Preparing the collar for cooking

1. Place the knife at the center of the collar and bear down, cutting it in half.
2. Cut away the membrane at the base of the collar.
3. Cut away the membrane, blade facing up (*sakasabocho*) on the inside of the bone.
4. Cut the collar away from the connecting bone.
5. The areas around the gills are inedible; cut them away.
6. Cut away the parts around the gills.

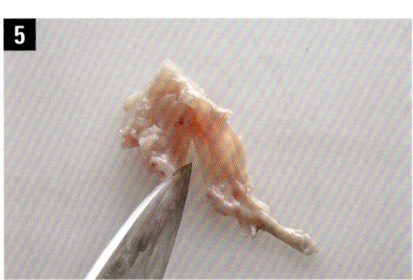

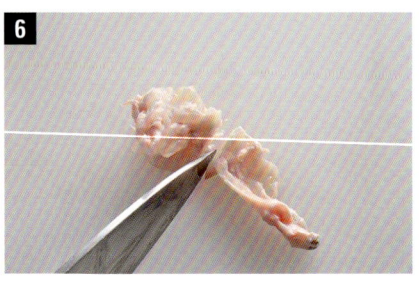

The separated bones of the collar (*kaeru-bone*). The way the pieces are cut may differ depending on whether they will be used in a hot pot, deep-fried, or grilled.

from page 167

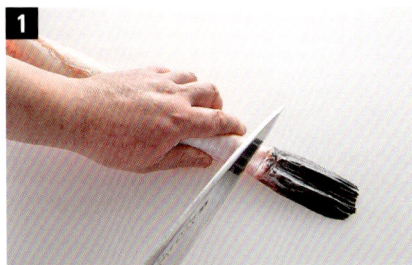

Cutting flesh in three pieces / Removing the muscle

1 Place the well-washed flesh with the tail to the right, dorsal-side up, and place the knife at the base of the tail.

2 Cut the tail off.

3 Now place the head end to the right. Insert the knife from the head end over the center bone as shown, cutting so as to leave some meat on the center bone.

4 Cut all the way to the base of the tail and remove the fillet.

5 Turn over the fish so that the center bone is facing down and again cut from the head end to the base of the tail, leaving some meat on the center bone.

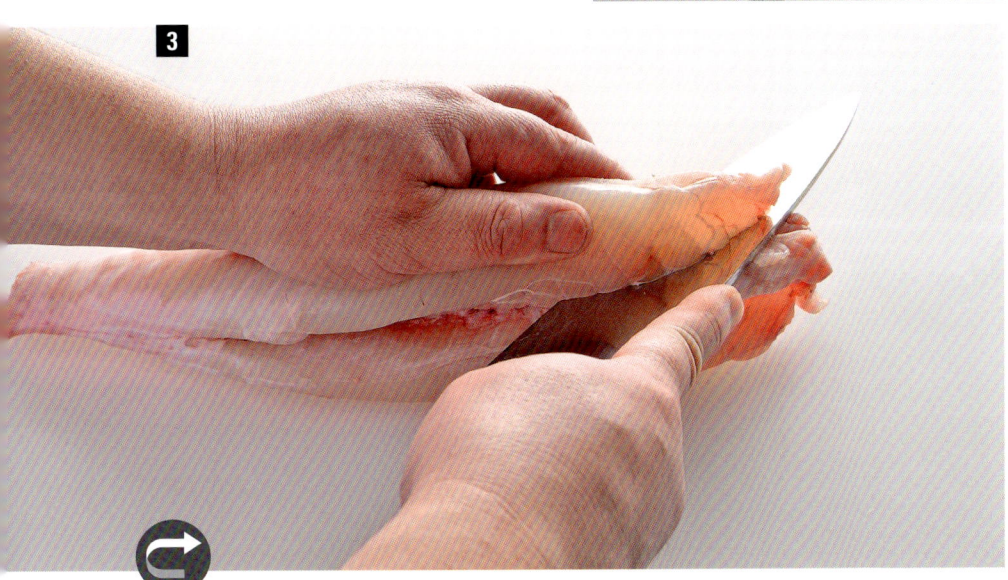

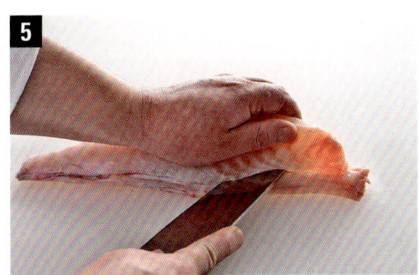

The *fugu* flesh cut into three pieces. Some flesh is intentionally left on the center bone (center) in order to enjoy it in hot pot, grilled, or deep fried.

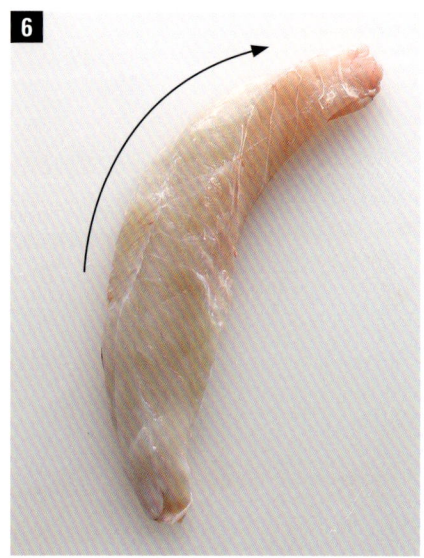

6 Remove any remaining tough muscle. It may be easier to remove it by curving the fish slightly.

7 Change to a *yanagiba* knife and slice off the tough muscle.

8 Muscle part after slicing.

Removing the *mikawa* skin from the flesh

1 Place the fillet with the tail end to the left. Close to where it is connected to the tail, the flesh is quite hard. Lay the knife down and slide it diagonally over the hard flesh and between the skin and soft flesh of the fillet.

2 Leaving the skin connected, flip the piece of hard flesh out to the left.

3 Turn the fillet around so that the tail end is toward the right. Insert the knife at the spot where the hard flesh was turned over.

4 Leaving the knife lying flat, cut toward the head end, sliding the blade up and down in small strokes over the *mikawa* ("fleshy skin"). Bring the knife to a halt just before the head end.

5 Lift the flesh and open it out to the left, as shown.

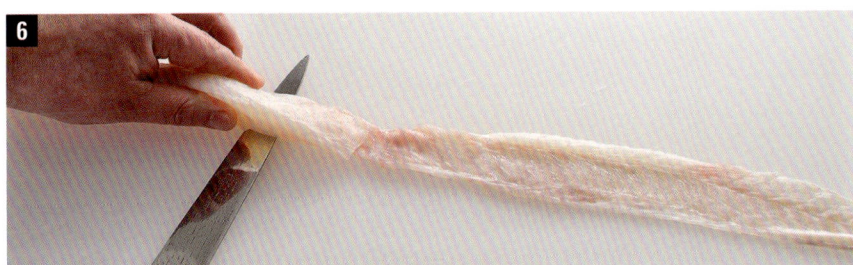

6 Remove the skin from the fillet in the same way.

Skin removed from the flesh. The skin will be blanched and used in cooking. When blanching, the skin will be easier to handle if it has not been completely cut away.

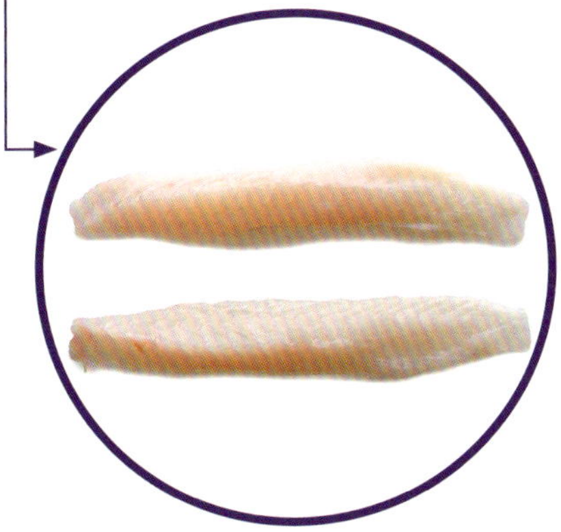

completed upper (*uwami*) and lower (*shitami*) fillets

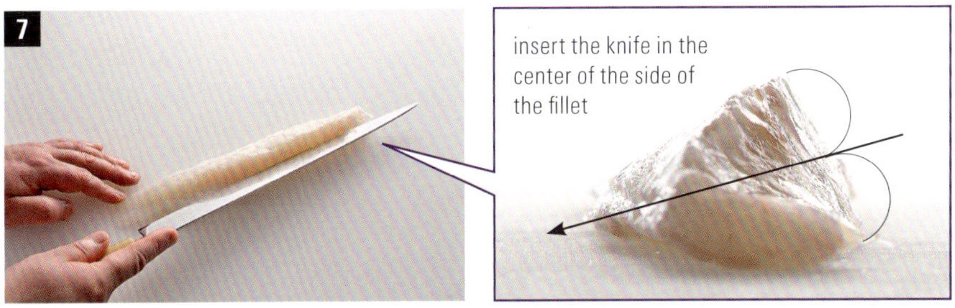

7

insert the knife in the center of the side of the fillet

7 Insert the knife at an angle in the center of the lower fillet in order to cut two equal-sized blocks. Place the fillet belly side to the right and insert the knife on a slant into the fillet (shown at right). To cut the upper fillet, place the tail end facing you; for the lower fillet, the head end should be toward you.

lower fillet cut into two *saku* blocks

from page 159

white ventral skin (above), black dorsal skin (below)

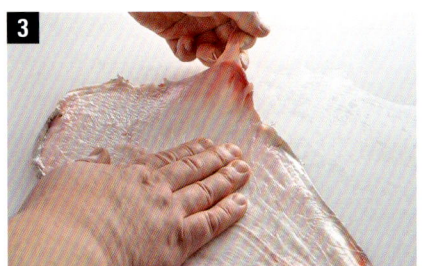

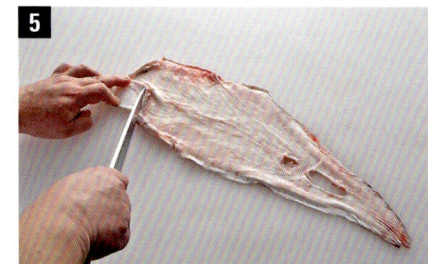

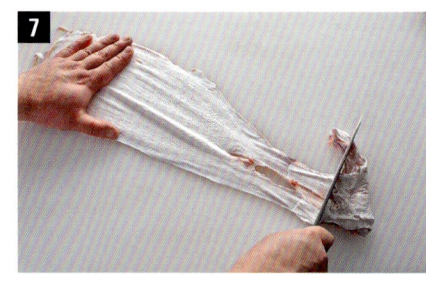

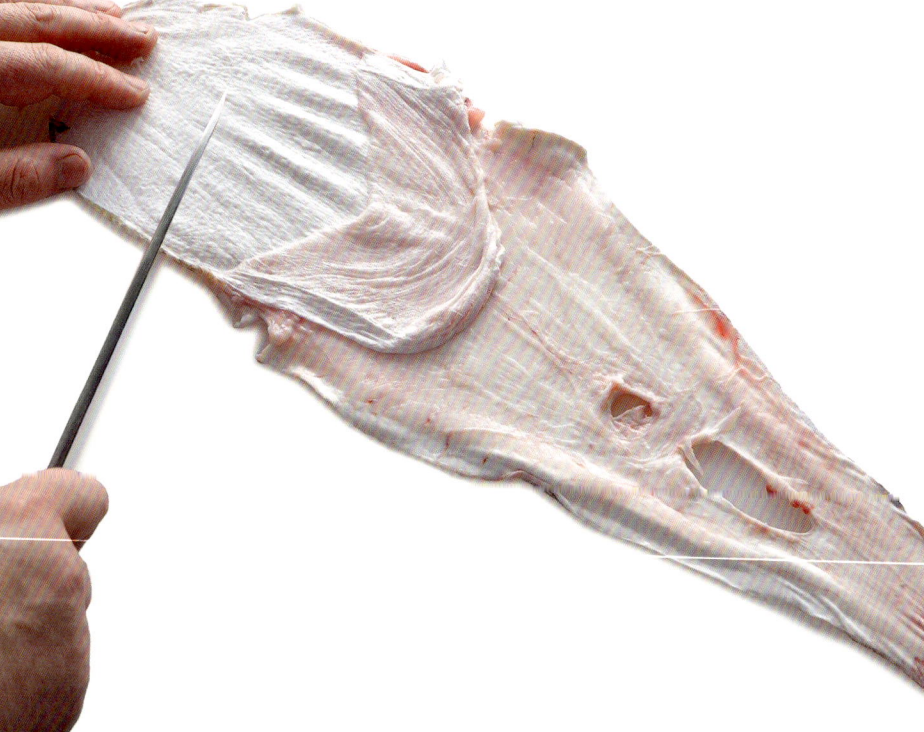

Removing the inner skin (*totoumi*) and rough skin (*samegawa*)

1 Place the white skin with the tail end to the right and the inside up. It is easier to peel off the *totoumi* inner skin if the wide part is to the left. Pinch the attached membranes and pull them out.

2 Pull the membranes back toward the tail.

3 Carefully pull off the membranes around the edges.

4 To strip off the inner skin, insert the *deba*
5 knife in a slit at one edge to get started.

6 While holding the outer white skin with
7 the left hand, strip away the inner skin with the knife to below the throat.

8 The white ventral skin (foreground) and its inner lining. The inner lining has a gelatin-like texture that gains a pleasant crunchy quality after blanching.

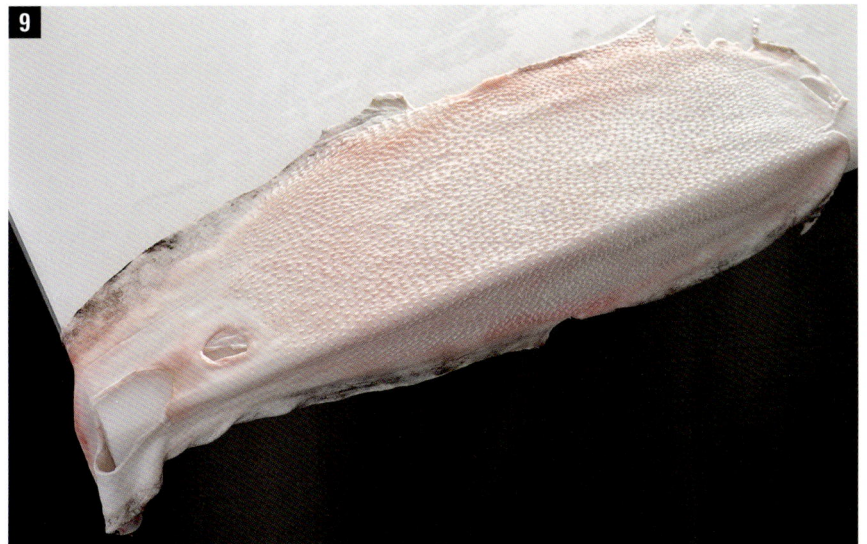

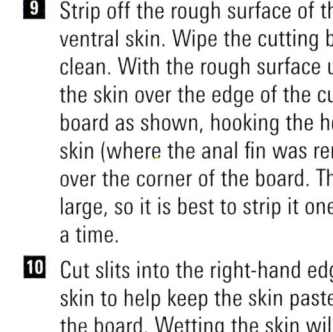

9 Strip off the rough surface of the white ventral skin. Wipe the cutting board clean. With the rough surface up, drape the skin over the edge of the cutting board as shown, hooking the hole in the skin (where the anal fin was removed) over the corner of the board. The skin is large, so it is best to strip it one half at a time.

10 Cut slits into the right-hand edge of the skin to help keep the skin pasted flat to the board. Wetting the skin will make it stick to the board better.

11 As you cut, fit the skin so it will lie perfectly flat on the board, without forming air bubbles.

12 Insert the knife flat into the left side of the rough skin.

13 With the blade horizontal and facing right (*sakasabocho*), move it in a sawing motion to strip off the rough skin portion that lies flat on the cutting board.

14 Stretch the entire ventral skin over the cutting board after the first rough skin portion has been removed.

15 Strip off the rest of the rough skin in the same way as seen in steps 12 and 13.

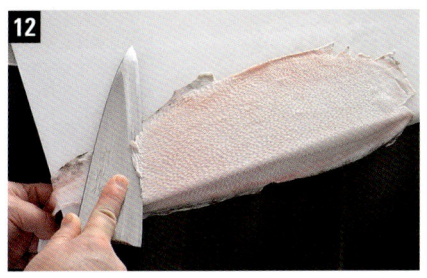

The ventral skin after removing the rough skin (*samegawa*). The rough skin is inedible, so check to make sure that none remains.

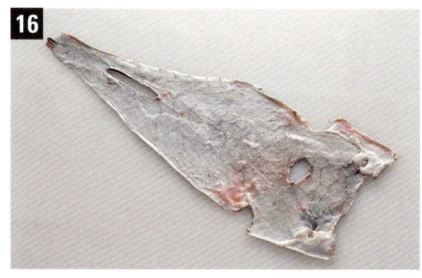

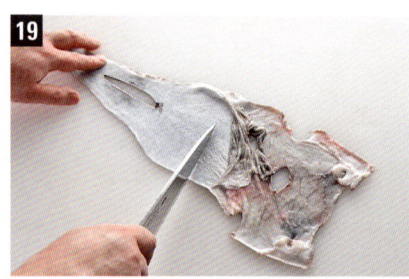

16 Remove the *totoumi* inner skin of the black dorsal skin. Place the skin with the tail end to the left and the inside up.

17 Striking the area at the tail of the skin with the blade of the knife will open up the layers.

18 Use the knife to separate the layers.

19 As in step **6** for the white ventral skin, pull back on the black skin while stripping away the inner skin with the knife.

20 When stripped up to the location of the eye holes, cut off the inner skin. The skin beyond the eyes is rough, so will not be used.

21 The black skin (below) and the inner skin.

22 Strip off the rough layer of the black skin. Wipe off the cutting board. With the rough side up, place the tail end of the skin to the left. Hook the hole (where the dorsal fin was cut off) over the corner of the cutting board. The black skin is about half the width of the white skin and can be stripped in one pass.

23 Strip off the rough skin, as explained in step **13** for the white skin.

the dorsal skin after removing the rough skin

to page 180

from page 155

Treatment of the fins

1 Sprinkle salt on the fins and rub them lightly.

2 Place fins in a bowl of water and wash them carefully to remove the mucous film.

3 Cut into the cartilage in the thick part of the fin (in dotted lines, photo below) with the knife.

4 Lift up on the cut flap of cartilage with the left hand.

5 Open up fin with butterfly cut. Lay out with the inner part down in a glass or metal tray. Sun-dry well to kill bacteria.

cartilage

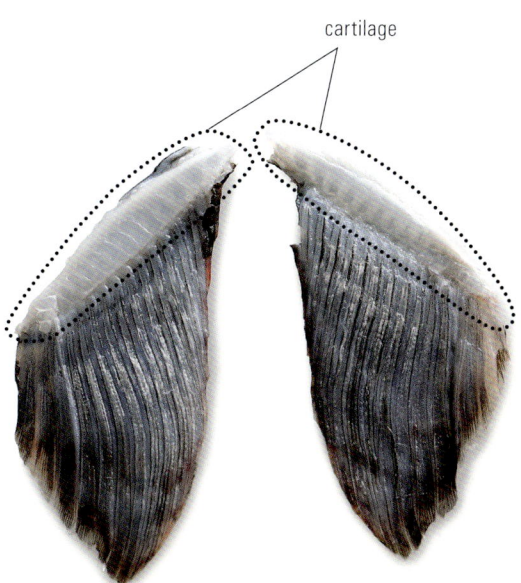

After sun-drying the fins, slightly toast them and place in a glass of sake to enjoy pufferfish fin sake (*hirezake*). The toasting will completely dry out the fin and remove any unpleasant smell.

Kikka-zukuri

Thin-sliced (*usu-zukuri*) pufferfish sashimi is called *tessa*. Freshly filleted pufferfish retains a large amount of water and is not easy to slice. So when serving as *usu-zukuri*, it is refrigerated for one day before cutting. Not only does the flesh become easier to slice, but it loses excess moisture and matures, enhancing its umami taste.

Preparing pufferfish
kikka-zukuri

1 Use the *yanagiba* knife. Place the fillet block at a 45-degree angle with the thicker part facing you, as shown. First cut away the lumpy end of the block.

2 Pressing the fillet lightly onto the cutting board, cut into the fillet, drawing the knife straight toward you. For the most attractive slice, appearing slightly thicker at the tip when served, it is desirable that the slice be about 3 mm (⅛ in.) when the knife enters the block and about 1 mm (¹⁄₁₀ in.) when it cuts through.

3 Take up the slice from the knife and turn it over.

4 Fold the part of the slice that extends beyond the width of the knife over the back of the blade, as shown.

5 Pinch the folded part lightly so that it will stand up and place the slice on the plate slightly overlapping the slice next to it. Place the slices in a circle starting at the outside of the plate and spiraling inward. This forms an arrangement like a chrysanthemum (*kiku*) flower. Having the folded tips stand up keeps the slices from sticking to the plate so that they are easier to pick up and eat.

Chrysanthemum-style Pufferfish Sashimi

pufferfish blanched skin	carrot curls
asatsuki chives	chrysanthemum petals
aka-oroshi	*sudachi*

from page 176

Preparing pufferfish skin

1 Use the *yanagiba* knife. Plunge the previously prepared white skin in boiling water. Place on the cutting board with the tail end to the left and cut off the blackish part from the area around the anal fin hole.

2 Cut the rest of the skin in half crosswise.

3 Stack the two halves.

4 Trim around the pieces so that both are the same size.

5 From one end, cut the two layers of skin into 3 mm (⅛ in.) strips.

6 Cut in half the blackish part of the skin cut off in step **1**.

7 From one end, cut 3 mm (⅛ in.) strips.

8 Plunge the previously prepared black skin into boiling water. Place the piece with the tail end to the left and cut away the black part.

9 Roll the black portion into a cylinder and cut the cylinder in half crosswise.

10 Cut each cylinder half into 3-mm (⅛-in.)

11 slices, starting at one end.

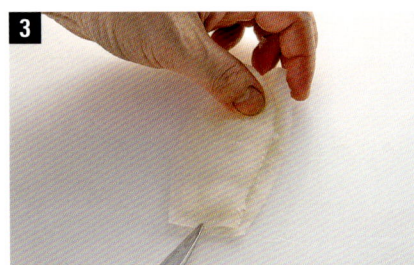

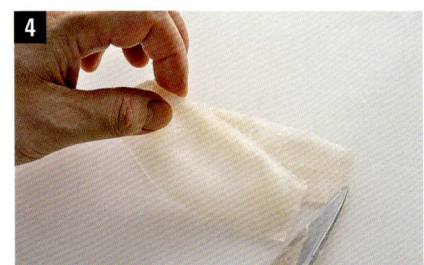

Grilled Pufferfish

Yaki Fugu

Grilled pufferfish uses parts of the fish with flesh on the bones such as the collar bone. Served in an Unge ware parching pan, the dish is topped with maple leaves and other seasonal decorations. The juice of the *sudachi* squeezed over the just-grilled meat gives it a refreshing tang.

roasted ginkgo nuts
sudachi

Grilled Pufferfish Milt

Yaki Shirako

Pufferfish milt, a delicacy renowned for its rich flavor and creamy texture, is wrapped in a thin skin, and the milt is very soft, nearly a liquid. Immediately before preparing, it should be placed in a 2 percent brine for about an hour to draw out the blood and fishy odor.

When grilling, it should be cut before placing over heat. If not cut, the sac holding the milt will break and the contents will spill out. The pieces should be well grilled until their delicious aroma signals that they are cooked through. *Shioyaki*—roasting after dusting with salt—is the ideal way to enjoy the distinctively soft texture of the milt. This simple seasoning allows the full enjoyment of the milt's essential flavor.

sprinkling of *ichimi-togarashi* chili pepper
sudachi

Suppon

SOFT-SHELLED TURTLE

Pelodiscus sinensis

Class Reptilia, order Testudines, family Trionychidae. The *suppon* turtle is distributed widely over tropical and temperate freshwater habitats in east and south Asia, Africa, and North America. Distinguished from other turtles by its soft carapace, it also has a long, elastic neck and a long, thin snout. Larger specimens may grow to a carapace length of thirty to forty centimeters.

Nearly all *suppon* used in cooking are farm-raised, given their scarcity in the wild. Their bite is powerful, and they are, moreover, very aggressive, meaning that chefs must be careful when handling them in the kitchen. These turtles hibernate at water temperatures of 59°F (15°C) or lower; they are considered to be most appetizing from late autumn to early winter, when they are approaching or have just entered into hibernation. Males have a longer tail and are more favored for their flesh than females, which lose weight while carrying eggs.

Rich in calcium, amino acids, and other nutrients, *suppon* boasts health and antifatigue properties and has a long history in Japanese gastronomy. *Suppon* dishes are often touted as being rich in collagen, which derives from the cartilage along the periphery of the shell. In the Kansai (Kyoto-Osaka) area *suppon* is also known as *maru*, from the nearly round (*maru*) shape of the shell; *maru-nabe*, or *suppon* hot pot, is a classic preparation method that brings out the appeal of this top-class ingredient to the fullest.

CUTTING THE SOFT-SHELLED TURTLE

Removing the head

1. Turn the live turtle over on its back (a soft-shelled turtle is very wary and unlikely to come out of its shell, but will do so more easily if turned upside down). When its head emerges, grasp it quickly with the right hand at the neck (from both sides of its throat, which is a vulnerable spot). Be careful to avoid its bite. If it does bite, it will relax its grip upon being lowered into water again.

2. Wash the turtle while keeping a firm grip on its neck. It is difficult to clean the base of the neck by hand, so use a natural-bristle scrub brush.

3. Turn the turtle over and wash the belly.

4. Grip the neck from the underside (so that the neck is gripped inside the fist) and hold it firmly.

5. Stand the turtle up, gripping firmly around its neck from above. Pull the neck over to the belly side and place the *deba* knife blade inside the carapace at the base of the neck.

6. Make an incision in the skin where you placed the knife in step **5**. Then sink the tip of the knife in deeply along the line of the carapace.

7. Push in the tip of the knife until it touches the joint between the carapace and the neckbone, and then cut through the joint completely (only by severing the connecting joint can you assure that the neck will be completely stretched out before it is cut off).

8. Pull out the joint at the base of the neck and insert the knife across it.

9. Then, pressing the turtle down on the cutting board, insert the knife at the base of the neck and cut in a scooping motion as indicated by the arrow.

10. Detach the head. Place the body in a bowl neck end down.

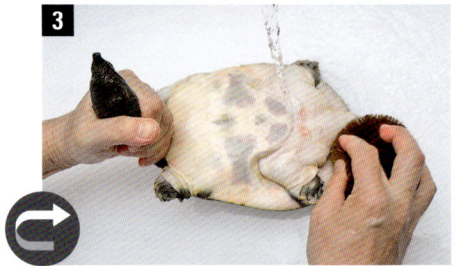

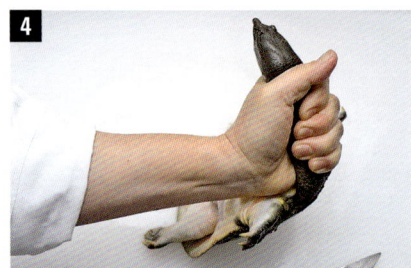

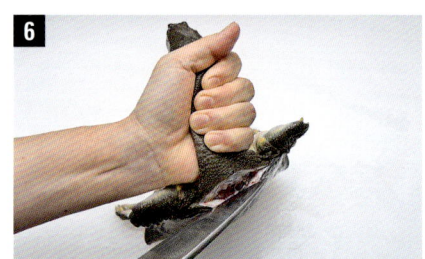

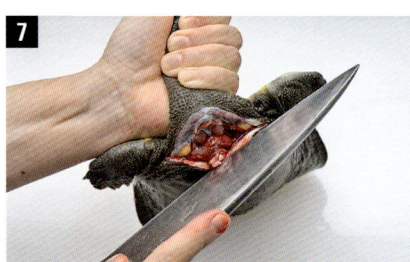

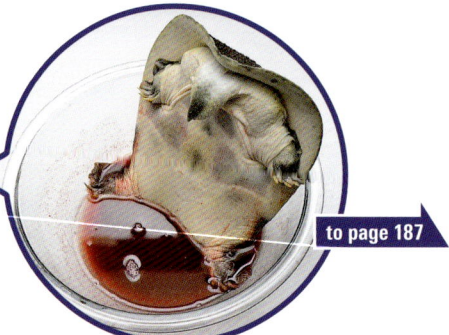

to page 187

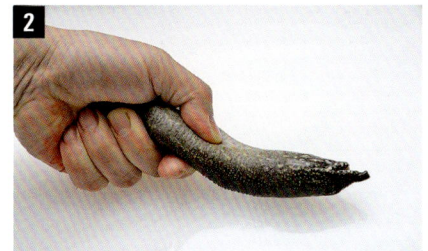

Carving the head

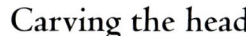 Hold the neck of the turtle with the head facing to the right.

2 Pulling the skin back with the thumb makes cutting easier.

3 Cut slits in a V shape along both sides of the triangular cartilage of the lower jaw. First cut diagonally through the skin along one side of the cartilage.

4 Then cut along the cartilage on the opposite side.

5 Cut in to form a V-shaped slit.

6 Place the knife at the tip of the slit.

7 Cut into the tip of the slit and lift up the cartilage (be careful not to cut the cartilage off).

8 Insert the knife at the base of the raised cartilage.

9 Cut the head off at the base of the cartilage.

10 The head removed.

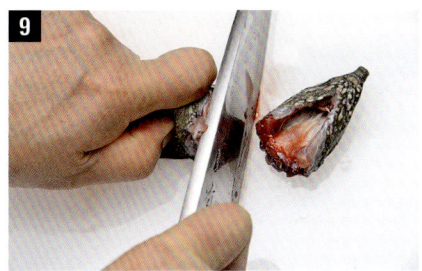

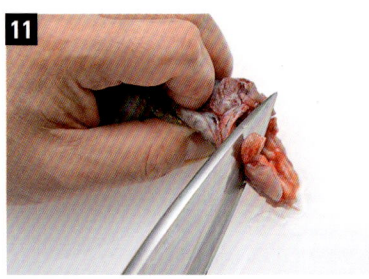

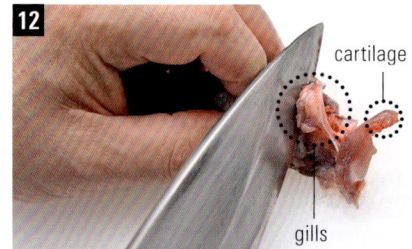

cartilage

gills

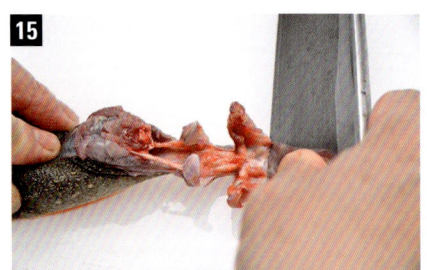

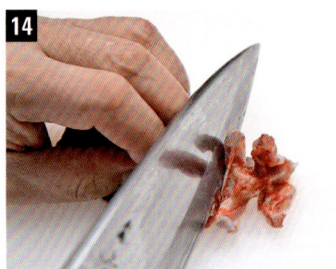

11 Pry out the cartilage on both sides with the knife.

12 Behind the cartilage are the gills; pry them out as well (without prying out the gills, it is not possible to pull out the esophagus).

13 Cut the tissue connecting the gills to the neck on one side.

14 Cut the tissue connecting the gills to the neck on the other side.

15 Holding down the cartilage at the end with the knife, pull the neck meat as shown.

16 With the cartilage end held down with the knife, pull back on the neck meat held in place with the left forefinger and pull out the esophagus.

17 Cut into the middle of the neck meat.

18 Cut neck meat into two pieces.

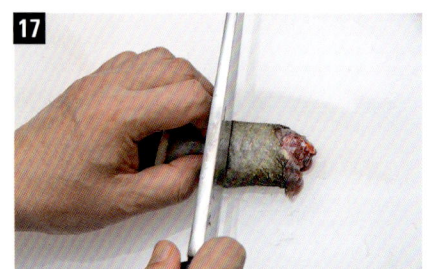

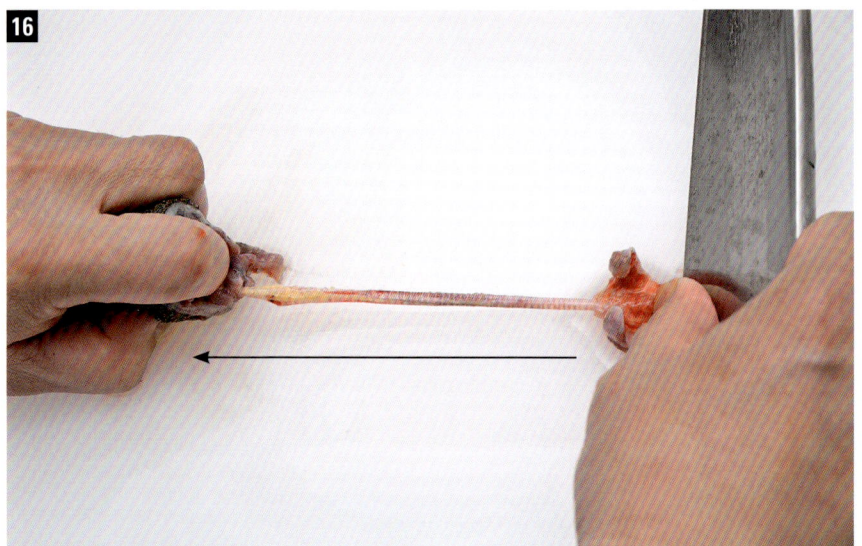

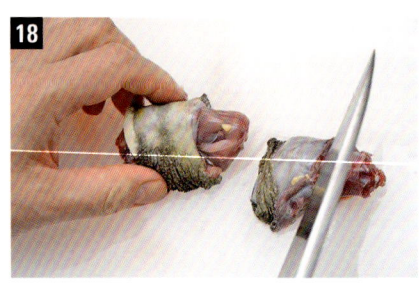

neck pieces

head

esophagus

The esophagus, gills, and cartilage are inedible and should be disposed of.

from page 184

Draining out the blood
Removing the carapace

1 Most of the blood will have drained out while the body was left standing in the bowl. Add about an equal amount of sake to prevent the blood from coagulating.

2 Continue to let stand until blood has drained out completely.

3 Wash the turtle with a scrub brush carefully, cleaning away the blood.

4 Blot dry with a cloth. Swab out the blood from the cavity where the head was removed.

5 Place on the cutting board with the head end to the left.

Cut along the dotted line around the edge of the hard carapace that covers the center of the turtle's back. The soft area surrounding the carapace is edible.

6 With the knife, make an incision across the back of the turtle at the edge of the hard carapace.

7 With the tip of the knife, cut from the incision made in step **6** around the perimeter of the hard carapace in the direction of the head.

8 Keep cutting around to where the carapace joins the neck.

9 Turn the head end to face you. Cut around the carapace above the base of the neck.

10 Turn the head end to the right. Continue cutting around the carapace toward the tail.

11 Insert the tip of the knife under the edge of the carapace and cut around to dislodge it.

12 Insert the tip of the knife under the carapace.

13 Cut away the tissue connecting the carapace to the pelvic girdle (hip bones).

14 After cutting the connecting tissue, lift the dislodged carapace to reveal the internal organs.

15 Put the carapace back in place and, holding the knife horizontally, insert it deeply inside to sever the tissue connecting the carapace to the left foreleg bones.

16 Turn the body so the head end is facing you. Turn the knife over and insert into the left corner to sever the tissue connecting to the other leg.

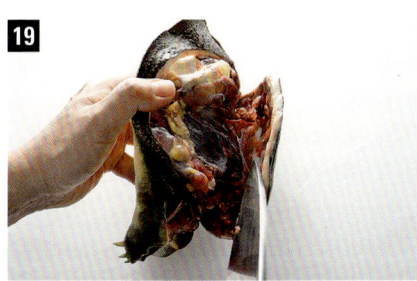

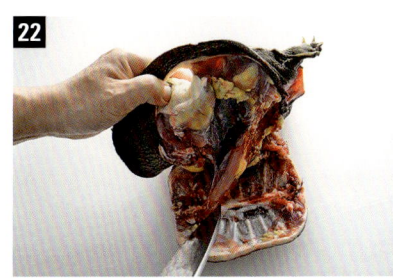

17 The body with the base of the leg bones cut on both sides.

18 Hold the turtle with the head end up, the left fingers clasping the edge of the soft carapace. Cut in with the knife between the hard carapace and the body as far as the backbone.

19 Turn the body so that the tail end is up and again cut in with the knife between the carapace and the body to free the carapace.

20 Connect the cuts made in steps **18** and **19**.

21 Holding the edge of the soft carapace with the left hand, press down and to the right with the knife on the hard carapace.

22 Pull the head end out with the left hand to separate the body from the hard carapace.

carapace removed
The yellow parts in the body are fat.

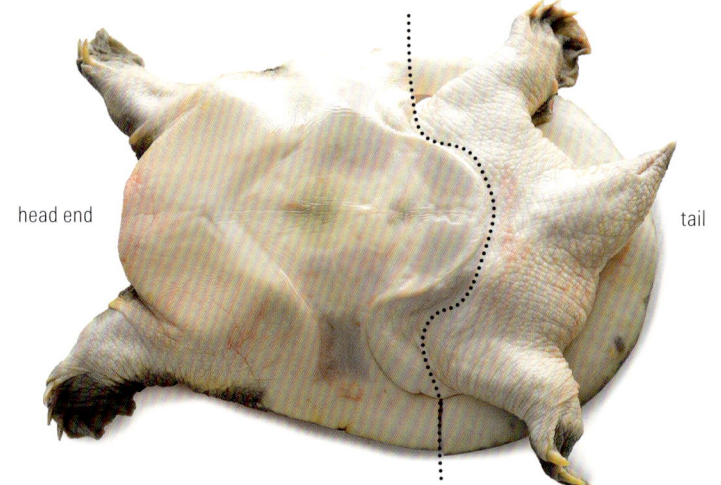

head end

tail

Removing the plastron (ventral shell)

1 Place ventral side up.

2 Make an incision in the skin from outside the base of the right rear leg in the direction of the plastron.

3 Stand up the body with the head end to the right and the belly facing you. While holding the tail end with the left hand, cut in toward the plastron.

4 Cut around the back of the plastron.

5 Now place the head end to the right and the belly side up. Make an incision from outside the base of the left rear leg in the direction of the plastron.

6 Cut around the edge of the plastron as far
7 as the base of the tail.

8 Holding the tail down with the left thumb, stand the body up, belly facing to the right.

rear legs side

forelegs side

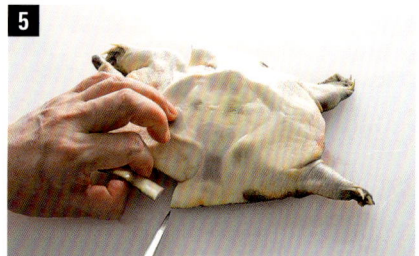

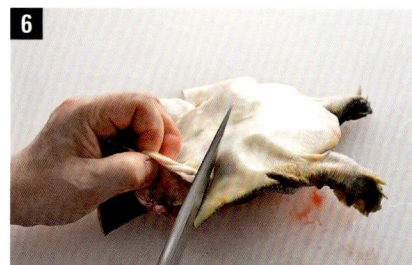

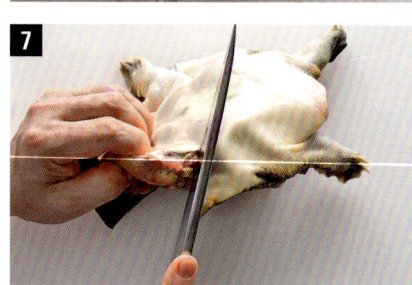

tail

9 Insert the knife at the curve of the tail end of the plastron.

10 Keeping the tail pinned down, cut under the plastron.

11 Slice through to meet the cuts made in steps 3 and 6.

12 When the cuts meet, use the knife to steady the plastron.

13 Pull out on the body with the left hand.

14 While pulling the body out to the left, separate the plastron to the right.

15 The internal organs will remain attached to the side with the rear legs, while the plastron remains connected to the forelegs.

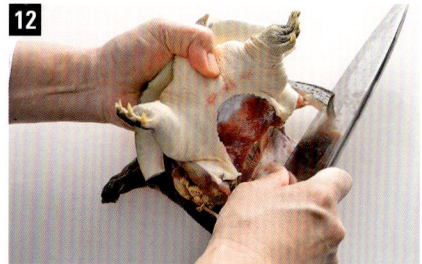

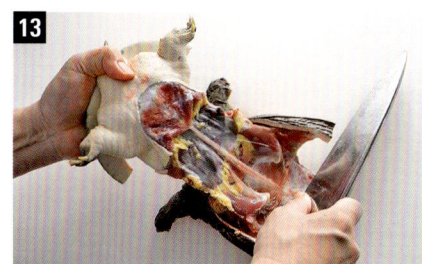

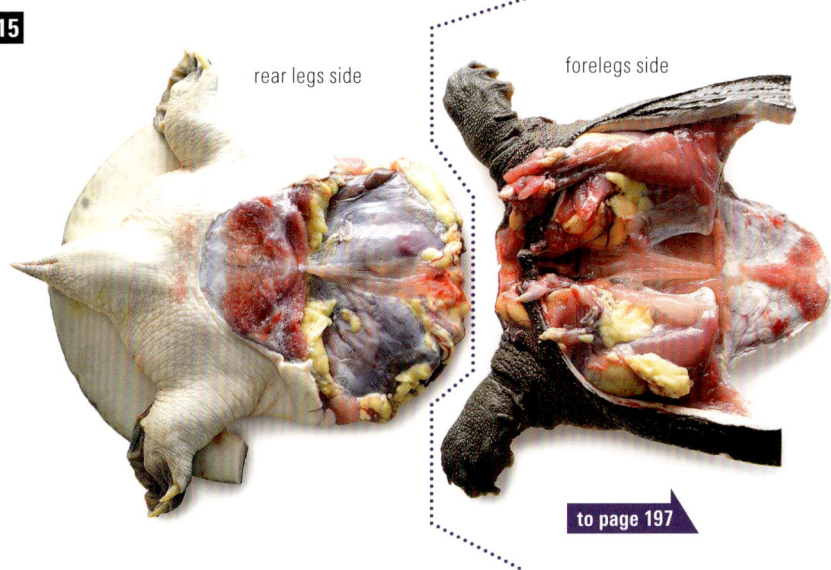

rear legs side

forelegs side

to page 197

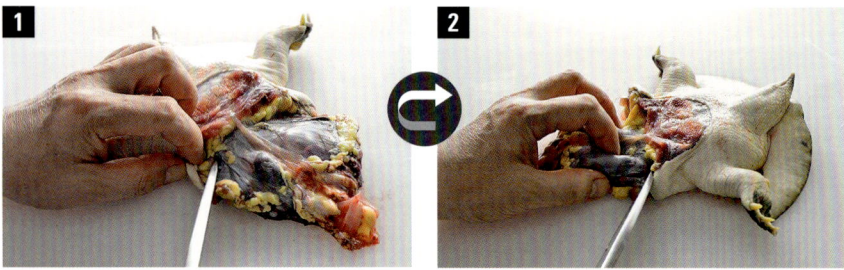

Removing the internal organs

1 Place the rear part of the body belly up and cut around the edge between the organs and pelvis.

2 Cut around the pelvis on the other side.

3 Both sides cut (internal organs still attached). At the base of the pelvis is the urinary bladder. Pull out at the base of the bladder and cut it off at the base (work carefully, since leakage from the bladder will foul the dashi).

4 With the tail to the left, hold the pelvic girdle with the left hand.

5 Steadying the body, press down on the internal organs with the knife.

6 Pulling firmly on the pelvis with the left hand, detach it from the organs.

7 The rear legs side and the detached organs.

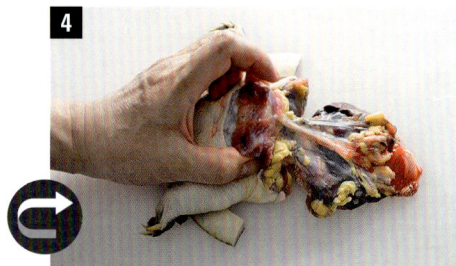

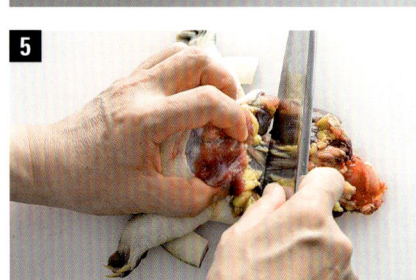

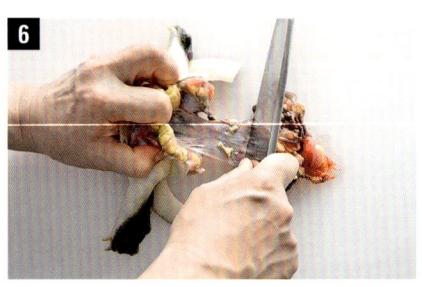

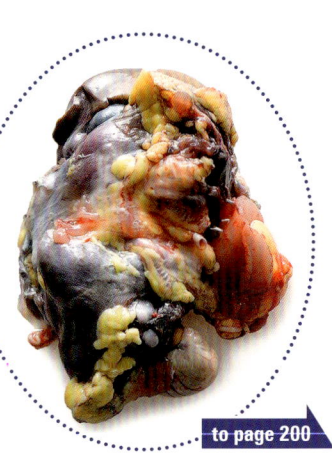

to page 200

detached organs

rear legs side

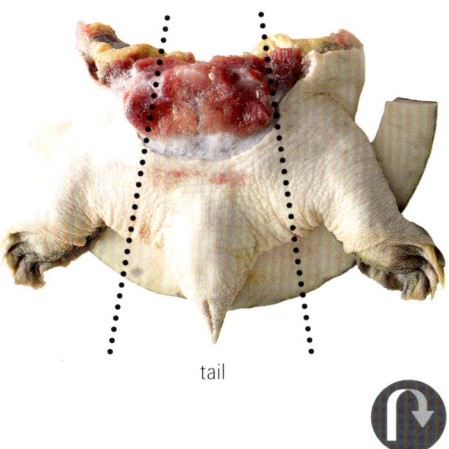

tail

Dividing the rear legs section

1 With the tail end away from you, cut in at the side of the pelvic girdle.

2 Cut as far as the joint where the right rear leg connects with the pelvic girdle.

3 Cut through the joint.

4 With the blade vertical and about equidistant between tail and leg, cut off the right rear leg (thus including more of the tail meat with the leg).

5 Shows the tail part (left) and the right rear leg (right) cut apart.

6 Now divide the tail side. With the tail toward you and the belly facing up, cut into the base of the other leg.

7 Angle the knife and cut into the pelvic joint.

8 Hold the knife vertically and cut through between the pelvic girdle side and the left rear leg.

9 Pelvic girdle side (left) and left rear leg (right).

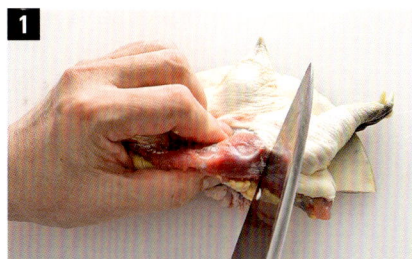

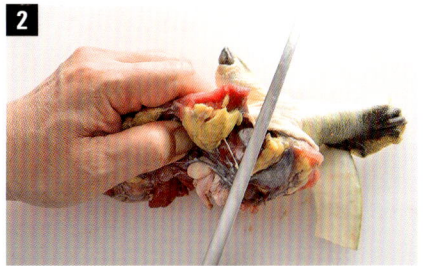

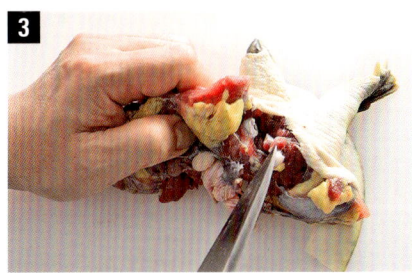

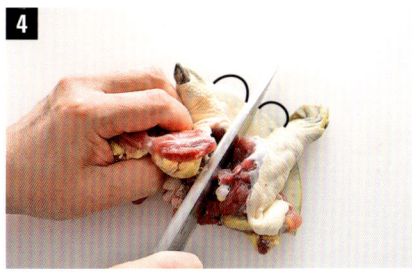

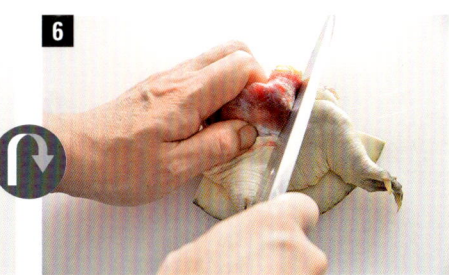

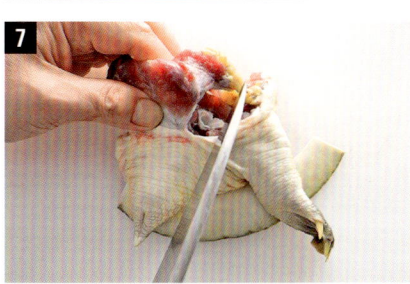

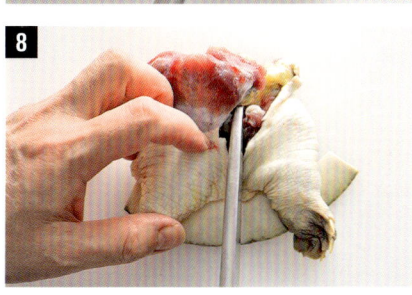

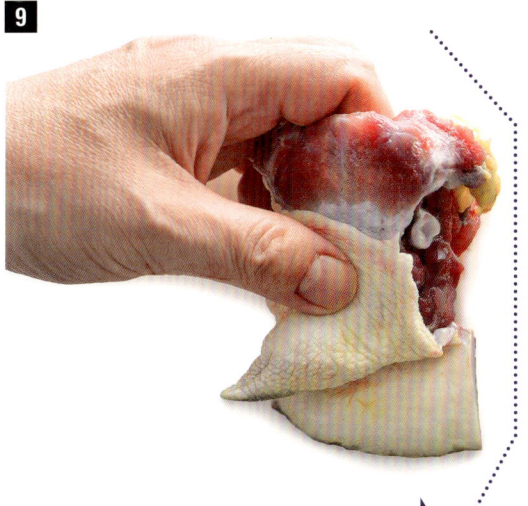

to next page (top)

to next page (bottom)

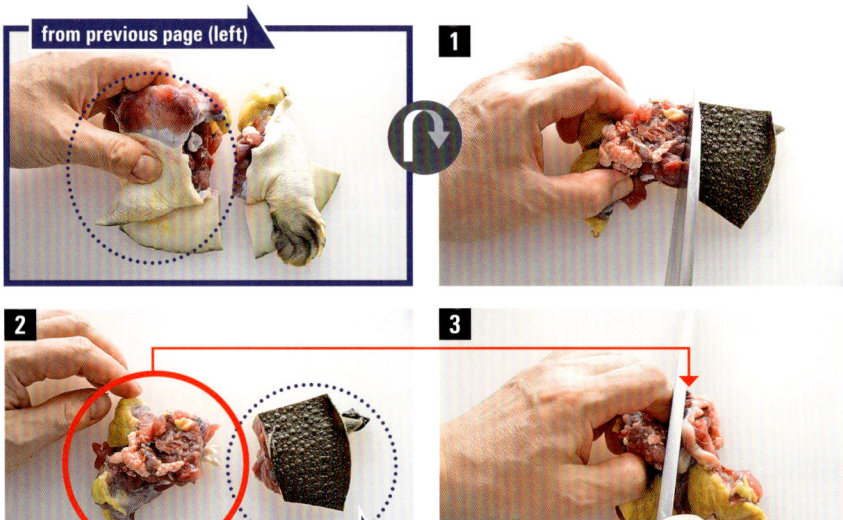

from previous page (left)

Separating the pelvic girdle and tail

1 To separate the pelvic girdle from the tail bones, locate the hard place at the edge of the soft carapace where they connect and cut the joint.

2 The tail separated from the pelvic girdle.

3 Stand the pelvic girdle part on end and cut it in two equal parts in the ventral-dorsal direction.

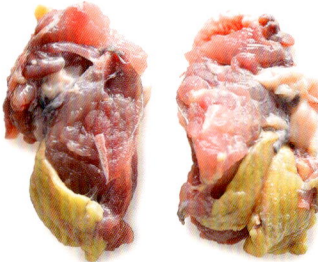

to page 196

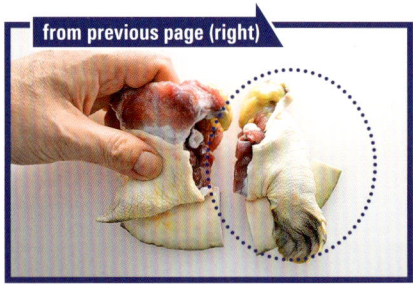

pelvic area after cutting in two
(two loin cuts)

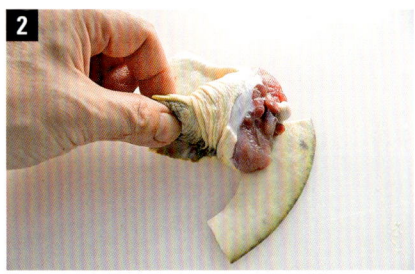

from previous page (right)

Cutting the rear legs

1
2 To locate the joint between the two leg bones, hold out the left rear leg, then with the thumb, push in on the foot, causing the joint to fold (it will naturally unfold when released).

3 The bent knee will protrude through the flesh.

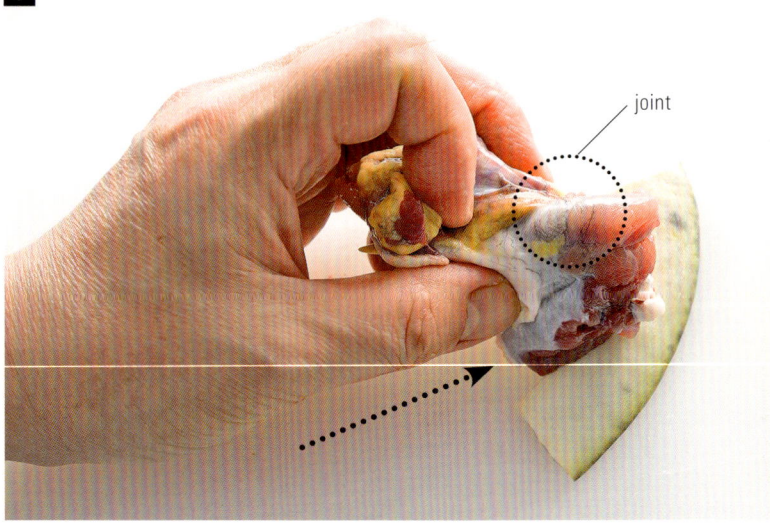

joint

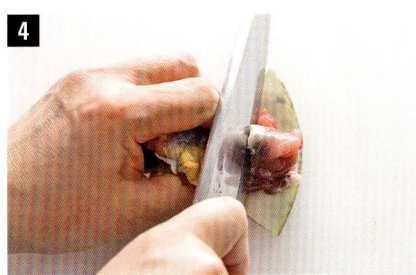

4 Cut through the joint.

5 Without removing the knife, tilt the blade and cut the flesh into two roughly equal parts.

6 The rear leg cut into two parts.

7 Place the leg with the foot facing right and cut off the foot at the joint. Divide the right rear leg in the same way.

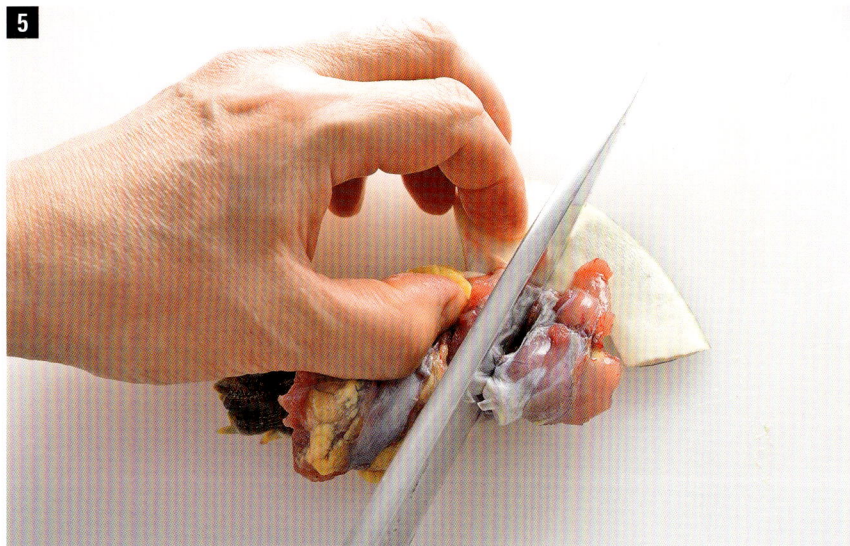

foot cut away from the rear leg

The feet have claws and are inedible, so are discarded.

from page 194

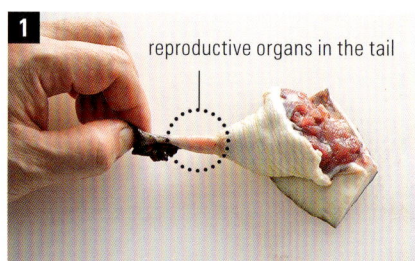

reproductive organs in the tail

Dividing the tail

1 The male reproductive organs located in the tail are inedible and are removed. Pull out on the tail.

2 To remove the bones running through the center of the tail (the reproductive organs are attached to the bones), first cut the skin at the side of the tail bones.

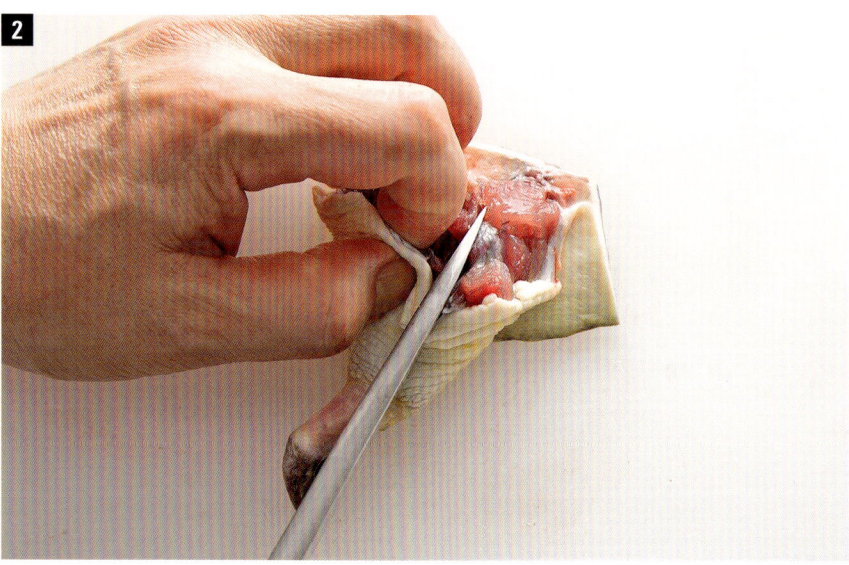

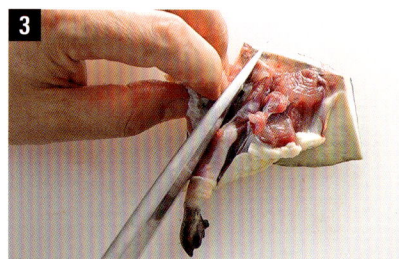

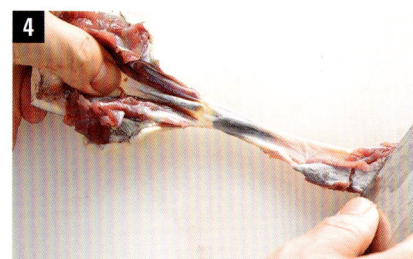

3 Cut along the other side of the tail bones.

4 Holding down the tail bone with the knife, pull the flesh away with the left hand.

5 Cut away the tail end.

6 Cut the base of the tail with the knife.

7 With the belly (white) side of the tail meat to the right, cut the tail meat in half.

8 The tail meat cut in half.

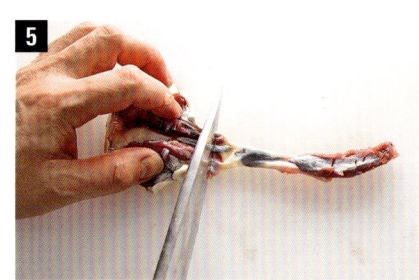

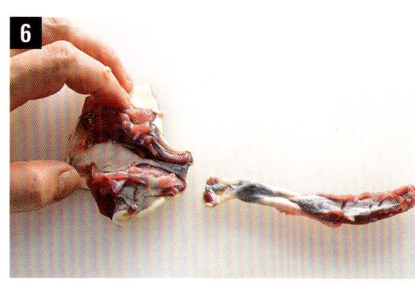

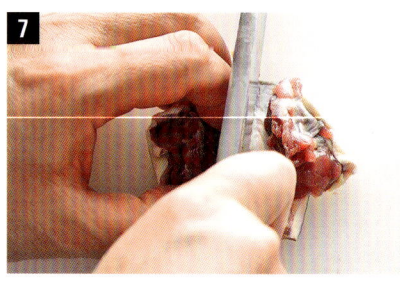

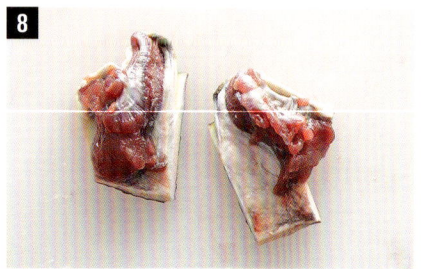

from page 191

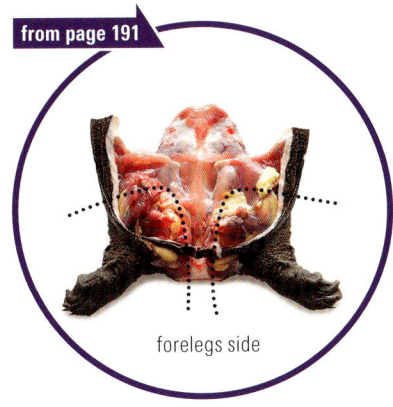

forelegs side

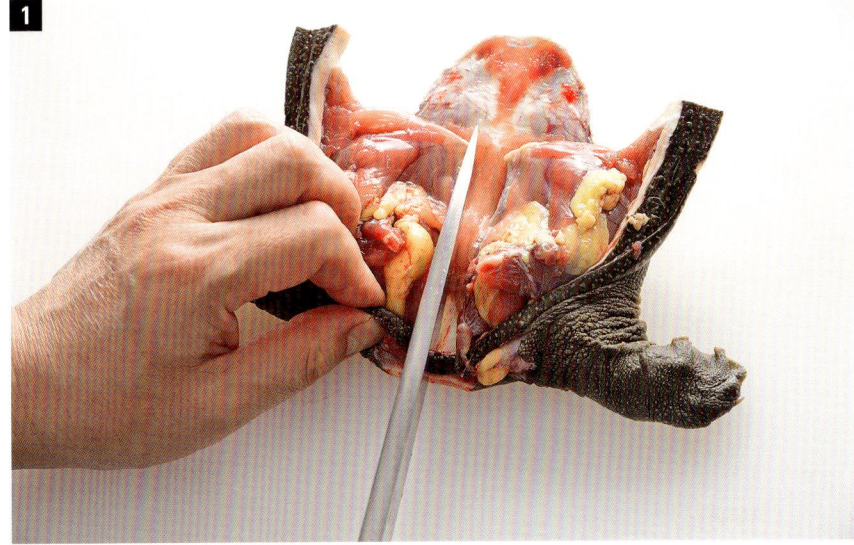

Dividing the forelegs section

1 Cut into the center of the part where the
2 neck was attached, all the way to the
plastron.

3 Pulling up on the right foreleg, cut the
border between the plastron and the leg.

4 Continue cutting back along the edge of
the plastron toward the back.

5 Cut the right foreleg off from the edge
of the plastron, as shown in the photo
below.

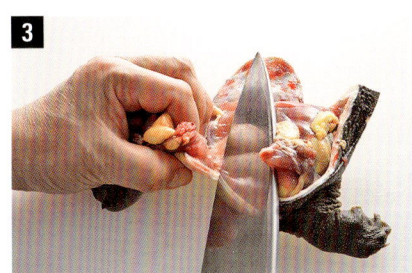

right foreleg cut away

6. For the left foreleg, likewise, lift up the leg and cut at the line between the plastron and the leg.

7. Continue cutting around the plastron in the direction of the tail end. Cut the leg off by pulling the knife toward you.

8. Cut the leg away at the edge of the plastron.

9. Shows the left leg cut away.

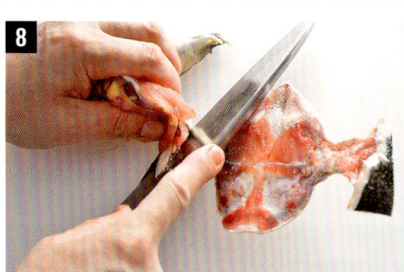

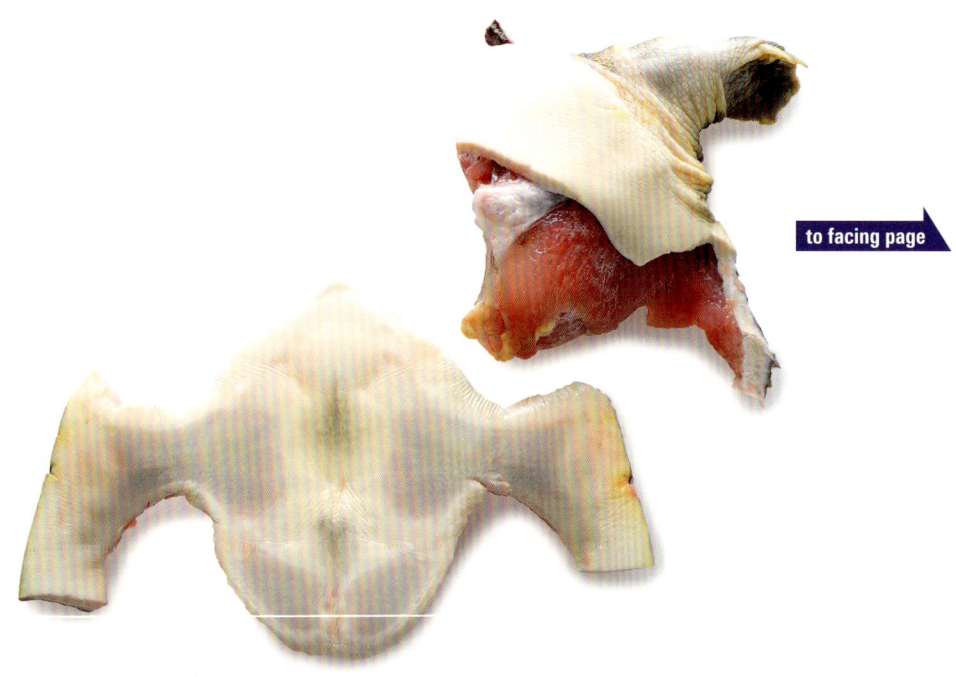

to facing page →

plastron (bottom) and left foreleg (top)

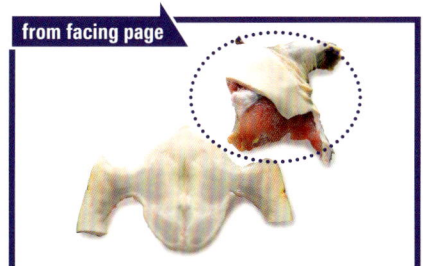
from facing page

Cutting the parts of the left foreleg

1 Probe for the joint between the three-pronged shoulder bones and the upper foreleg bone and place the knife at the joint.

2 Cut into the center of the joint.

3 Slant the knife and position the blade behind the joint.

4 Avoid the bone directly under the knife by slanting the knife to the right in a scooping motion.

5 The left foreleg and flesh cut away.

6 Push the foot into the skin so that the

7 knee joint protrudes.

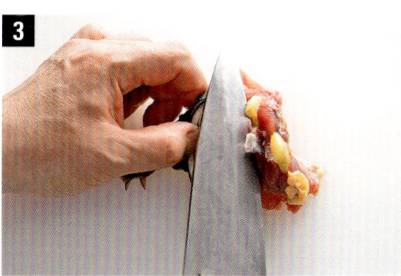

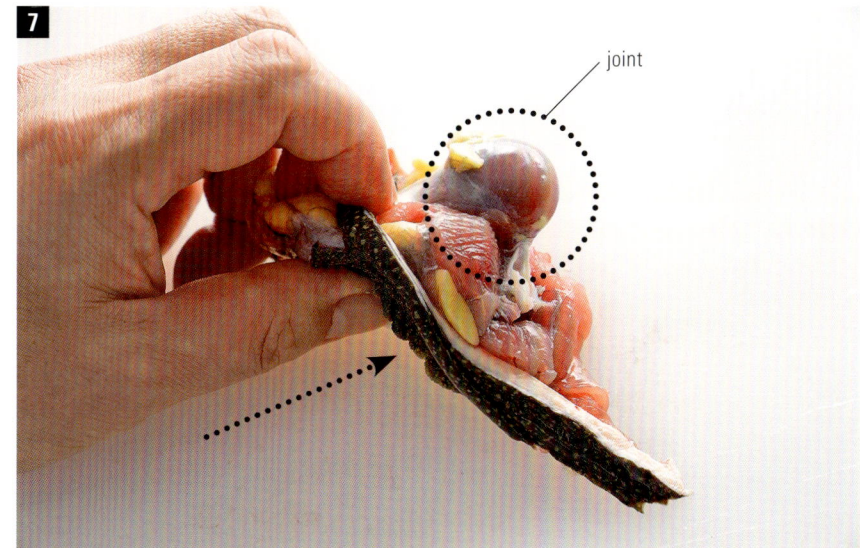

joint

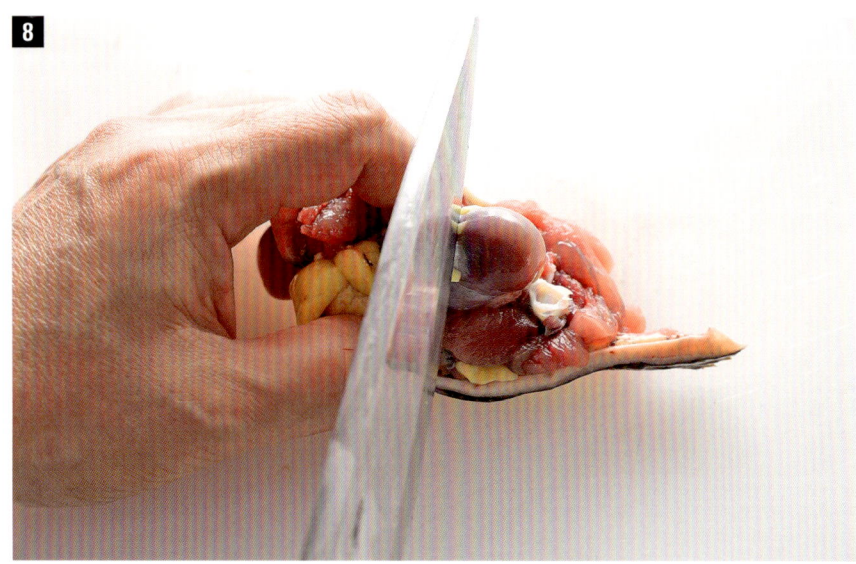

8 Position the knife midway in the joint, as shown.

9 Cut through, dividing the leg into two.

10 Shows the two parts of the leg, with the foot pulled out once more.

11 Position the knife at the joint between the leg and the foot.

12 Cut off the foot. Divide the right leg in the same way.

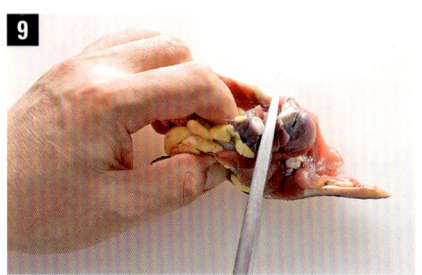

foot cut away from the foreleg
The foot is discarded.

from page 192

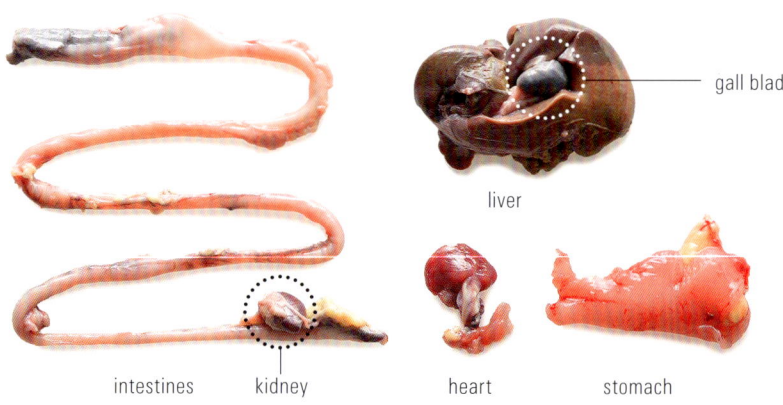

intestines   kidney   heart   stomach   liver   gall bladder

LEFT: Intestines with the kidney attached to the lower end. Top RIGHT: The black ball seen inside the liver is the gall bladder. Carefully remove to prevent puncturing and spreading its bitter contents. All the internal organs are edible except for the gall bladder.

Head, carapace, plastron, and parts of the body divided. There are sixteen parts with flesh attached. The head is used in making dashi.

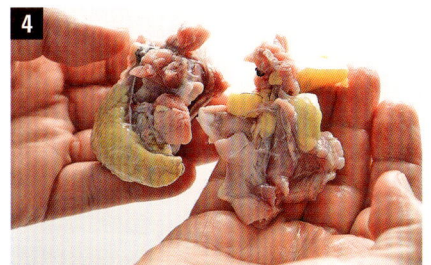

Pretreatment of internal organs and body parts

1 Place all the body parts, the carapace, and plastron in a large bowl. Soak in 175–185°F (80–85°C) water (the temperature is important: if the water is too hot the skin will melt and be difficult to peel off, and it will also be difficult to remove if the water is too cool).

2 Peel the outer skin off the hard and soft carapaces.

3 The hard carapace and skin. These are hard and inedible.

4 Only the shoulders are without part of the outer skin.

5 Peel the film-like outer layer off the skin.

6 An outer layer also covers the white skin parts; remove that as well.

Suppon Turtle Hot Pot
Maru-nabe

For turtle hot pot, the soup is not strained but enjoyed after removing only the head and carapace. The collagen-rich and tasty soup as well as the plump, gelatinous flesh can be enjoyed to the last drop.

Serves 8

Turtle soup

| 1 *suppon* turtle about 1 kg. (2¼ lbs.)

| About 2 L (2.1 qt.) water

| 1.2 L (1.3 qt.) sake, divided

| 20 g (⅔ oz.) Rishiri kombu

| 1 tsp. salt

| 2 Tbsp. *usukuchi* shoyu

24 4-cm (about 2 in.) length *naganegi*

4 cm (about 2 in.) x 4 cm (about 2 in.) x grilled *mochi*

8 pieces of tofu, each 5 cm (about 2¼ in.) x 3 cm (1¼ in.)

160 ml (⅔ cup) sake

4 tsp. ginger juice

Directions

1 Place water, ⅓ of the sake to be added (see below), and a strip of kombu in a large pot and bring to a boil over high heat. The sake should be added in three stages (if added all at once, the alcohol will saccharify and make the dish too sweet). Add the skinned pieces of flesh and the soft carapace and cook over high heat for about 20 minutes. Skim off any froth that forms.

2 After all the froth has been skimmed off, remove the strip of kombu and add another ⅓ of the sake.

3 Turn the heat to low and simmer for 40 minutes. Add the remainder of the sake midway in simmering.

4 Add salt while simmering.

5 Add *usukuchi* shoyu while simmering. After the 40 minutes, turn off the heat. Leave the soup as it is overnight (this allows the turtle meat to mature, increasing its umami taste; in order to keep the meat from drying out, the soup should not be removed).

Make the hot pot

Place the soup in a pottery *nabe* cookpot and bring to a boil. Add tofu and *naganegi* and simmer. Just before it is ready, add grilled *mochi*, ginger juice, and sake.

Anko
MONKFISH
Lophiomus setigerus

Monkfish, the general term used for members of the family Lophiidae, order Lophiiformes, and in Japanese *anko*, is a deep-sea fish widely found from the tropics to the temperate zone. The two main species found in Japanese waters are called *kutsu-anko* and *ki-anko* but are ordinarily not distinguished since they are very similar. The rather grotesque-looking fish is about a meter long and flattish with a wide head and massive mouth filled with very sharp teeth. The dorsal fin takes the shape of the distinctive "lure" the fish dangles to bring prey within reach.

Monkfish is in ample supply from late autumn through winter and in the Kanto region is prized as much as pufferfish for its taste; it is a leading winter fish. Other than the jawbone and spine, almost the entire fish is edible, so there is little waste. In addition to liver (*ankimo*), renowned for its richness, breast meat, and the skin, which is full of collagen, the gills, fins, stomach, and ovaries are also considered delicacies, each with its own flavor and texture. The leading way of enjoying monkfish is as hot pot, with vegetables added together with these "seven parts" (*nanatsu dogu*) of the fish (see p. 219).

The body of the monkfish is rather flabby and soft and is covered with mucous film, making it almost impossible to handle on a cutting board, so it is carved while hanging by a hook inserted into its lower jaw. The fish also retains a large amount of water, which drains out in the process of cutting, so it must be hung in a place suitable for this drainage.

CUTTING MONKFISH

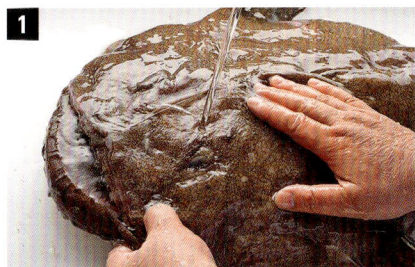

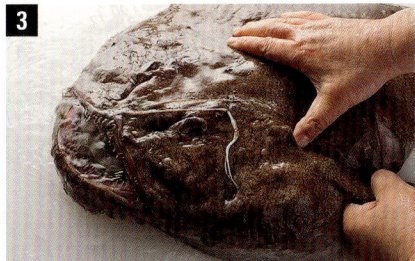

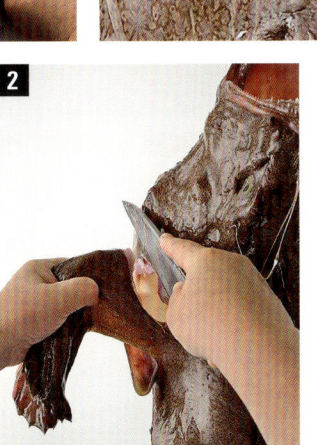

Preparatory trimming

1 First wash away the mucous film covering the surface of the fish, rubbing it down from head to tail and using a brush to remove the mucus from the tail fin.

2 Run water into the mouth as well, taking care not to cut yourself on the sharp teeth.

3 Press on the back of the fish to flush the water out of its mouth, washing out the inside of the belly. Run water into the mouth and flush out again, repeating until the water runs out clean.

4 Hang the fish from its lower jaw on a suspended hook strong enough to hold the fish's weight.

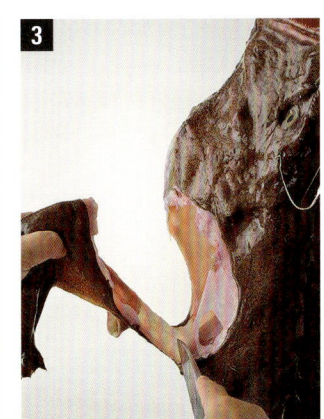

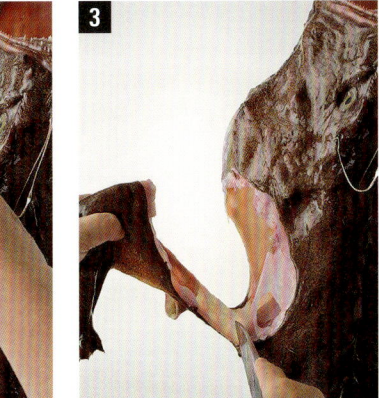

Removing the pectoral and ventral fins

1 Pull out one of the pectoral fins and insert the *deba* knife at its base.

2 Chop down forcefully on the cartilage and cut through.

3 Cut off the entire fin at its base.

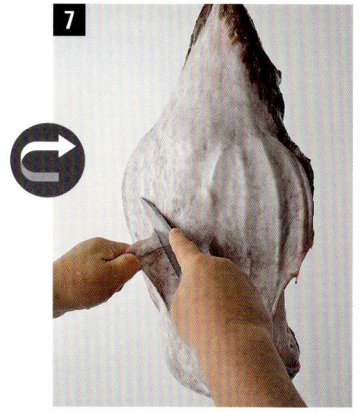

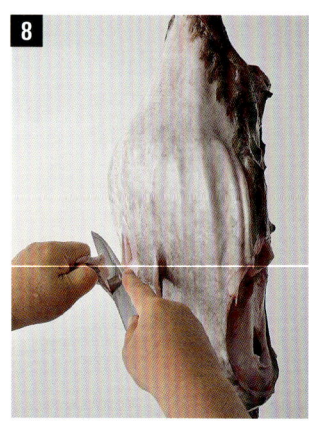

4 Insert the knife at the base of the pectoral fin on the other side.

5 Again, chop down firmly with the knife to cut through the cartilage, and remove the fin.

6 The fish with both pectoral fins removed. Place the removed fins in water to soak.

7 To remove the ventral fins, turn the fish so that the belly is facing you and insert the knife at the base of one of the ventral fins.

8 Cut downward and remove the fin.

9 Insert the knife at the base of the ventral fin on the other side. Cut downward and remove the fin.

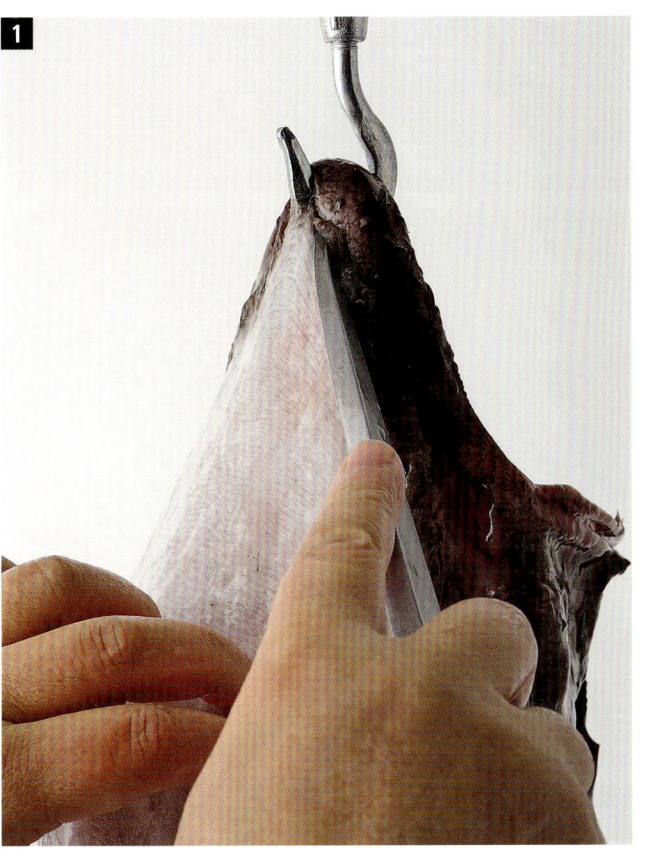

Removing the skin

1. Turning the belly (ventral) side of the fish to face you, insert the tip of the knife at the peak of the lower jaw.

2. Steady the fish with the left hand. Slowly rotating the body away from you, draw the tip of the knife down along the edge of the jaw, cutting through the skin only.

3. Rotate the dorsal side of the fish slightly to the left, as shown, and likewise slit through the skin around the edge of the upper jaw.

4. With the knife facing right, make a shallow incision from the left side of the jaw, cutting just the skin while rotating the fish carefully.

5. When the dorsal side of the fish is directly in front of you, turn the knife over and cut from the right side toward the center.

6. Rotate the body slightly to bring the ventral side in front of you and cut down from the peak of the jaw to meet the cut made in step 5.

7. Now the skin should be slit entirely around the edge of the upper and lower jaws.

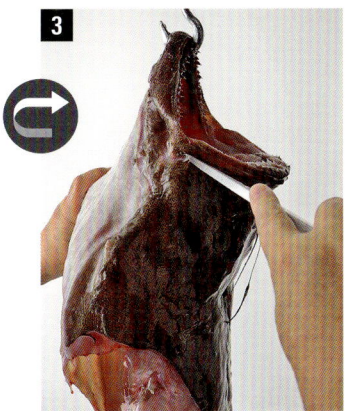

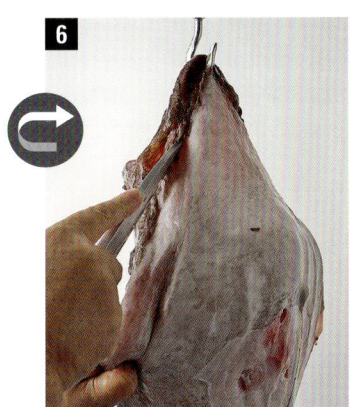

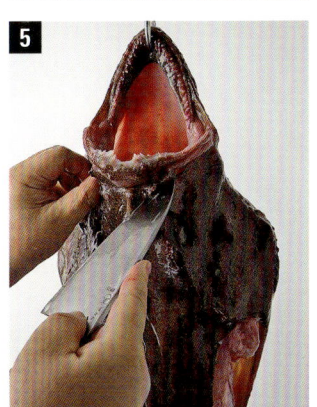

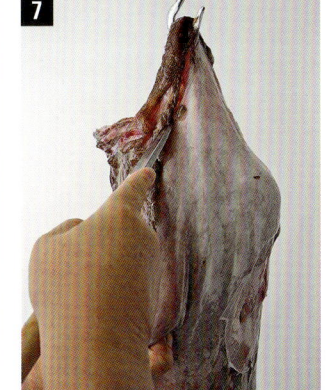

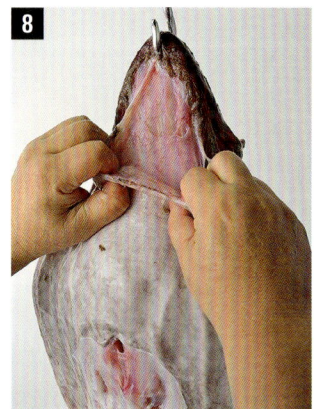

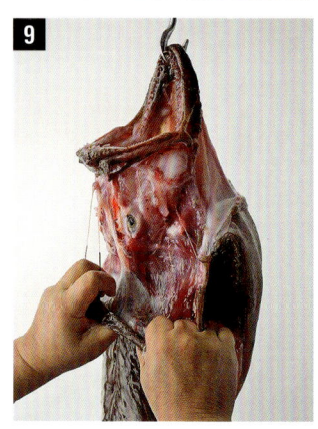

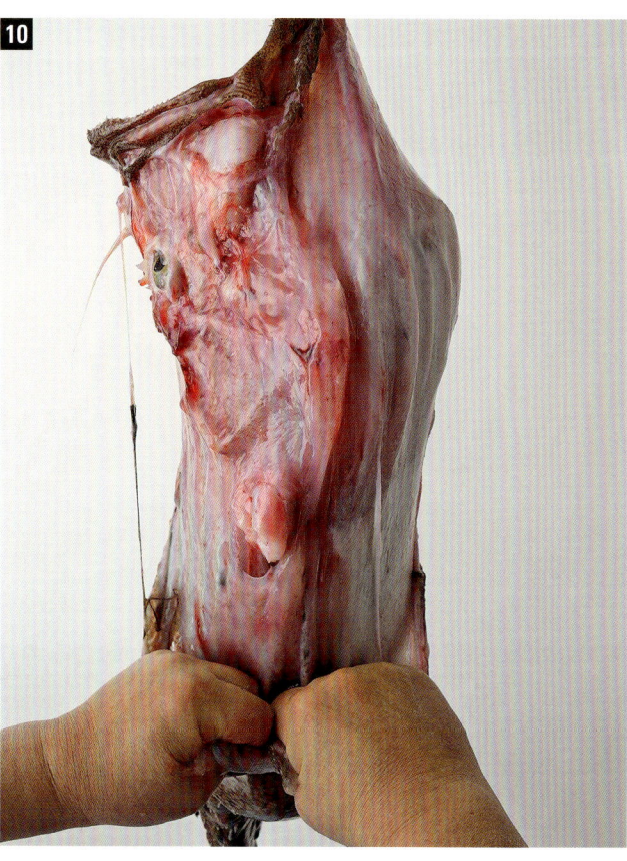

8 **9** Rotate the body so that the belly is facing you. Grasp the edge of the skin at the slit at the lower jaw with both hands and pull down on the skin, stripping it away from the body.

10 Rotating the body as needed, pull down on the skin a little at a time on all sides.

11 When the skin has been pulled off as far as the tail fin, cut it away at the base of the tail.

12 The entire fish with the skin removed. Place the removed skin in water to soak.

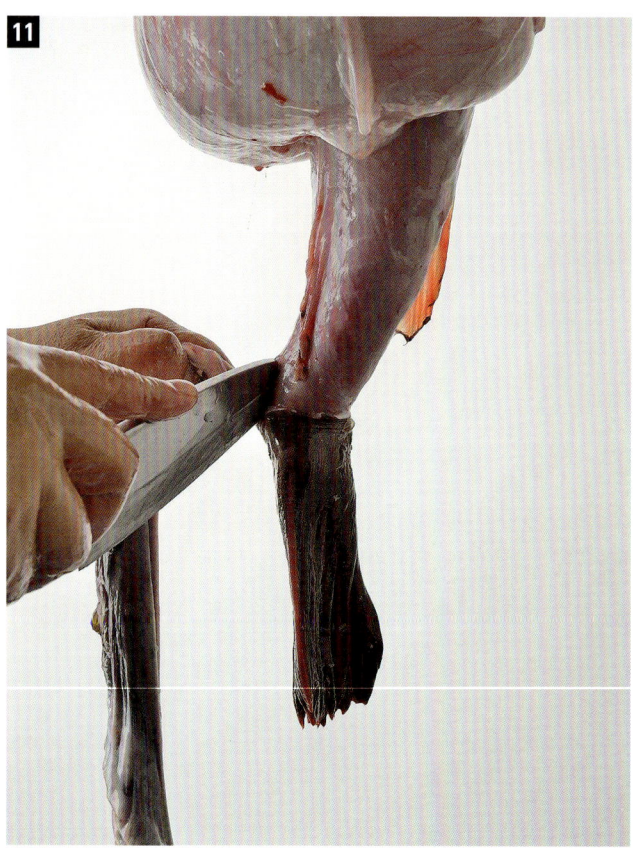

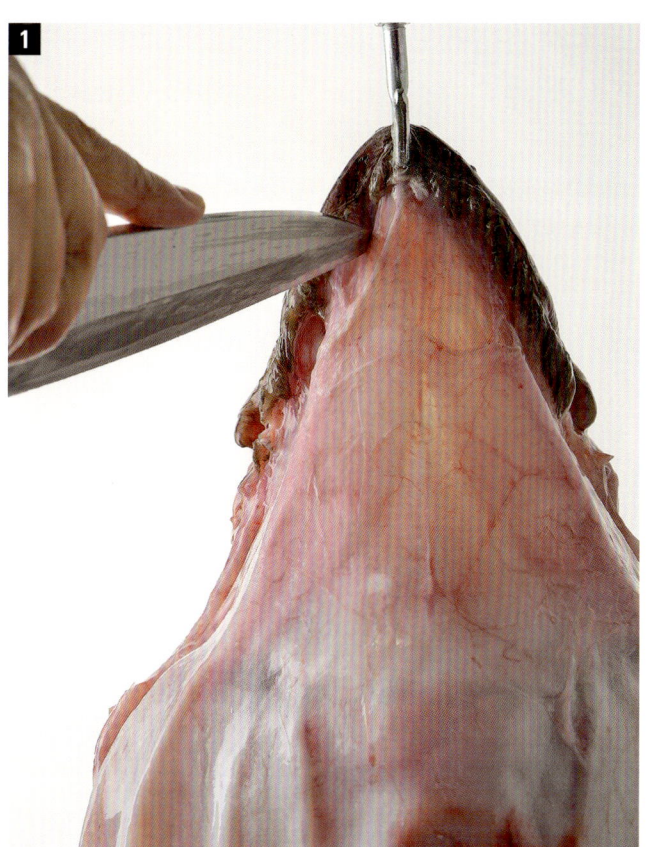

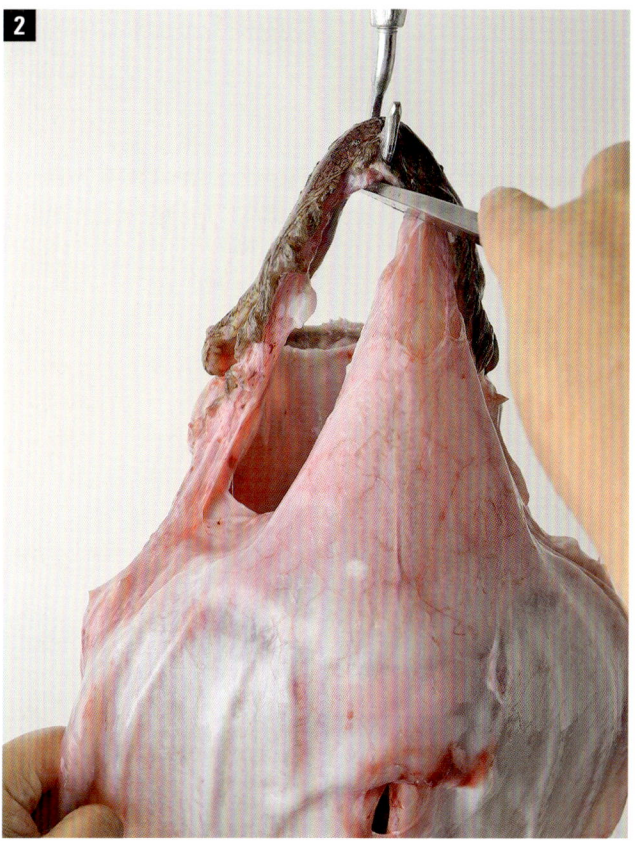

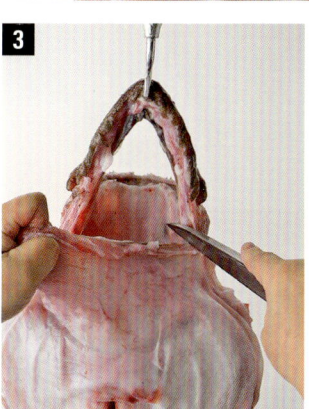

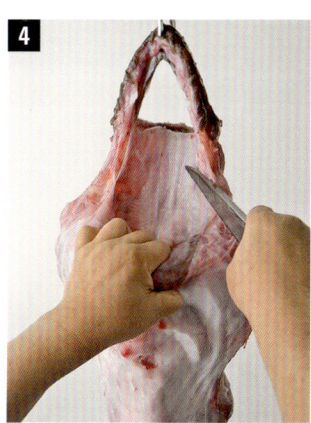

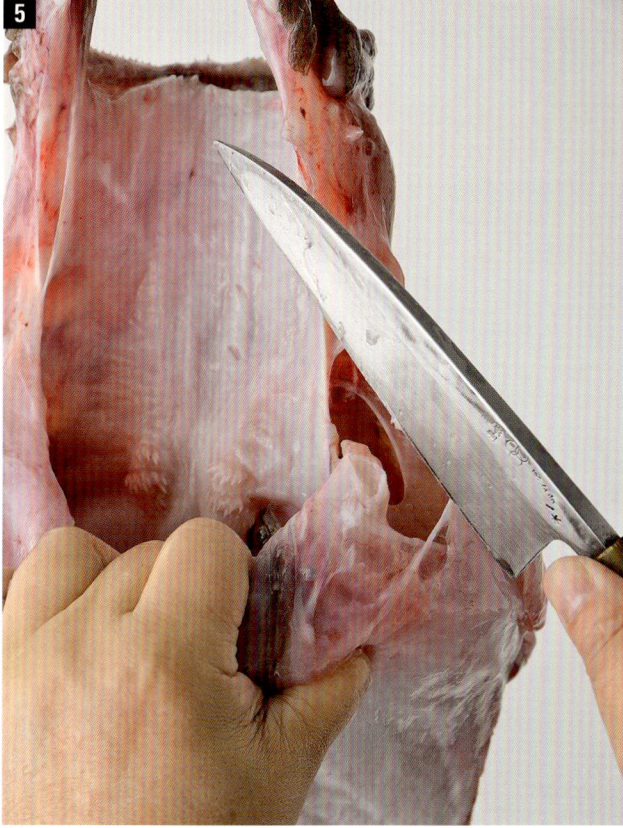

Opening the belly and removing the gills

1 Position the belly to face you and insert the knife along the edge of the lower jawbone. Cut through the remaining skin and flesh attached to the jaw. Cut down along the bone to where the upper and lower jaws join.

2 Cut through the skin and flesh along the other side of the lower jaw.

3 Cut down further on both sides, extending the opening until the knife strikes bone.

4 Grasp the cut-out part in order to steady the fish.

5 Chop through the bone struck by the knife in step **3**. Likewise chop through the bone on the other side.

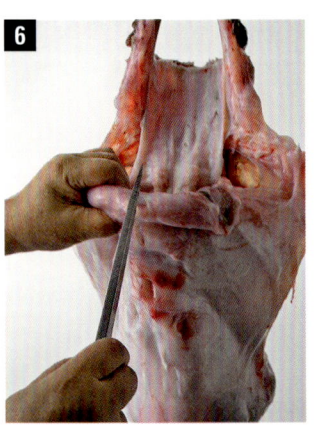

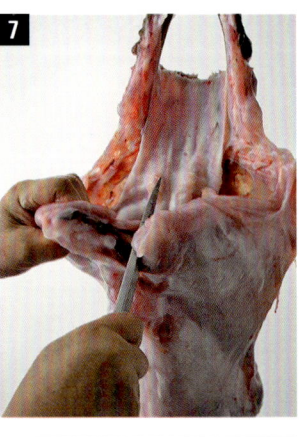

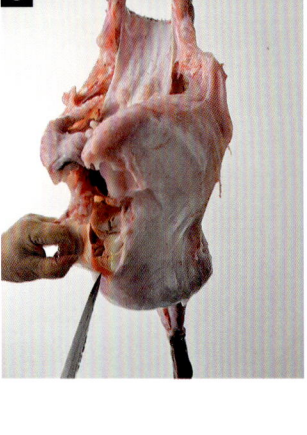

6
7 Insert the knife at the center of the breastbone and cut right through.

8 Slit the membrane over the liver, taking care not to damage the liver.

9 Grasp the gills on either side and pull apart so that the inside of the fish is visible.

10 With the knife facing up, cut the spot (upper black circle in photo **9**) where the cartilage is attached to the gills.

11 Cut the spot (lower black circle in photo **9**) on the lower side where the gills are attached to the cartilage.

12 Cut out the gills and the cartilage on the left. Likewise, cut out the right side.

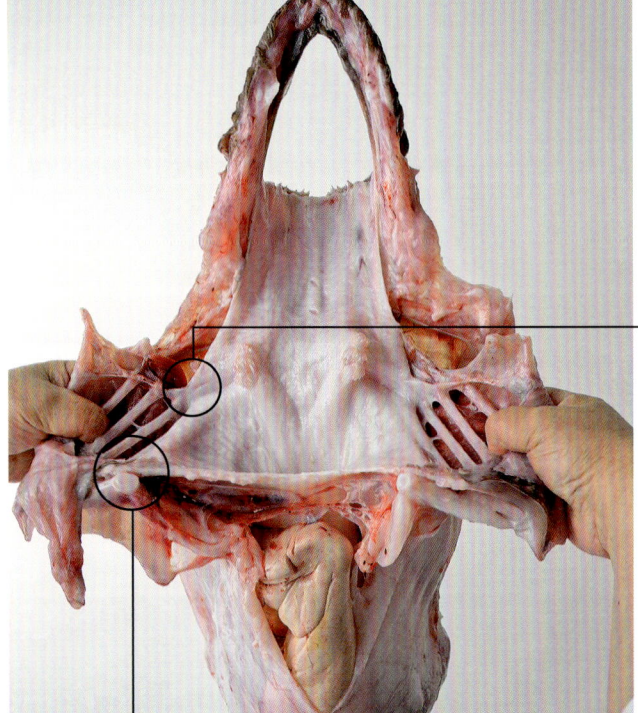

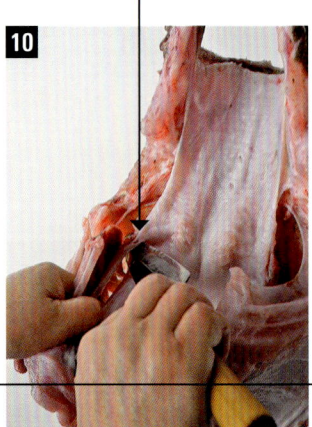

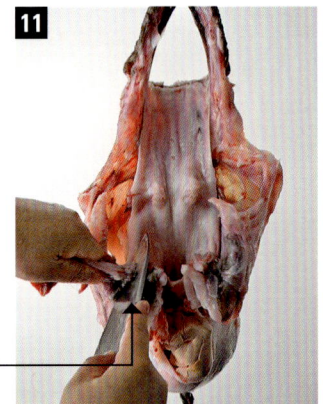

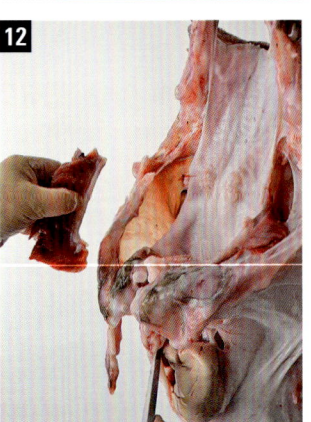

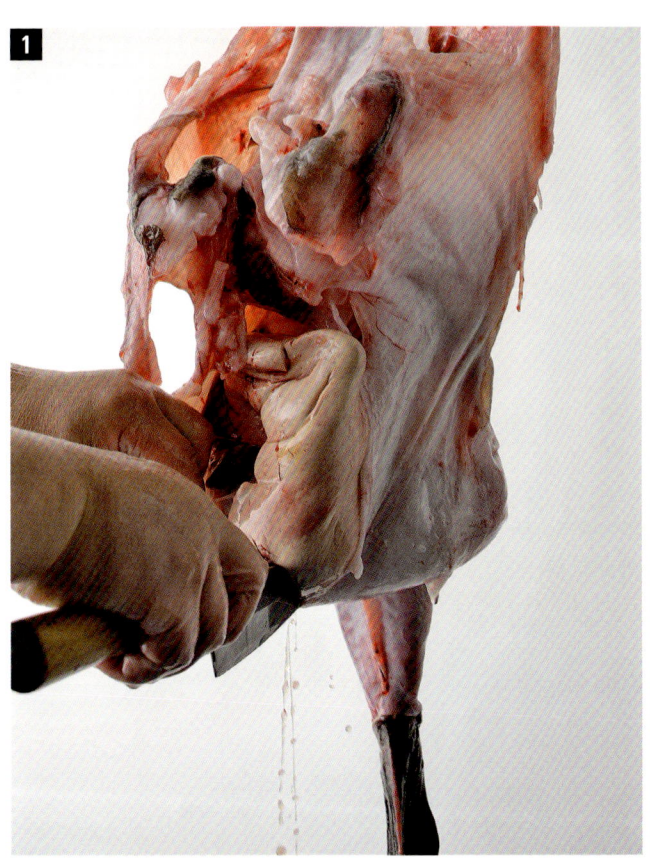

Removing the liver

1 Taking care not to damage the internal organs, cut the sides of the belly down to the tail fin and drain out the cavity.

2 Holding the liver with the left hand and taking care not to damage the stomach, carefully cut through the membranes connecting the liver to the body.

3 The body after removing the liver.

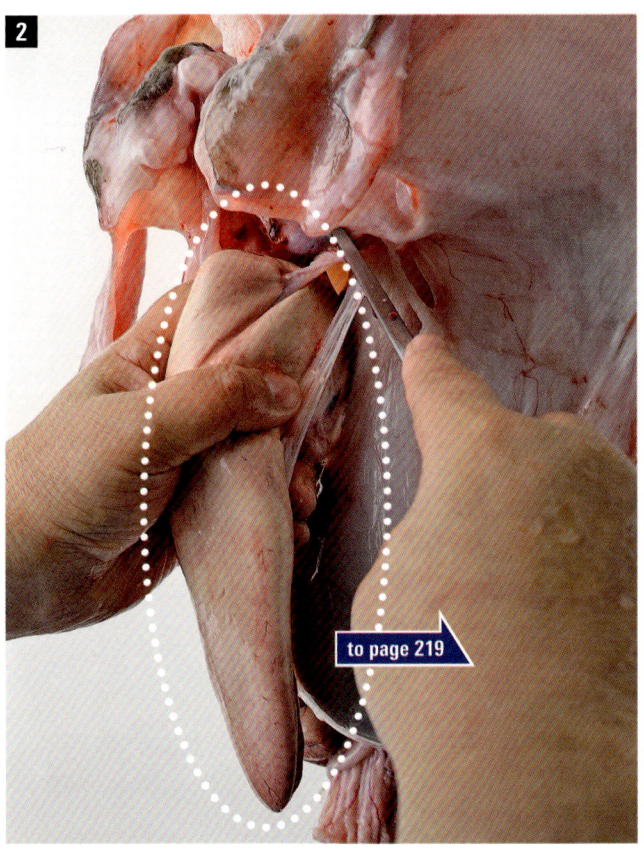

to page 219

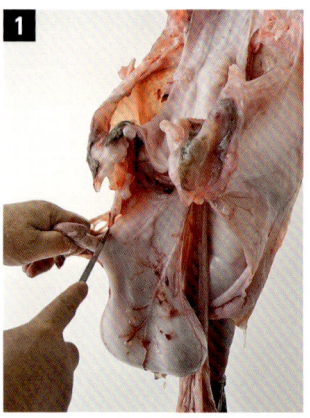

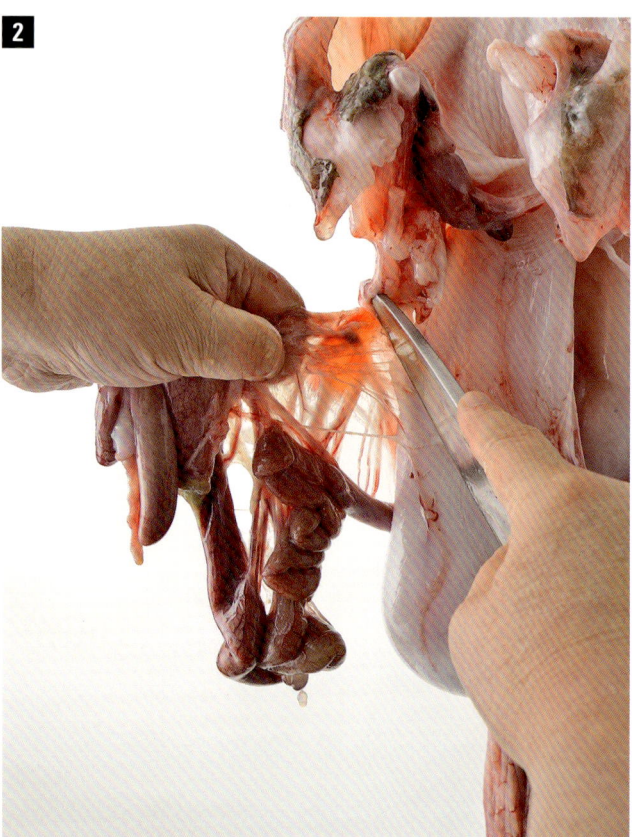

Removing the intestines, stomach, ovaries, heart, and rib cage

1 Cut away the intestines.

2 Cut the membranes connecting the intestines to the cavity.

3 Grasp the stomach sac and position the knife at the entrance to the stomach. Cut off the stomach. Empty the contents of the sac.

4 Grasp the ovaries (or in the case of a male, the testicles), the creased organs hanging behind the stomach. Place the knife at the base of the ovaries (or testicles) and cut them off.

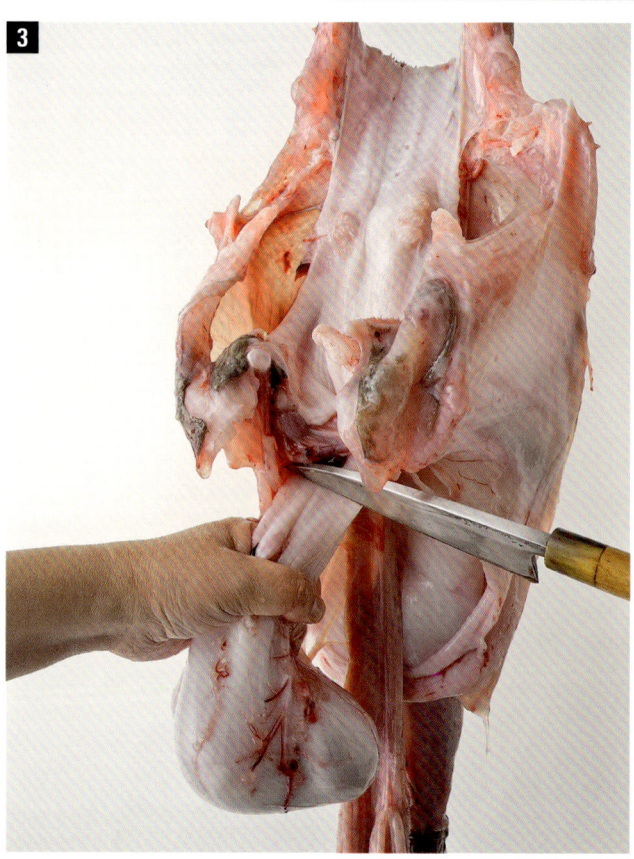

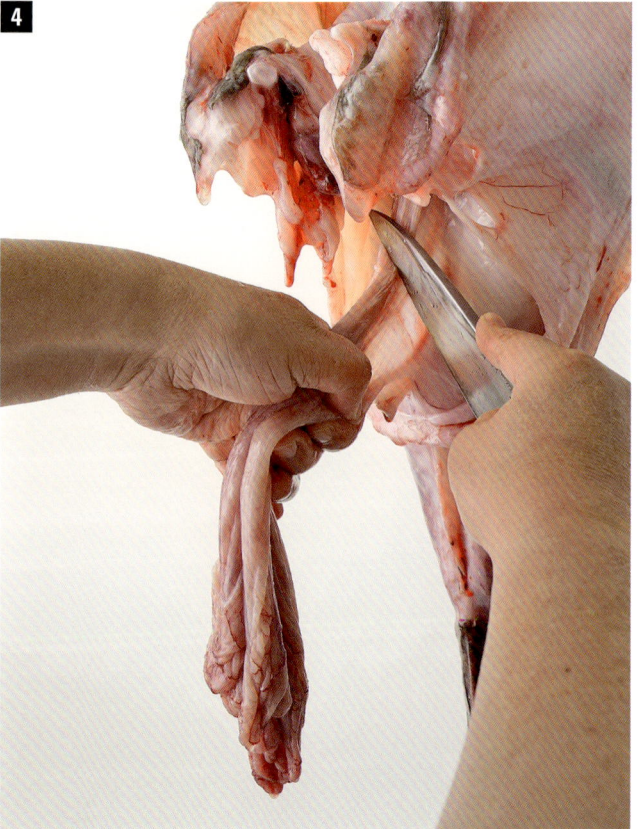

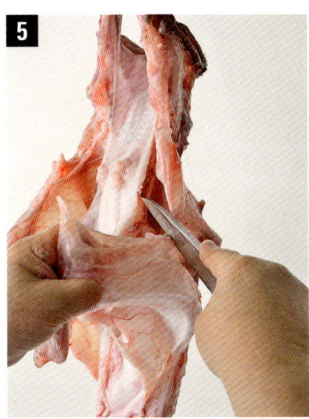

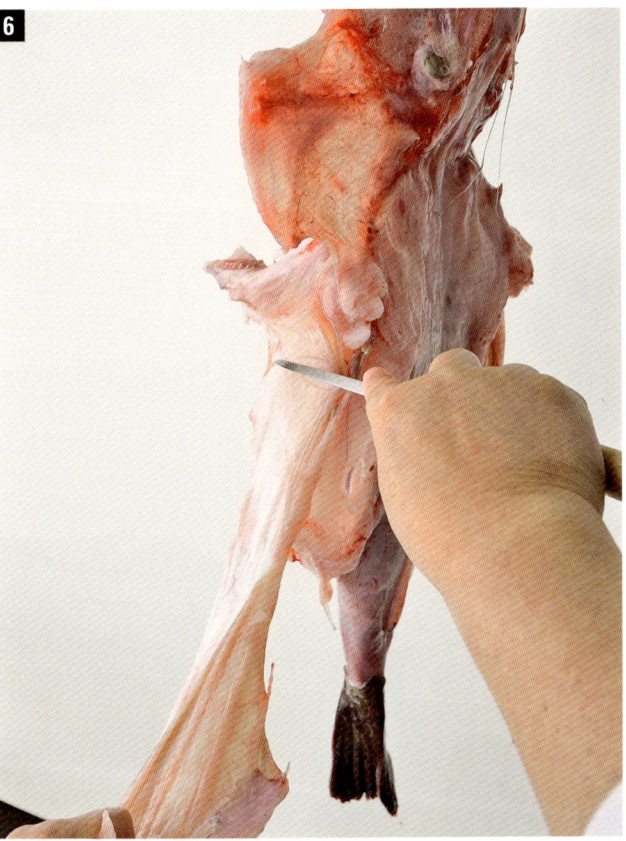

5 Grip the right-hand rib bones with the left hand and insert the knife at the base of the rib cage as shown.

6 Continue cutting downward and cut the rib cage away from the body; pull it off together with the membranes attached to it.

7 Rotate the body, grip the left-hand rib bones, and insert the knife at the base of the rib cage.

8 After cutting through the base of the rib cage, pull the rib cage off together with the membranes attached to it.

9 Cut off the heart, which is located close to the center.

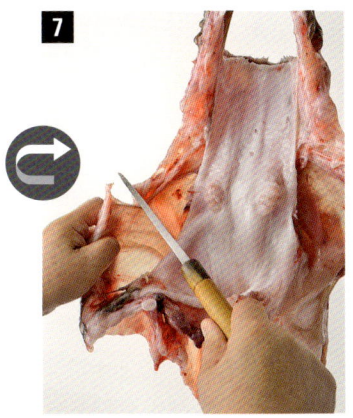

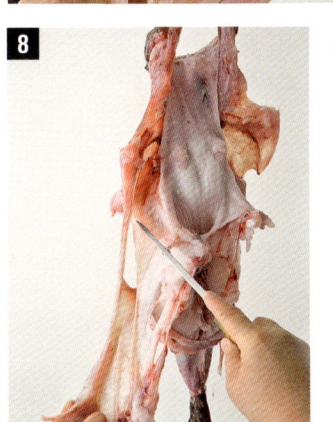

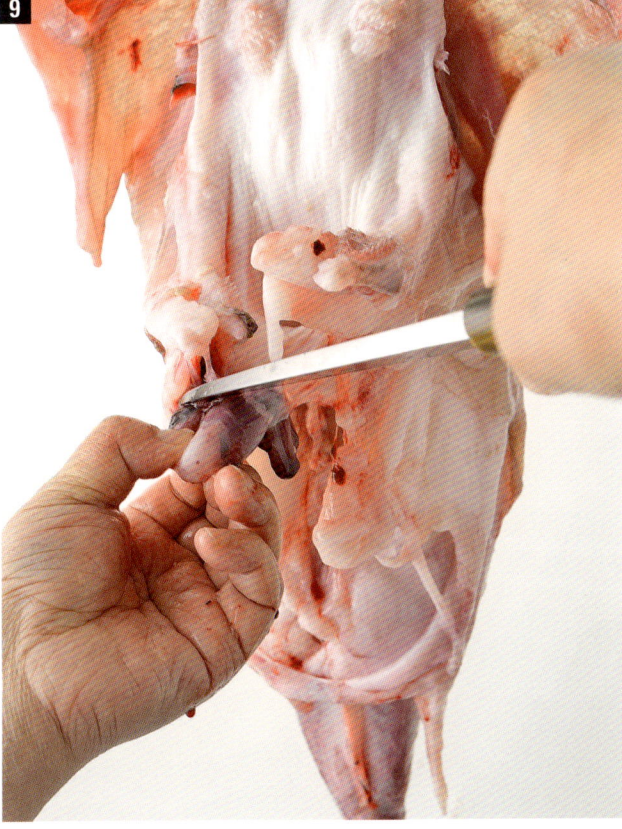

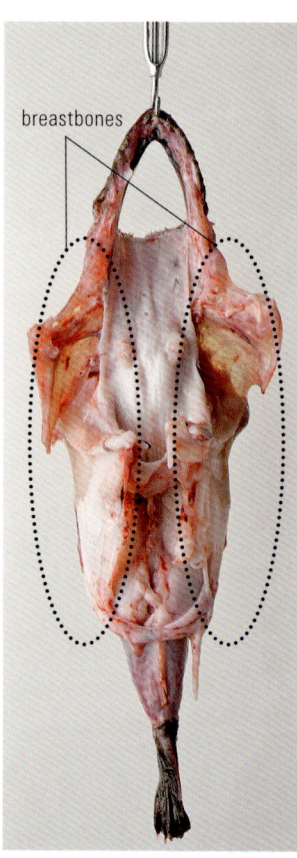

breastbones

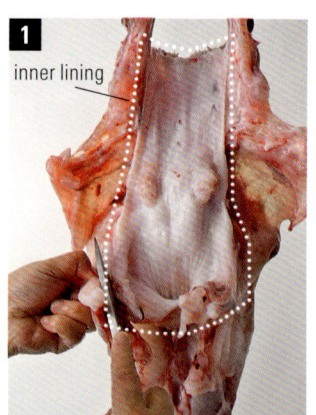

inner lining

Removing the abdominal lining, breastbones, and kidneys

1 To cut away the lining of the abdominal cavity, insert the knife into the tissue connecting the lining to the body.

2 Cut through the tissue, separating the lining from the body.

3 Insert the knife into the tissue
4 on the other side; continue cutting the lining loose.

5 Grasp the part of the lining that has been separated from the body and insert the knife with the blade facing upward; slice upward until the knife cuts through at the jaw.

6 Locate parts of the lining remaining and carefully trim them off. Holding the entire lining, pull it off.

7 The body with the lining of the abdominal cavity removed.

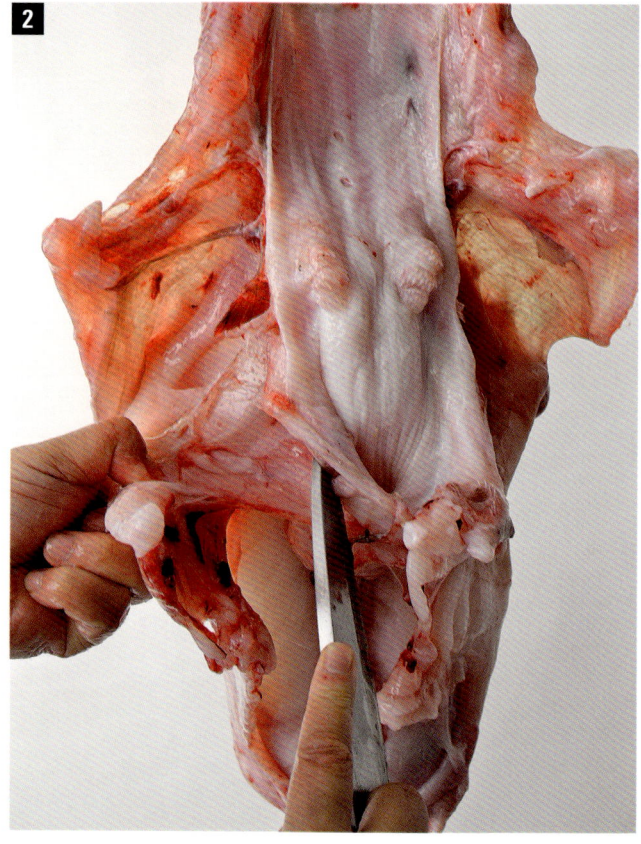

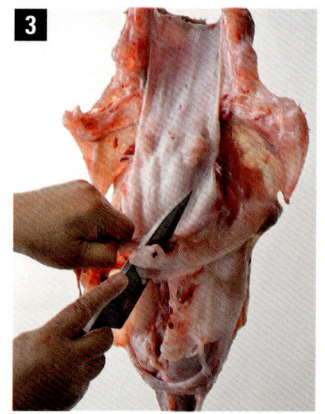

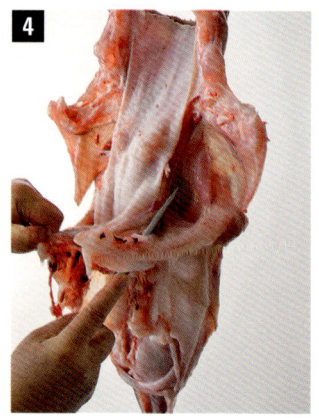

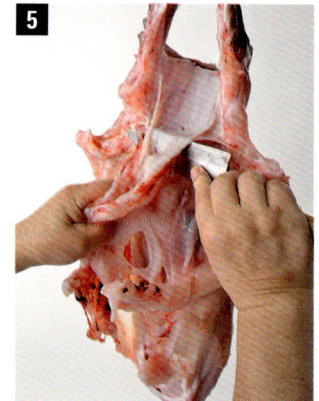

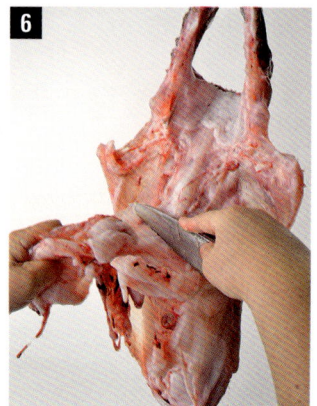

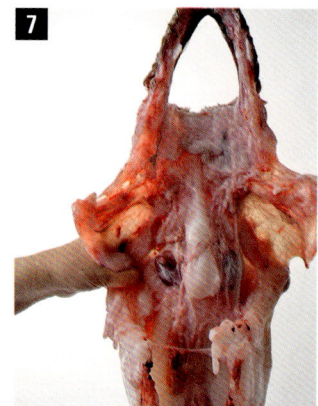

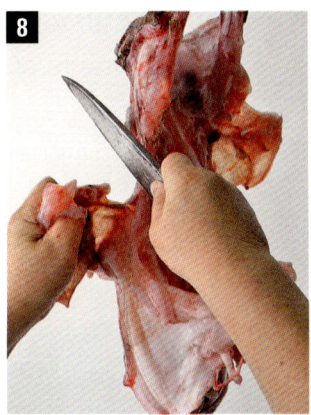

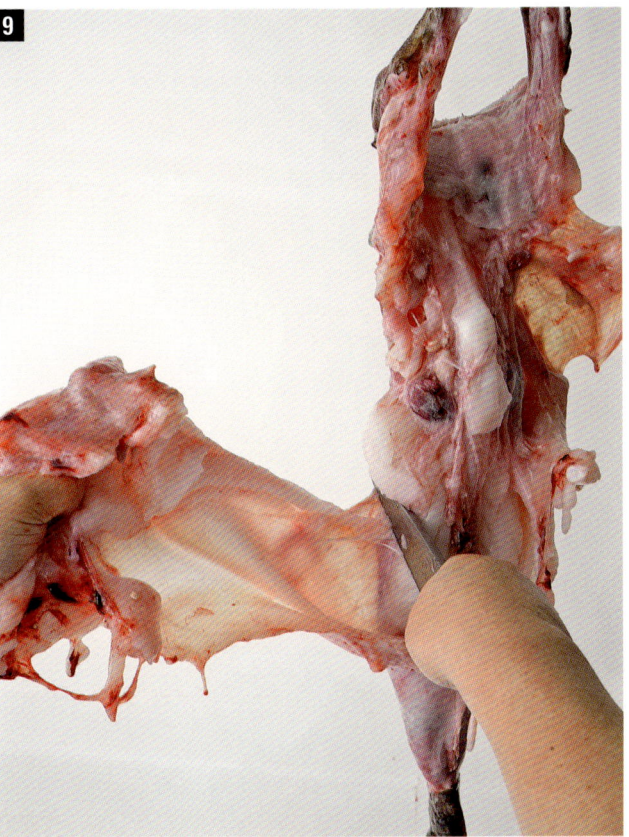

8 Insert the knife perpendicularly into the joint between the head and the divided breast-bone on the left side and start cutting it away from the base of the head.

9 Cut away the left breastbone together with the membranes attached to it.

10 Likewise, position the knife at the base of the breastbone on the right side.

11 Start cutting downward and cut away the right breast-bone together with the membranes attached to it.

12 Remove the kidneys on both sides.

13 The body with the two halves of the breastbone and kidneys removed.

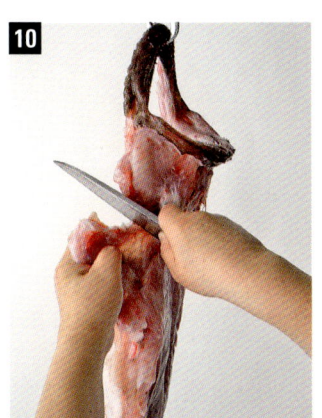

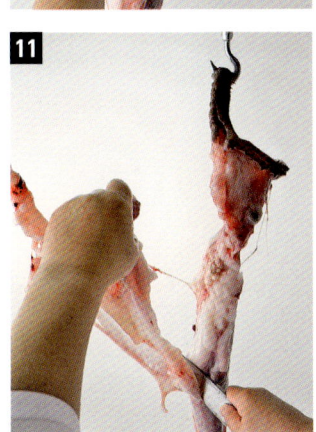

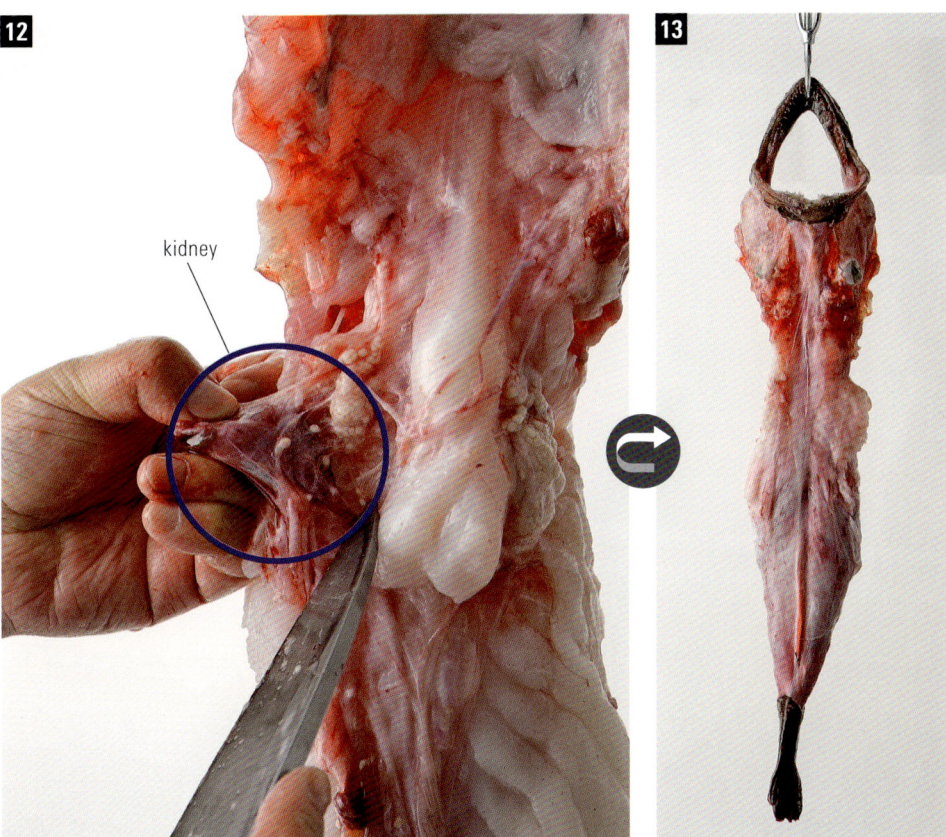

kidney

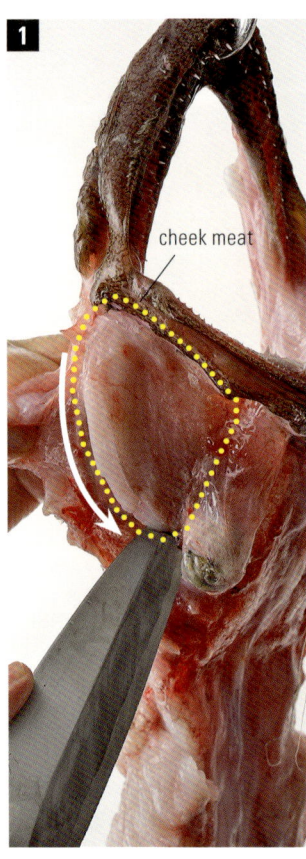

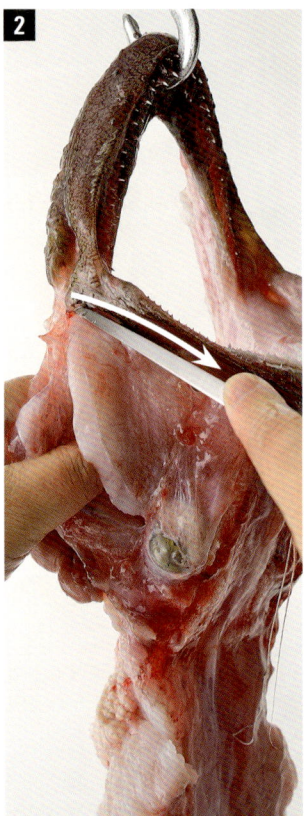

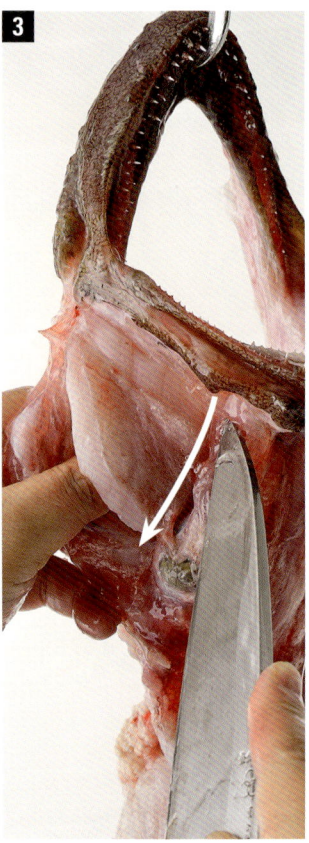

Removing the cheek meat

1 Leaving the skin on the inner side, make shallow cuts around the three sides of the triangular cheek meat on the left side. Make the first cut along the edge of the jawbone.

2 Then slit the side of the triangle directly under the mouth.

3 Finally cut along the remaining side of the triangle.

4 Press the cheek out from the inside and peel it away from the skin behind. Follow the same procedure for the other cheek.

cheek meat

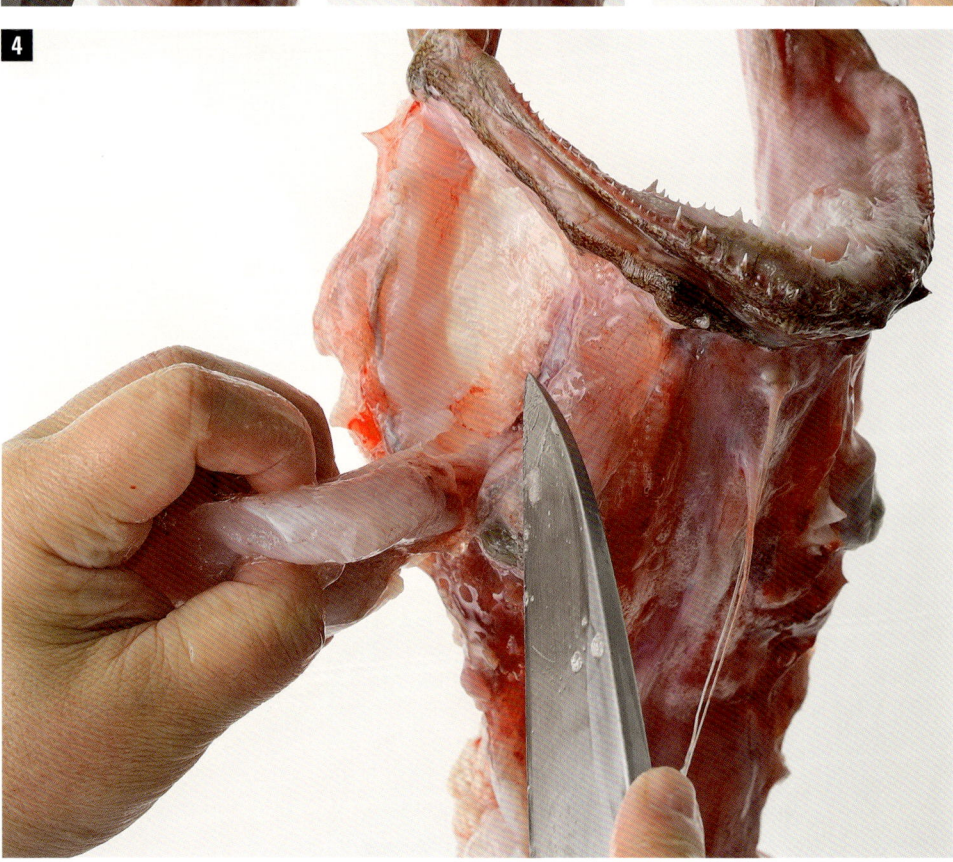

1

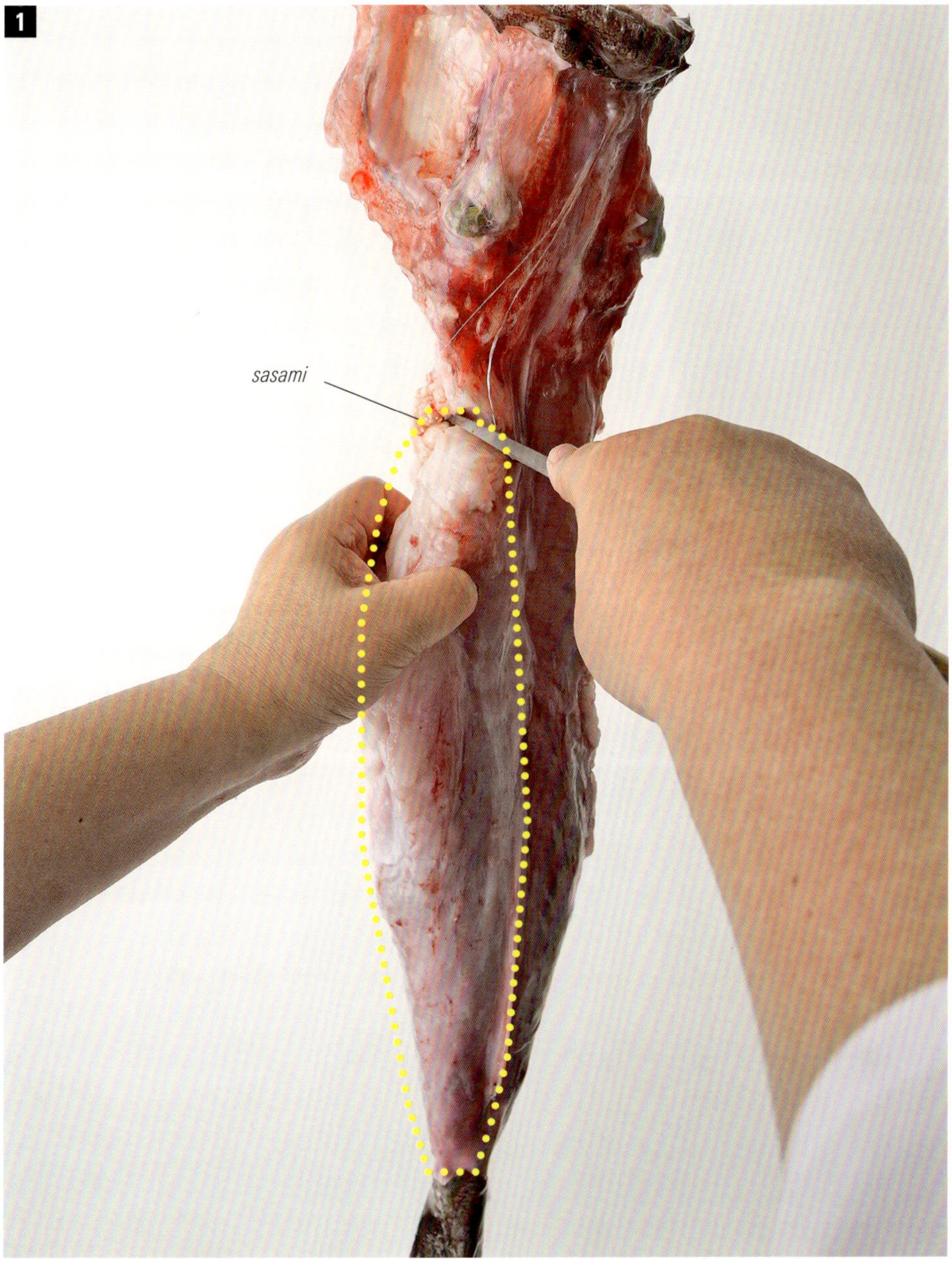

sasami

Removing the breast meat (*sasami*)

1 To cut away the breast meat (dotted-line part in photo **1**), steady the flesh with the left hand and make a shallow cut at the top of the breast to both sides of the spine.

2
3 Gripping the flesh with the left hand, cut all the way down along the spine.

4 Cut off at the base of the tail. Follow the same procedure for the breast meat on the other side.

5 The fish after the cheeks and breast meat are removed.

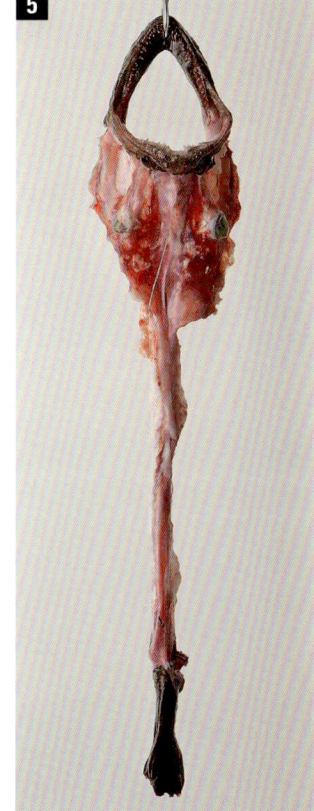

2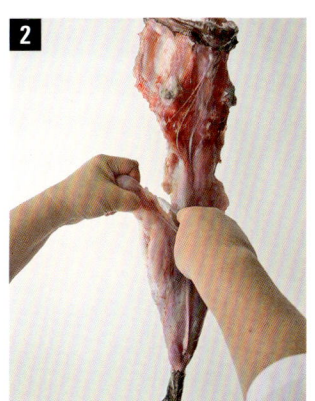

3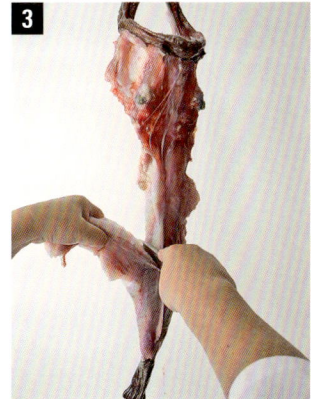

4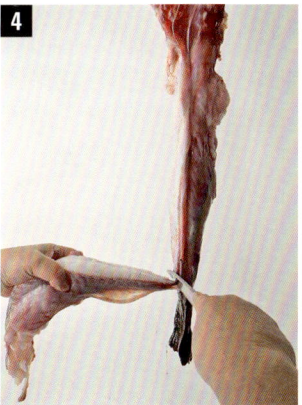

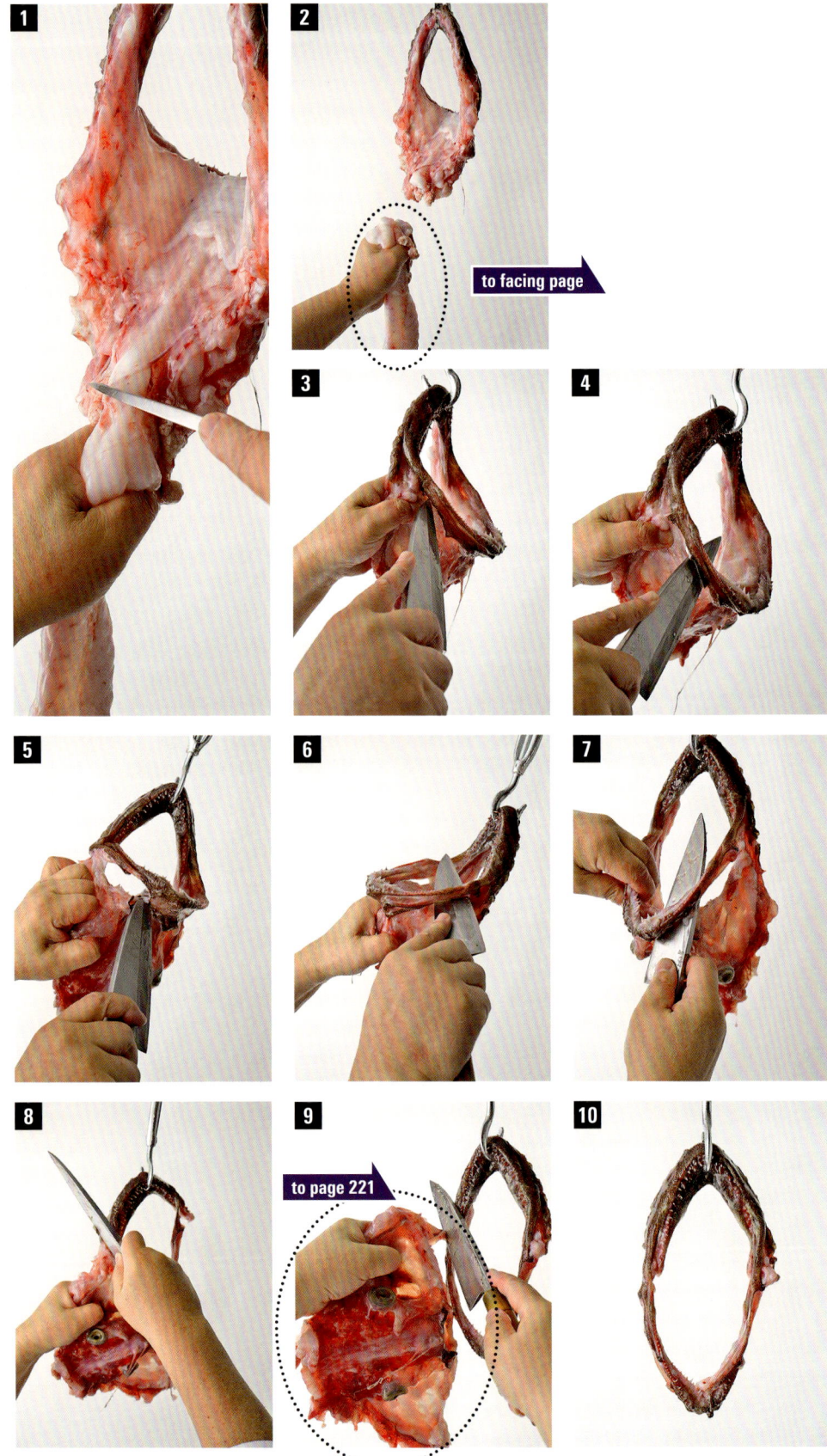

to facing page

to page 221

Removing the spine and headbone (face) from the jawbone

1 Rotate the fish so that the belly side is facing you and place the knife at the joint connecting the spine to the head.

2 Push in the knife forcefully to cut through the spine (continue to facing page).

3 Cut off the rest of the fish, leaving only the jawbone. Be careful of the sharp teeth. Grasp the skin where the cheeks were attached and place the knife on the skin at the jawbone.

4 Start cutting around the inside of the jawbone.

5 Grasp the flesh of the headbone with the left hand and continue cutting around to the center of the upper jaw.

6 On the other side as well, cut through the cheek skin and along the jawbone.

7 Cut along the line between the headbone and the jawbone and sever the connection at the middle of the jawbone.

8 Cut any remaining tissue connecting the headbone to the jawbone.

9 Separate the headbone from the jawbone.

10 Only the jawbone remains on the hook.

PREPARING THE "SEVEN PARTS" FOR COOKING

The edible parts of the monkfish, including the liver, fins, and so forth laid out on this page are dubbed the "seven parts" (*nanatsu dogu*) in the nomenclature of Japanese cuisine. The taste and texture of each of these parts differ and are enjoyed for their distinctive qualities.

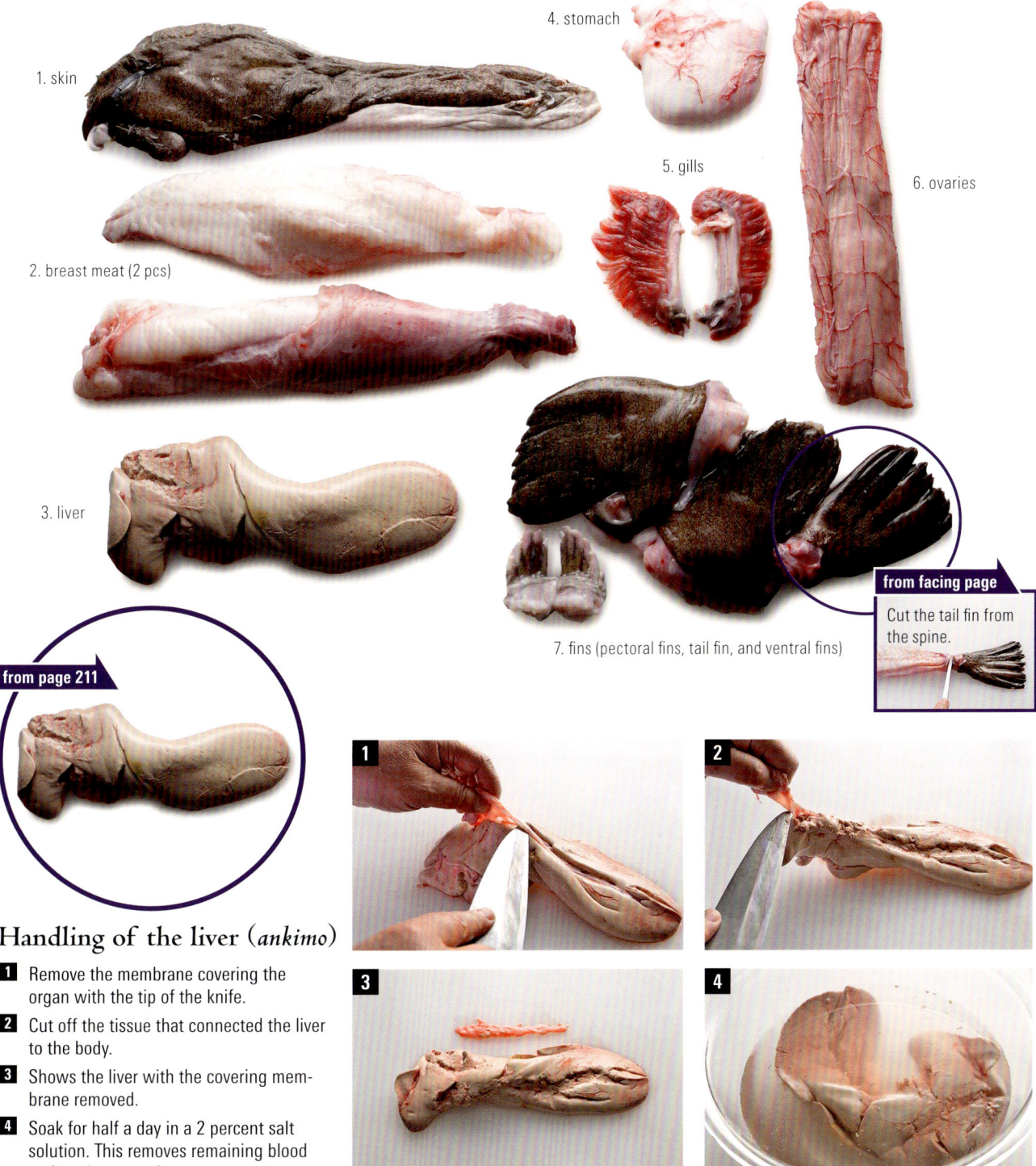

1. skin

2. breast meat (2 pcs)

3. liver

4. stomach

5. gills

6. ovaries

7. fins (pectoral fins, tail fin, and ventral fins)

from facing page
Cut the tail fin from the spine.

from page 211

Handling of the liver (*ankimo*)

1 Remove the membrane covering the organ with the tip of the knife.

2 Cut off the tissue that connected the liver to the body.

3 Shows the liver with the covering membrane removed.

4 Soak for half a day in a 2 percent salt solution. This removes remaining blood and unpleasant odor.

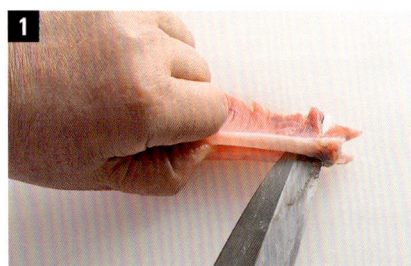

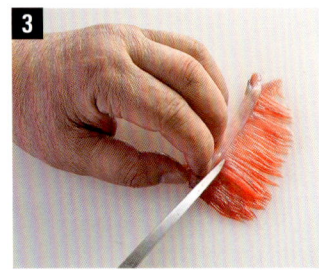

Treatment of the gills

1 Place the tip of the knife, blade facing to the right (*sakasabocho*). Cut the cartilage joint at one end.

2 Cut the cartilage joint at the other end, and separate gill layers.

3 Holding down the cartilage with the fingers of the left hand, use the blade of the knife to scrape the blood and liquid out of the gill tissue.

4 Follow the same procedure on the back of the gills; when they are clean and white, wash well in water.

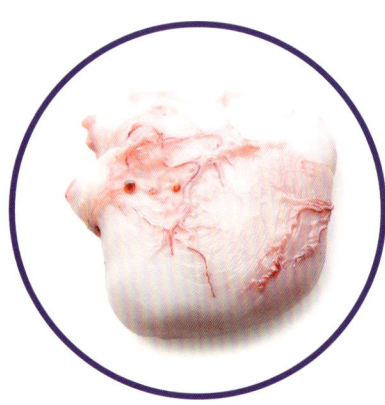

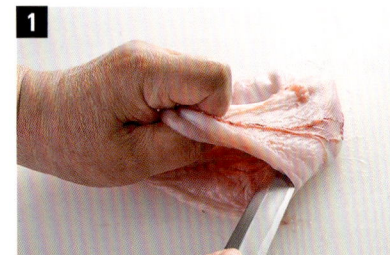

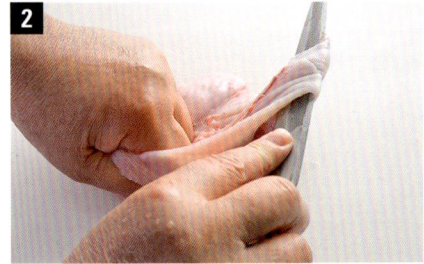

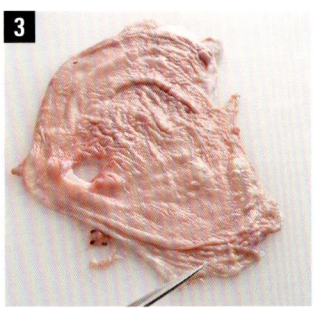

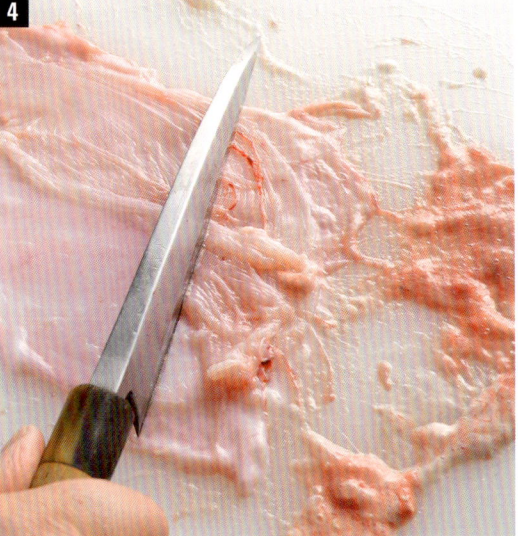

Treatment of the stomach

1 Insert the knife into the stomach sac.

2 Open it out from the inside.

3 Stretch the sac out over the cutting board, inside out.

4 Gripping the sac with the fingers of the left hand, move the blade of the knife in left-to-right strokes to smooth out the folds of the sac. Turn the sac over and follow the same procedure on the outside. Place in salt water to soak for about 30 minutes.

Treatment of the breast meat

1 Insert the knife under the reddish blood vessels visible on the back side of the breast meat. Carefully pull off the vessels away from the flesh.

2 Pull and cut away the membrane covering the flesh.

3 Place the tip of the knife, blade facing to the right (*sakasabocho*). Cut off the membrane.

4 Cut flesh into easy-to-eat pieces.

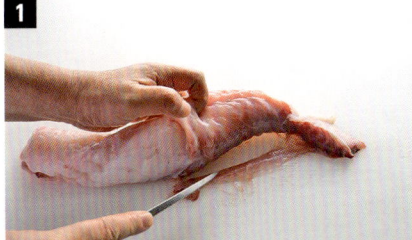

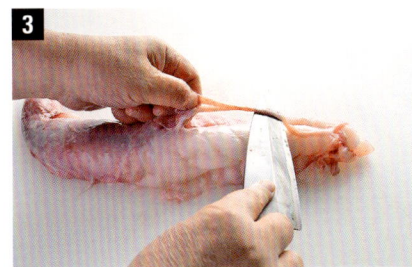

from page 218

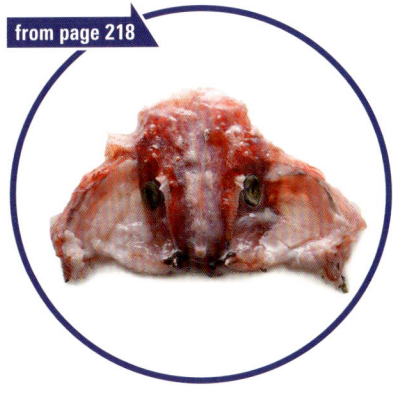

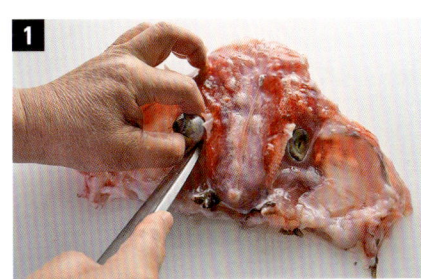

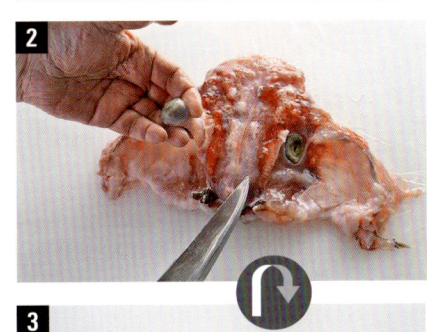

Cleaning of the headbone or face (*ara*)

1 Insert the knife under one of the eyes.

2 Cutting around the edge, remove the eye. Follow the same procedure for the other eye.

3 Turn the headbone over.

4 Cut into bite-sized pieces and wash well in water.

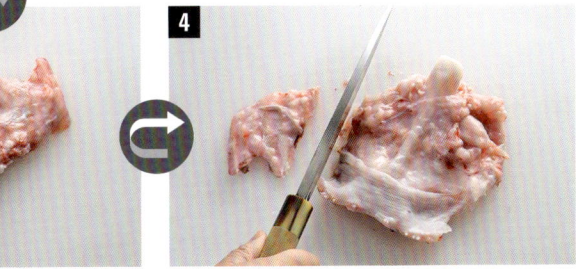

Monkfish Liver Hot Pot

Anko-nabe

The best way to enjoy monkfish down to the last morsel is in a hot pot. The meat and other parts of the fish are first blanched in hot water (*shimofuri*) to remove fishy odor and then simmered together with vegetables in a rich soup flavored with the monkfish liver. The flesh is light and not fatty. It will become hard if overcooked, so is best eaten early in the simmering. The headbone pieces and skin, by contrast, are rich in collagen and, if slowly cooked, will soften to a jelly-like consistency.

Make the liver hot pot soup

1
4 Bring water to a boil and turn off heat; plunge the pectoral fins, stomach sac, skin, and ovaries into the water for 5 seconds (*shimofuri*), then plunge into in ice water (which removes mucous film and blood) and cut into bite-sized pieces.

5 Make the liver paste. Roast the liver until it is heated through and whir in a food processor to make a paste. For about 220 g (about 7 oz.) of liver, mix with 70 g coarse graind miso (*ara miso*). Blend in 40 ml (scant ¼ cup) sake a little at a time; add 2 Tbsp. of mirin and mix in well.

Pour water in the hot pot and add a piece of kombu (about 5 g per 1 L of water); place over medium heat. Remove the kombu just before the pot boils. Dissolve the liver paste a little at a time in the liquid and adjust the taste with *usukuchi* shoyu. Add the other "seven parts" and simmer (about 10 minutes), then add the vegetables and tofu and again simmer (about 5 minutes).

Monkfish Liver Hot Pot

hakusai (Chinese cabbage)

spinach

shiitake mushrooms

enoki

aonegi

daikon

carrot

Koi
CARP
Cyprinus carpio

Family Cyprinidae, order Cypriniformes, carp are freshwater fish with two pairs of whiskers. The body is short and its shape more or less cylindrical. Those generally used for cooking are black-brown in coloring.

Carp readily adapt to different environments and are easy to farm, so they have been pond raised for a long time and are an important source of protein for landlocked areas. Carp lives are long, frequently several decades. Colorful carp kept for ornamental enjoyment are popular in Japan; the brocade carp (*nishiki-goi*) is celebrated as the national fish.

In Japan, carp is mainly served as *arai* (sashimi that has been firmed up by soaking in ice water), as a soup called *koikoku* made from the head and bones, and as *koi uma-ni* simmered in a sweet-salty sauce made with shoyu and sugar. In recent years, the custom of eating carp has generally faded, and the fish is not commonly stocked in fish markets.

Since carp that is not fresh quickly starts to produce an odor, chefs generally purchase live carp. After the dish is spiked, it is quickly filleted without removing the scales.

CUTTING CARP

Removing the head and the internal organs

1 Place the head to the right and the dorsal fin facing you. With the blade facing right (*sakasabocho*), insert the *deba* knife at the rear end of the dorsal fin.

2 Make a shallow cut, slicing continuously over the dorsal fin. Cut toward the head, with the tip of the knife sliding over the central bones.

3 Keeping the blade facing to the right, continue cutting up to the head.

4 At the head, remove the knife, reverse direction (blade facing left), and cut in further over the central bones along the length of the fish, separating the flesh from the bones.

5 Continue cutting in all the way to the tail.

6 Lift the flesh to check the path of the knife and make repeated passes to separate the flesh from the bones.

7 Holding the body firmly with the left hand, insert the knife at the line extending from the gill cover to the pectoral fin and cut the flesh between the gill cover and the incision made in steps **1** to **6**.

8 Lift the upper part of the fish and insert the knife to cut the belly bones away from the flesh.

9 Taking care not to damage the internal organs with the tip of the knife, slide the blade over the spine and cut the flesh from the bones in the direction of the tail.

10 Continue cutting the flesh away to the base of the tail.

11 Place the tip of the knife, blade facing to the right (*sakasabocho*). Cut away the intestines and remove the internal organs.

12 Remove all of the internal organs, taking special care not to puncture the gall bladder (located just under the heart; see next page), which could cause its bitterness to flavor other parts of the fish.

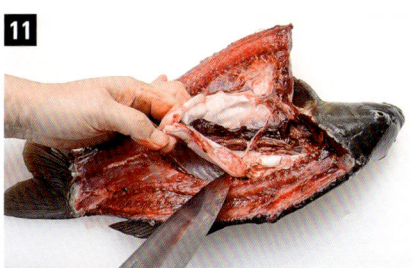

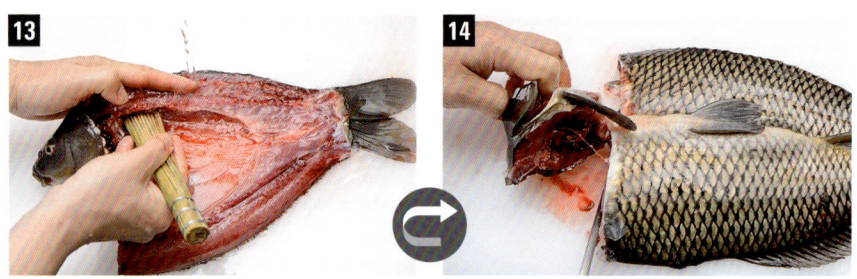

13 Wash the fish carefully in running water, using a *sasara* or other stiff-bristled brush to clean out the cavities. Blot dry with a cloth.

14 With the head to the left, skin-side up, cut off the head.

internal organs and head removed

gall bladder

Removing the spine and central bones

1 Place the fish skin-side up with the tail to the right and place the knife horizontally above the dorsal fin.

2 Steadying the fish with the left hand, make a shallow cut toward the head end.

3 Lift the flesh with the left hand and, checking the location of the tip of the blade, cut in further, sliding the knife over the central bones. Cut the connection between the belly bones and the spine and cut in further, sliding the knife over the central bones and cutting the flesh away.

4 Make repeated passes to cut through the connection of the belly bones to the spine.

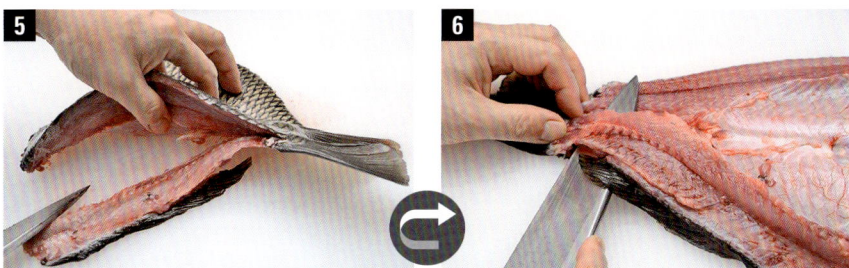

5 Leaving the central bone section attached to the base of the tail, separate the flesh from the dorsal fin and the bones.

6 Turn the fish over (skin-side down). Insert the knife under the spine at the base of the tail, angle the blade down, and cut the tail off at the base.

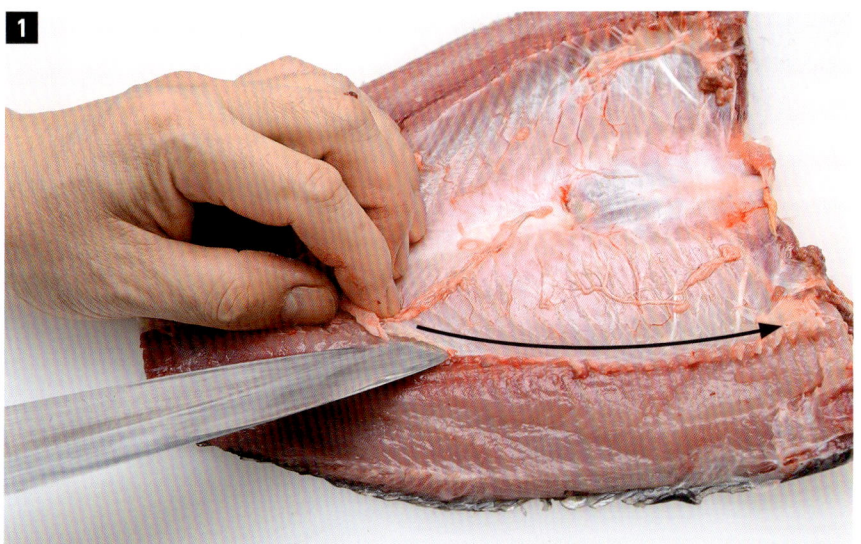

Removing the belly bones

1 Place the fish with the tail end to the left, skin-side down. With the blade of the knife facing right (*sakasabocho*), insert the tip about 1 cm (½ in.) under the base of the belly bones. Cut forward toward the head end and separate the belly bones from the flesh.

2
3 Insert the knife tip under the belly bones on the other side and cut toward the head end in the same way, as shown. Continue cutting and separate the belly bones from the flesh.

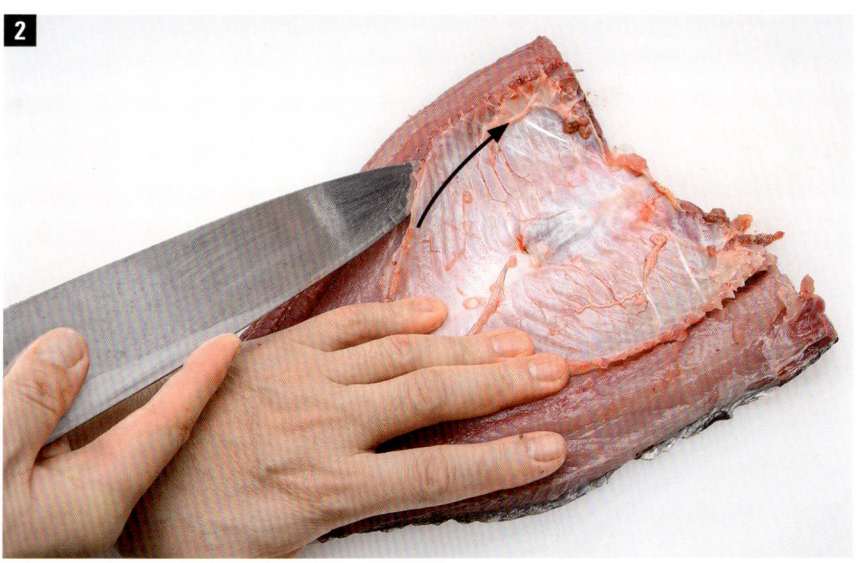

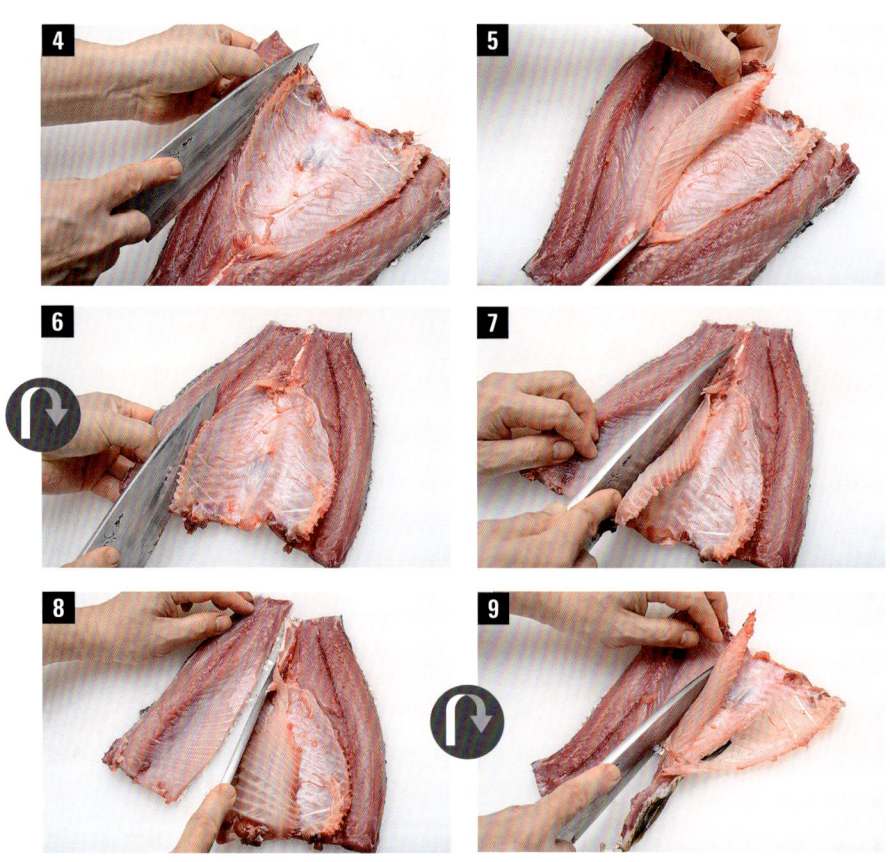

4 Pulling out on the flesh with the left hand, press out the belly bones with the side of the knife and cut under them, sliding the blade along the bones.

5 Separate the belly bones from the flesh, scraping them away to their base.

6 Turn the fish around so that the tail end is away from you and insert the knife under the belly bones on the other side.

7 Continue cutting under the belly bones toward the tail end.

8 Once the belly bones have been scraped off as far as their base, insert the knife along the center line of the back and cut off the left fillet.

9 Place the tail end facing you and cut off the other fillet on the opposite side, leaving the belly bones attached to the skin at the center.

upper fillet (*uwami*)

central bones (*nakabone*)

head

belly bones, ventral fins, and anal fin

lower fillet (*shitami*)

Removing the skin

1 Leaving the scales attached, place one of the fillets skin-side down with the tail end to the left. Switch to a *yanagiba* knife and, with the knife facing right (*sakasabocho*), insert the blade between the flesh and skin.

2 The skin is slippery with mucus, so grip with a cloth and cut toward the head end, moving the knife back and forth to remove the flesh from the skin.

3 When the blade reaches the head end, sever the skin-flesh connection.

fillet and removed skin

Arai

The *arai* method of firming up the flesh of thinly sliced carp by chilling it in ice water is one technique in preparing sashimi. It also draws out some of the fat, enhancing the flavor of the fish. Although mainly used for carp and bass, the *arai* method is well suited to fish that is on the fatty side.

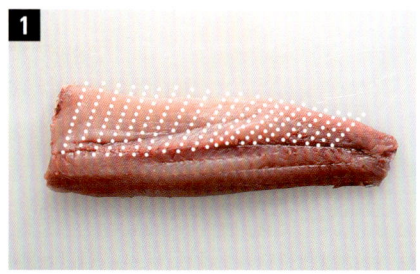

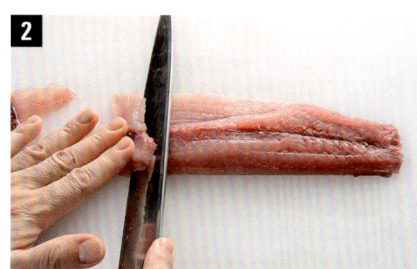

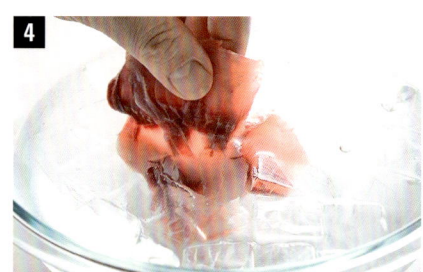

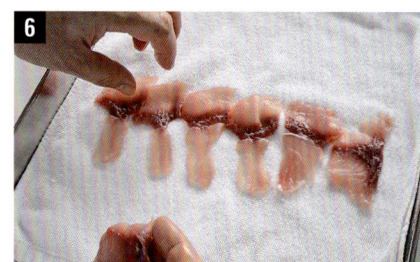

1 Place a carp fillet skin-side down with the head end to the left and start slicing at an angle from the head (dotted lines in the photo), cutting through the flesh and bones.

2 Supporting the flesh with the left hand, insert the *yanagiba* knife near the heel of the blade and at an angle to the block, as shown.

3 Draw the blade toward you from heel to tip, cutting slices about 5 mm (¼ in.) thick. Cut the flesh and bones together.

4 Drop the slices into ice water.

5 Swish the pieces well in the water to chill them thoroughly.

6 Line up the chilled pieces on a clean, dry cloth.

7 Cover with another cloth to soak up extra moisture. Arrange in a serving dish and add garnishes.

Chilled Carp

julienned daikon and cucumber

cucumber curls

shiso flowerets

red *shiso* buds

benitade

wasabi-dai (cucumber cup for wasabi)

wasabi

Grilled Carp with *Sansho* Sauce
Sansho Tare-yaki

This dish is made with well-fattened carp flavored with a grilling sauce and served with a generous helping of chopped *kinome* (*sansho*) leaves. The tender flesh is scored to make the bones edible when the fish is grilled on skewers.

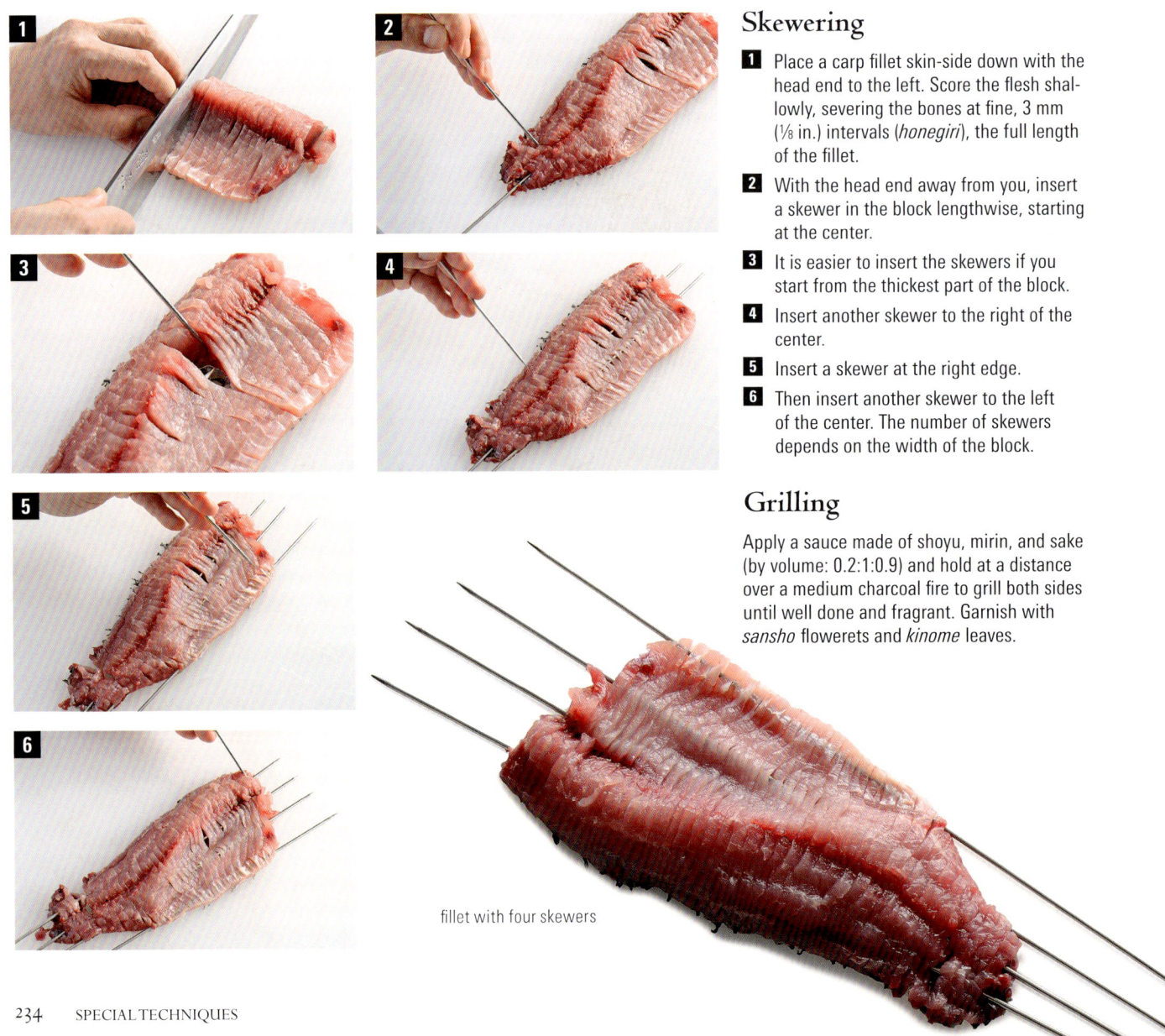

fillet with four skewers

Skewering

1 Place a carp fillet skin-side down with the head end to the left. Score the flesh shallowly, severing the bones at fine, 3 mm (⅛ in.) intervals (*honegiri*), the full length of the fillet.

2 With the head end away from you, insert a skewer in the block lengthwise, starting at the center.

3 It is easier to insert the skewers if you start from the thickest part of the block.

4 Insert another skewer to the right of the center.

5 Insert a skewer at the right edge.

6 Then insert another skewer to the left of the center. The number of skewers depends on the width of the block.

Grilling

Apply a sauce made of shoyu, mirin, and sake (by volume: 0.2:1:0.9) and hold at a distance over a medium charcoal fire to grill both sides until well done and fragrant. Garnish with *sansho* flowerets and *kinome* leaves.

Grilled Carp with *Sansho* Sauce

sansho flowerets

kinome

A tuna about to be carved at the fish market. Tuna from Japan's coastal waters and other parts of the world and auctioned to the highest bidder. Later they are cut into their various parts and sold to fish shops and restaurants.

Maguro
TUNA

Thunnus

Tuna is a general term for the genus Thunnus, family Scombridae, order Perciformes. With great, spindle-shaped bodies, tuna (*maguro*) grow from one to three meters in length and are found in the temperate and tropical waters of the world. Bluefin tuna, called *kuromaguro* (or *honmaguro* or simply *maguro*) in Japanese, is the leading type; the species that migrates the farthest north, it reaches the greatest size at some three meters, and can weigh up to more than 400 kilograms. Catches sell for exceedingly high prices at auction, sometimes for newsworthy figures.

The body of the tuna is divided into three parts—from head to tail, the *kami* (upper), *naka* (middle), and *shimo* (lower). The dorsal part of the *kami* is *sekami* (upper back), the ventral part of the tail is the *harashimo* (ventral lower), and so forth. Tuna on the market is sold in these parts (the block in the photo is a *haranaka* or "ventral middle" block). The taste differs depending on the amount of fat, and there are three grades: *akami* (lean), *chutoro* (medium fatty), and *otoro* (extra fatty). The red meat, of which there is the greatest quantity on the fish, is found in the area of the spine and the dorsal meat. It is low in fat and has both umami and a slight bitter flavor. The well-known succulent *otoro* meat is found in the *harakami* (ventral upper) and *haranaka* parts. High in fat, it has a whitish cast and a texture that melts in the mouth; the fat has a faint sweetness. *Chutoro* comes mainly from the *haranaka* and *harashimo* parts; it has a rich and mellow taste, along with the light bitterness of the *akami* red meat and the sweetness of fat. In general, the *kami* (upper) and *naka* (middle) parts are the more highly priced.

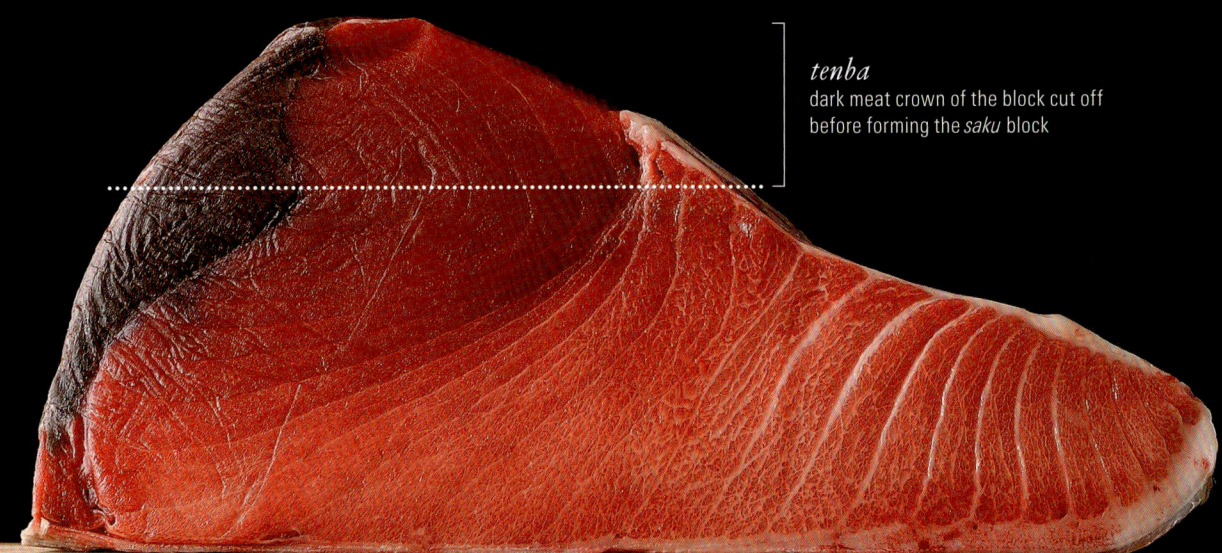

tenba
dark meat crown of the block cut off
before forming the *saku* block

CUTTING TUNA

to facing page

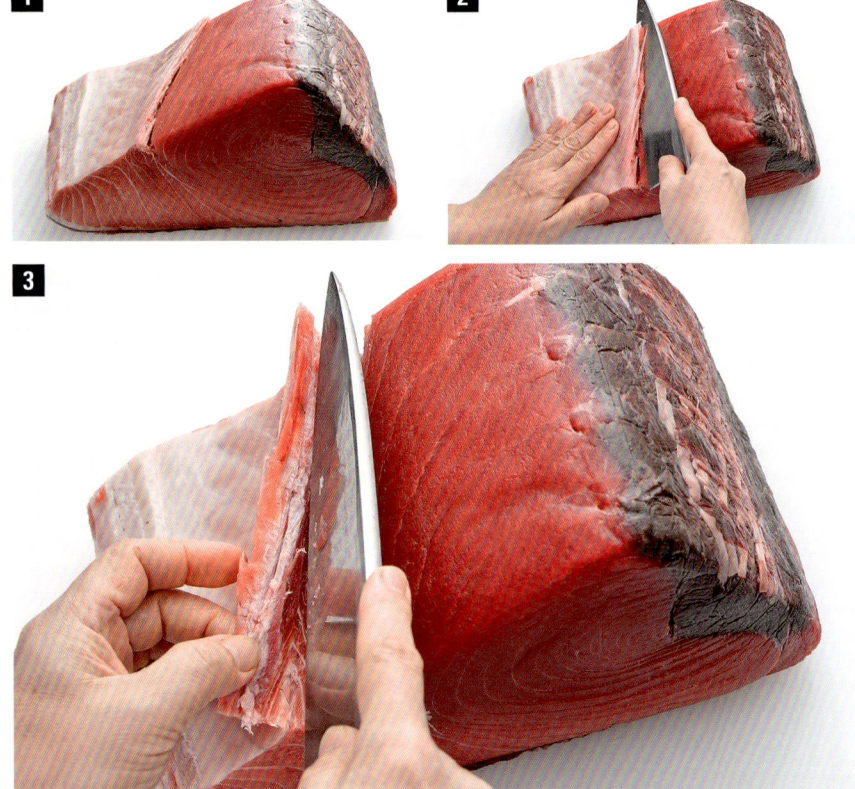

Removing the belly bones and the crown (*tenba*)

1 Place the *haranaka* block with the skin-side down and the dark-meat side (*chiai*) to the right.

2 Insert the *deba* knife under the belly bones.

3 Inserting the knife repeatedly, separate the belly bones from the flesh.

4 Block with the belly bones removed.

5 The block becomes fragile if the dark meat (*chiai*) has been trimmed off first, so it is left on for cutting the *tenba*. Change to a *yanagiba* knife. Place the block with the skin-side down and the dark-meat side to the right. Insert the knife horizontally at the point where the dark meat is thickest (when viewed from the cross section, where the grain of the flesh looks like circular tree rings, known as the *nenrin*). Leaving the *nenrin* whole would result in sashimi slices with too much tough tissue, so it is customary to cut through the *haranaka* block in the center of the *nenrin*.

6 Cut straight through and remove the *tenba* (crown part of the *nenrin* from the center up).

block with the *tenba* cut off

to page 240

Cutting *saku* blocks from the skin side of a cut of *maguro*

1 Place the skin-side down and the dark meat (*chiai*) on the left.

2 Insert the knife at the line between the dark meat and red meat.

3 Steady the dark meat with the left hand and cut through, separating it from the block.

4 If any dark meat is left on the block, trim it off in thin layers.

dark meat (*chiai*) cut off from block

The red meat (*akami*) is nearest the dark meat (*chiai*); next to it is the medium fatty (*chutoro*) and succulent extra fatty (*otoro*) meat.

akami   chutoro   otoro

5 Insert the knife vertically on the top side of the block at the left edge and cut down to the skin.

6 With the knife facing right (*sakasabocho*), insert the blade over the skin from the left side and cut to meet the vertical cut made in step **5**.

7 Insert the knife again from the top about 2 cm (about 1 in.) to the right and cut down vertically to the skin (adjust the width of the block depending on the purpose).

8 Cut the block away from the skin as in step **6**.

9 Make the *saku* blocks of equal width.

to page 242

9 Repeating steps **5** through **8**, continue cutting the block into 2 cm (or appropriate) widths and slicing them away from the skin. As the remaining block becomes smaller, insert the knife at a slight angle. In this way the width of the *saku* blocks will remain equal.

the *saku* blocks cut from the skin

from page 238

Cutting the *tenba* into *saku* blocks

1 Place the *tenba* with the dark-meat (*chiai*) side to the left. Insert the knife along the line of the dark meat as shown.

2 Continue cutting down, separating the dark meat from the block.

3 Shows the dark meat separated from the *tenba* block.

4 Place the block from which the dark meat has been removed with the sloping side (belly side) to the right. Cut off the *akami* meat nearest the dark-meat side in a rectangular block.

to facing page

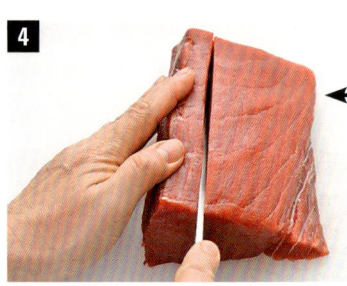

The rectangular block is set aside for tuna marinade (*zuke*), and the remainder is reserved for *tekka* tuna roll and other miscellaneous uses.

from facing page

Marinated Tuna Sashimi *Zuke*

Lean-meat tuna marinated in a mixture of shoyu and other seasonings is called *zuke*. The marinade draws out some of the excess moisture from the flesh and gives it a soft and chewy texture. Originally, *zuke* was made only with tuna, but sometimes salmon and other fish are marinated as well.

Marinade

Mix together de-alcoholized sake, shoyu, and mirin (proportions 1:2:1) and marinate a block of *akami* tuna for about 30 minutes. Or slice only the part to be eaten immediately and marinate for about 10 minutes.

Tuna *Nigiri-zushi*

An array of marinated *akami*, *chutoro*, and *otoro* tuna sashimi. A dish to savor the diverse flavors of tuna sashimi.
(see p. 245)

Hira-zukuri

The leading method of serving tuna as sashimi is to cut them into rectangular pieces called *hira-zukuri* (see also p. 54). For this fish, the pieces are cut fairly thick.

from page 240

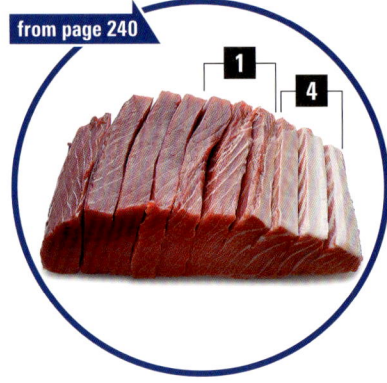

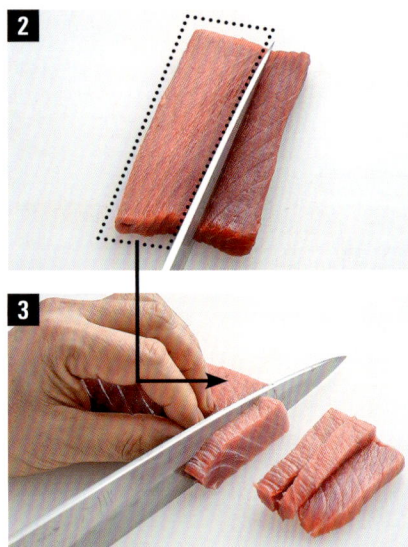

1 A *chutoro* and *akami saku* cut from the block. Insert the knife between the tough muscle (*suji*) and the flesh and slice the tough muscle off from the edge of the block.

2 Divide the *chutoro* (dotted line) and *akami* parts of the block.

3 With the *chutoro* part flat, rest the heel of the knife on the cutting board and insert into the flesh vertically, cutting the block into slices 1 cm (½ in.) thick.

4 Likewise trim the tough muscle from the *otoro* block.

5 Lightly steadying the flesh, tip the knife at an angle to cut slices of about 1 cm (½ in.) thickness.

Rectangular Cut Tuna Sashimi

carrot and *udo* curls
pine-needle-cut *udo*
"whirlpool" daikon
hamabofu
wasabi leaf
sakuraso flowers
wasabi

APPENDIX

Ichiban Dashi
[p. 134]

Yields about 5.5 L (5.7 qt.)

7.2 L (7.2 qt.) water

120 g (4 oz.) Rishiri kombu

200 g (about 7 oz.) katsuobushi
(*honkarebushi*) flakes

Place water and kombu in a large pot.
Heat over low heat, slowly raising temperature to 140°F (60°C). Once liquid has reached
140°F (60°C), simmer for 1 hour, adjusting
heat to maintain even temperature. This step
brings out maximum umami.
    Remove kombu and raise temperature to
185°F (85°C) over high heat. When temperature reaches 185°F (85°C), remove pot from
heat and add katsuobushi flakes. Wait for
the katsuobushi flakes to thoroughly soak up
water. 10 seconds later, strain liquid through
a fine-mesh cloth and leave to drain naturally,
without squeezing the cloth.

Warijoyu
dipping sauce for all sashimi dishes

Yields about 120 ml (½ cup)

100 ml (scant ½ cup) *ichiban* dashi

2 Tbsp. plus 1 tsp. *tosajoyu* (see below)

3 g katsuobushi flakes

Place dashi and *tosajoyu* (below) in pan and
heat over high heat. When it boils, remove
from heat and add katsuobushi. Strain after
cooling.

Tosajoyu
**optional dipping sauce for sashimi dishes
[p. 82]**

Yields about 400 ml (1⅔ cups)

100 ml (scant ½ cup) de-alcoholized sake

200 ml (scant 1 cup) *koikuchi* shoyu

100 ml (scant ½ cup) *tamari* shoyu

Dash of mirin

20 g (⅔ oz.) katsuobushi flakes

10 g (⅓ oz.) kombu

Combine all ingredients except katsuobushi
in pan and place over low heat. When liquid
boils, remove from heat and add katsuobushi.
Cool, then strain, squeezing liquid out of
katsuobushi.

Basic Vinegar Flavoring
[p. 57]

Yields about 720 ml (about 3 cups)

400 ml (1⅔ cups) *ichiban* dashi

4 Tbsp. plus 1 tsp. *usukuchi* shoyu

2 Tbsp. plus 1 tsp. *koikuchi* shoyu

juice from 8 large *sudachi* and 2 yuzu

Place all ingredients in a bowl and blend.

Tosa-zu
**optional vinegar flavorings for *kobujime*
sashimi like red sea bream and flounder**

Yields about 880 ml (scant 4 cups)

600 ml (2½ cups) *ichiban* dashi

200 ml (scant 1 cup) rice vinegar

4 Tbsp. plus 1tsp. *usukuchi* shoyu

1 tsp. sugar

5 g kombu

20 g (⅔ oz.) katsuobushi

Place all ingredients except katsuobushi
in a pan and heat over high heat. Add
katsuobushi just before the mixture boils and
remove from heat. Strain after cooling.

Pon-zu
**optional dipping sauce for white-fish
usu-zukuri sashimi like flounder, bartail
flathead, and pufferfish**

Yields 850 ml (about 3½ cups)

100 ml (scant ½ cup) sake

100 ml (scant ½ cup) mirin

420 ml (about 1⅔ cups) shoyu

2 Tbsp. water

360 ml (1½ cups) juice of two or more citrus
like yuzu or lemon.

Heat sake and mirin to evaporate alcohol.
Add shoyu and water and boil mixture briefly.
Add citrus juice and store in refrigerator for
2 days to allow flavors to blend. Strain and
refrigerate.

Sushi-zu
[p. 241]

Yields about 180 ml (¾ cup)

120 ml (½ cup) rice vinegar

1 Tbsp. plus 1 tsp. sea salt

75 g (2½ oz.) sugar

Combine all of the ingredients in a pan and
bring to a boil. Mix well, and when salt and
sugar dissolve, remove from the heat.

Sushi Rice
[p. 241]

Yields about 450 g (2½ cups)

210 g (generous 1 cup) rice

1 cup plus 2 Tbsp. water

2.5 cm (1 in.) square kombu

2 Tbsp. *sushi-zu* (recipe above)

Wash rice in two or three changes of cold
water and let drain in a sieve 30 minutes
before cooking. Combine kombu, water and
rice in a rice cooker and steam. Let the just-
cooked rice rest for 10 minutes and transfer
to a sushi tub. Pour the *sushi-zu* over the rice
and mix with a rice paddle using a gentle
slicing and tossing motion.

Cooking Utensils of the Japanese Kitchen

The cooking utensils described here are frequently used for Japanese cuisine and for the recipes in this book. They come in various shapes and sizes; those depicted here are standard versions.

Katsuobushi shaver
Katsuobushi-kezuriki
This box-shaped utensil is for making paper-thin shavings of katsuobushi, used mainly for dashi, from rock-hard, dried bonito fillets. The dried fillet is pulled against the blade at the top of the box, and the shavings fall into the box below.

Grater and brush
Oroshigane, burashi
Although graters can also be made of ceramic or glass, this one of metal, with tiny raised metal teeth is the standard type of grater in Japanese kitchens. A special grater-cleaning brush makes it easy to remove lingering bit, remaining in the teeth. Such brushes are usually made of bamboo.

Wasabi grater
Samegawa-oroshi
This grater, consisting of a piece of sharkskin glued onto a wooden base, is used mainly for grating wasabi into a fine paste. Grating wasabi against the textured sharkskin gives the paste a mellow tang and a fine aroma. The wasabi root tip should be held vertically against the grater and grated slowly in a circular motion.

Drop lid
Otoshibuta

A lid placed directly on top of ingredients being simmered or cooked. It is usually made of wood, and has a slightly smaller diameter than the pot it is used with. The lid acts to distribute flavor evenly and prevents foods from crumbling during cooking.

Fish scaler
Uroko-tori

Utensils for removing fish scales help remove scales more quickly than a knife and are also easy to use on large fish. Removing scales is difficult if the surface of the fish is dry, so it should be wetted first.

Bamboo brush
Sasara

Cleaning utensil made from narrow bamboo splints bundled together to form a brush. Used for clearing blood and debris left after fish has been cleaned, the *sasara* has bristles that can reach every crevice without damaging the flesh. Bamboo is not moisture-resistant, so the brush should be thoroughly cleaned and dried after use.

Fish-bone tweezers
Hone-nuki

Tweezers for kitchen use with a strong spring that facilitates deboning fish, whether the bones are large or small. Come in various shapes and sizes, and different ones are used depending on the size of the fish.

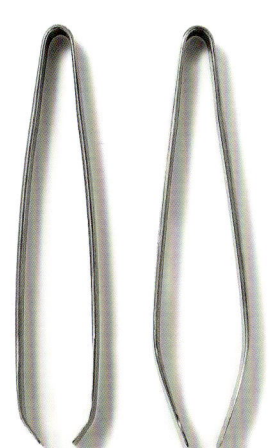

GLOSSARY

Aka-oroshi

Daikon grated together with dried red pepper (with a chopstick, make holes in daikon, insert 3 or 4 deseeded dried red peppers, and grate). Adds a refreshing bite to the usual grated daikon. Also called *momiji-oroshi*.

Ara

Head, central bones, collar, tail, and other bones remaining from the filleting of fish. Rich in umami, the *ara* are sprinkled with salt and eaten grilled or simmered, or used to make soup broth.

Arai

Method of removing excess moisture, fat, and strong odors from fish by thoroughly washing sashimi of very fresh fish, such as sea bream or carp, in ice water. The procedure gives the flesh a crisp and crunchy texture.

Arai-negi

Garnish made by chopping long onions (*naganegi*) or green onions (*aonegi*) in thin rounds, wrapping loosely in cheesecloth, swishing in water to rinse away sliminess, then wringing the cheesecloth lightly.

Ashirai

Composition and plating of dishes in a pleasing manner; handling and use of garnishes to bring out flavor, aroma, and color of dishes.

Chiai

Dark meat specific to fish, found in abundance especially in migratory fish that are very active. The dark meat is rich in iron and other nutrients but tends to have a strong odor. Its freshness decreases quickly, so it is usually removed from the flesh to be used for sashimi. The term *chiai* is also used for the area where blood collects along the central bones of the fish.

Daimyo-oroshi

A variant of filleting in three pieces. Cutting in from the dorsal side at the head end and slicing back over the backbone toward the tail, this technique enables the quick separation of the dorsal and ventral flesh from the central bones. The method gets its name because it allows for more flesh left on the bones, and is thus a more "lavish" way of preparing fish as would be

performed for a daimyo lord. It is used for fish with thick or soft and easily damaged flesh, such as *kochi* (bartail flathead) and *okoze* (devil stinger), or when the flesh is thin on the bones such as *kisu* (sillago) and *sayori* (halfbeak).

Engawa

Tough muscle along the base of the pectoral and ventral fin of flounder (*hirame*). The flesh is succulent and fatty, and since the amount found on one fish is small, it is considered a sashimi and sushi delicacy.

Enoki

Small mushrooms with long, thin stems and small caps, *enoki* have a faint aroma and a crunchy texture; well suited to stir-fried dishes and soups.

Gobo

Burdock root. This long root vegetable is rich in fiber with an aroma redolent of the earth. Pleasantly crunchy even after cooking, it is often used in simmered dishes, including *taki-awase* combinations.

Gomai-oroshi

Filleting a fish in five pieces. The fish is first cut along the line of the spine and then the flesh on either side cut away from the central bones, sliding the knife over the central bones from the spine toward the dorsal or ventral fin, respectively. This yields two ventral fillets and two dorsal fillets and the central bones as the fifth piece. This method is used especially for flat fish like flounder (*hirame* and *karei*).

Hamabofu

This vegetable of the parsley family (*Apiaceae*) has green leaves and slender, reddish stems; it has a distinctive aroma and a faintly astringent taste. A garnish often used with sashimi.

Hanamaru kyuri

An immature (around 3 cm or 1¼ in.) Japanese cucumber formed as the flower begins to bloom at the tip. Used mainly as a garnish with sashimi.

Ikejime

Method of spiking fish after capture, as preparation for transporting to the kitchen; spiking the brain and spinal cord extends the period before muscles stiffen and maintains the quality and freshness of the flesh.

Ji
Dashi seasoned with salt, shoyu, and other ingredients. Varieties include *suiji*, which is used for thin soups, and *happoji* (versatile base), which contains dashi, sake, mirin, or other ingredients and is used in preparing a wide variety of dishes. A combination of marinated ingredients in a seasoned liquid like this is called *jizuke*.

Jomi
Choice parts of fish or fowl after bones and inedible parts have been removed. For fish, the flesh that remains after filleting (see **sanmai-oroshi**) and the removal of ribs and other small bones.

Kappo
One style of serving Japanese cuisine. A *kappo* restaurant is centered around counter seating and features just-made dishes that the chef prepares in front of the customer(s). A variant of the open kitchen.

Katsuramuki
A 6–7 cm (about 2¼ in.– 2½ in.) cylindrical section of a vegetable—usually a daikon—peeled while rotating into a thin continuous sheet. This sheet may then be cut into long threads or into decorative forms.

Ken
Thinly cut strands of vegetable, usually daikon or carrot, used as a garnish or cushion for sashimi. Strands cut with the grain of the ingredient are called *tateken* and those cut across the grain are called *yokoken*.

Kobujime
This is a technique of curing whereby the umami of kombu is transferred to other ingredients such as white-fleshed fish (sea bream, flounder, etc.) by sandwiching or rolling up in strips of kombu.

Komi
Another name for *yakumi*, the term for garnishes used with sashimi to provide a refreshing piquancy or spice and bring out the flavor of the fish. Includes wasabi, grated daikon, and **arai-negi**.

Kuzu
A thickening starch made from the root of the kuzu vine, it is often used in Japanese cuisine because it does not change the taste or coloring of the food.

Kyuri
Japanese cucumber, averaging about 20 cm (8 in.) in length. The skin is thin and edible and the flesh is crunchy and juicy.

Myoga
Buds of *Zingiber mioga*, a plant in the ginger family. Traditionally used as a garnish for summer dishes, it has a crispy texture and a lightly piquant aroma. It is also eaten as a sweet pickle.

Naganegi
Allium fistolosum, a thick and long green onion similar to the leek that is native to China and other parts of Asia. The white part is generally sliced or chopped for use as a garnish. The upper portions, which are tougher and green, are used in soups and other dishes.

Nori
Seaweed sheet made from edible algae that has been pressed and dried. The standard product is packaged in square sheets, but also sold in small, bite-sized sheets, flakes, strips, and other forms.

Oigatsuo
Refers to the addition of more katsuobushi flakes to katsuobushi-based stock or **ji** stock in order to increase the umami. The flakes may be wrapped in a piece of gauze or other thin covering.

Ore-matsuba
This is a decorative trimming usually made with **yuzu** peel. It is made after removing the white spongy inner peel, which is bitter. The *matsuba* (pine-needle) shape is made by slitting a long slender strip of yuzu peel down the center, leaving about 5 mm (¼ in.) connected at one end. The *ore-matsuba* decorative cut, made by cutting the strip in thirds from opposite directions, imitates the look of two pine needles joined together.

Pon-zu

A lightly seasoned sauce made of dashi, soy sauce, and vinegar and seasoned with **yuzu**, *sudachi*, or other citrus juice.

Sakasabocho

Cutting with the knife blade facing upward or to the right. This technique is used when cutting fish, for example, in removing belly bones.

Sanmai-oroshi

Literally, "three-piece cutting," *sanmai oroshi* is the most basic of fish-dressing techniques. The head is removed and the body filleted, slicing off the "top fillet" (*uwami*) and the "lower fillet" (*shitami*), leaving the central bones (backbone and tail) as the third piece.

Sansho

Japanese pepper, *Zanthoxylum piperitum*. The dried seeds have the sharpness of pepper and leave a tingling sensation that lingers on the tongue. The young leaves, called *kinome*, are used as an aromatic garnish.

Sasami

Chicken breast meat that gets its Japanese name, *sasami*, from the shape of a bamboo grass (*sasa*) leaf; it is a light-tasting, tender, and low-fat cut.

Sebiraki

Butterfly cut. One method of carving a fish by cutting in along the dorsal side and slicing the flesh away from the central bones from the dorsal side.

Shimofuri

Blanching fish or meat by plunging briefly in boiling water, then immediately cooling in cold water, so that the surface turns white, leaving a pattern resembling frost (*shimo*). *Shimofuri* removes fishy or fatty smells and seals in the food's umami.

Shirako

Milt served as *sunomono*, grilled, and in soups. Cod *shirako* are also called *kumoko* ("cloud roe").

Shiso

Perilla frutescens, an herb belonging to the mint family, sometimes known as Chinese or Japanese basil. Red and green varieties both have culinary uses. Known for its anti-bacterial properties, green *shiso* is often served with sashimi.

Shitami

Lower fillet. Flesh of the fish on the underside when it is placed with the head to the left and the belly facing you (see **uwami**).

Sujiko

Term used for salted salmon roe in the sac. *Ikura* are salmon roe that have been released from the sac and salted.

Sukibiki

Method of scaling fish when the scales are small, fine, and overlapped by inserting the knife under the scales but over the skin to skim them from the surface.

Tataki

Method of preparing sashimi by searing the surface of the block briefly over a strong fire and then cooling down in ice water. Often used with bonito (*katsuo*). Note that *tataki* here means "seared," as contrasted with the chopping or dicing of fish such as seen in "chopped mackerel" (*aji tataki*).

Tosa-zu

A vinegar mixture made by blending dashi, shoyu or other ingredients, heating and adding **oigatsuo** to deepen the umami. With this richer umami, it makes a suitable dressing for salads containing light-tasting seafood.

Tsukejoyu

Shoyu prepared for dipping sashimi. Shoyu alone can be too strong, so restaurants may have a recipe for their dipping shoyu made by adding seasonings and dashi.

Tsukuri

Sliced sashimi. The term may also be used to denote the method of cutting *usu-zukuri* (p. 124) or *hoso-zukuri*. (pp. 56, 150)

Tsuma

One of the garnishes served with sashimi. The significance of the *tsuma* is primarily decorative and usually added to evoke the season. Examples are curled vegetable strips, *shiso* leaves, **hama-bofu** sprigs.

Tsuyu shoga

The juice of raw, grated ginger.

Udo

Aralia cordata. The stalk and young leaves of this indigenous Japanese mountain vegetable have a texture and a flavor resembling that of asparagus or celery with a faint licorice overtone.

Uwami

Upper fillet. The flesh of the fish on the upper side when the fish is lying with the head to the left and the belly facing you. After capture in Japan, fish is usually shipped to market with the head to the left and the belly forward, and because of the weight of the fish itself, the underside in this position is likely to lose its freshness most quickly. If shipping time is short, there is little difference between the two sides, but chefs often use the upper fillet for sashimi and the lower fillet for a simmered or grilled dish.

Wakame

A type of seaweed found in Japan and Korea; it is most commonly used in *aemono*-dressed salads and garnishi with sashimi.

Wakasa-yaki

Wakasa-style grilling. This is the leading preparation for tilefish (*amadai*). The fish is carved by the butterfly technique from the centerline of the back, sprinkled with salt, brushed with sake, and grilled slowly to prevent scorching.

Warijoyu

Shoyu that has been flavored with dashi and other seasonings. Used for dipping sashimi. See **tsukejoyu**.

Yori

Literally, "strings," these are spirals made by cutting vegetables in the **katsuramuki** peeling technique, then cutting the slices on the diagonal and soaking them in water until they curl up. Curled daikon, carrot, and **udo** are frequently used as decorative garnishes with sashimi.

Yuan-yaki

Sake, shoyu, and mirin are mixed to make a marinade (*yuan-ji*), in which fish, chicken, or other ingredients are soaked before grilling or frying. In some cases yuzu slices or citrus juice may be added to the marinade. *Miso yuan-yaki* is a version in which miso is added to the marinade.

Yuzu

A citrus cultivated in Japan since ancient times, the juice is quite sour, but the skin (zest) is favored as a garnish for its delicate fragrance and piquancy. Green yuzu is in season in August, bright yellow yuzu in November.

Zuke

Sashimi, typically tuna, that has been marinated in shoyu and other seasonings. The marinating draws out excess moisture and gives the fish a tasty and chewy texture as well as increasing its umami.

INDEX

Page numbers in *italics* refer to a recipe.
Titles of a recipe are also in *italics*.

CONVERSIONS

Standard U.S. measures are used in this book; the metric conversions in parentheses are also in accordance with U.S. standards.

1 cup = 240 ml (rounded up from 236.59 ml)
1 ounce = 30 g (rounded up from 28.349 g)

Please use the conversion table below as a guide.

Volume

Metric	USA
5 ml	1 teaspoon
15 ml	1 tablespoon
50 ml	3 tablespoons + 1 teaspoon
60 ml	¼ U.S. cup
80 ml	⅓ U.S. cup
100 ml	⅓ U.S. cup + 4 teaspoons
240 ml	U.S. 1 cup
400 ml	U.S. 1⅔ cups
480 ml	U.S. 2 cups = 1 pint
1000 ml (1 L)	U.S. 4 cups = 2 pints = 1 quart

Weight

Grams	USA
10 g	⅓ ounce
15 g	½ ounce
20 g	⅔ ounce
30 g	1 ounce
50 g	1⅔ ounces
100 g	3⅓ ounces
150 g	5 ounces
200 g	7 ounces

Length

Metric	USA
3 mm	⅛ inch
6 mm	¼ inch
1.25 cm	½ inch
2.5 cm	1 inch
5 cm	2 inches
6.25 cm	2½ inches
7.5 cm	3 inches
10 cm	4 inches

Temperature

Celsius (°C)	Fahrenheit (°F)
100°C	210°F
120°C	250°F
130°C	270°F
150°C	300°F
160°C	325°F
170°C	340°F
180°C	350°F
190°C	375°F
200°C	390°F

Publication Committee Chairperson: Nakata Masahiro, Japanese Culinary Academy
Publisher: Kiyota Junji, Shuhari Initiative
Project Manager: Tsukiji Masashi, Shuhari Initiative
Art Direction and Design: Miki Kazuhiko and Hayashi Miyoko, Ampersand Works
Editing: Kawakami Junko, Letras
Writing: Kawakami Junko and Kitagawa Yoshiko
Translation: Center for Intercultural Communication
Copyediting: Kim Schuefftan
Proofreading: Center for Intercultural Communication

PHOTO CREDITS

Saito Akira: pp. 2–3, 8–10, 15, 17–25, 27–29 and top 30, 31–32, 35, 40–62,
  64–71, 73–153, 155–243, 246 top left
Yamagata Shuichi: pp. 246 top right and bottom, 247
Kuma Masashi: Jacket

COOPERATION

The publisher thanks the following individuals and institutions for
  cooperation with photography for this book:
p. 13: Collection of the Tokyo National Museum, TNM Image Archives;
  p. 26: Takaosan Jingoji Temple, Kyoto; p. 37: KEYENCE CORPORATION;
  pp. 38–39: New World Transparent Specimens/Tomita Iori

CONTRIBUTORS

Fushiki Tohru, scientist: *Mukoita* and the Arts of Sashimi (pp. 10–11)
Kumakura Isao, historian: Knives in the History of Japanese Cuisine
  (pp. 12–13)
Nakata Masahiro, specialist in Japanese cuisine: The Hygiene for Food Eaten
  Raw (p. 14); Knives in the Japanese Kitchen (p. 16); Standard Techniques
  (p. 33); Spiking Fish (p. 40); Handling Pufferfish (p. 154)
Kawasaki Hiroya, scientist: The Secrets of *Tsukuri* (p. 34); Curing Fish (p. 63)
Matsumura Yasuki, scientist: The Merits of the *Yanagiba* Knife (pp. 36–37)

英文版 **日本料理大全** 向板 I
切る技法、魚のおろし方

2017年4月1日発行

監　　　修　　特定非営利活動法人 日本料理アカデミー
出版委員長　　仲田雅博

発 行 者　　清田順稔
制作責任　　築地　正
発 行 所　　シュハリ・イニシアティブ株式会社
　　　　　　〒104-0061　東京都中央区銀座2-11-2
　　　　　　info@shuhariinitiative.jp
　　　　　　shuhariinitiative.jp
　　　　　　Tel 03-6226-4833／Fax 03-6226-4835

印刷・製本　　大日本印刷株式会社